# Praise for *Fluid Leadership*

"Pietro Pazzi challenges the way we think about leadership in uncertainty. *Fluid Leadership* gives you real strategies for staying grounded, connected, and effective when everything around you shifts. It's a practical, human guide to leading with clarity and emotional intelligence through change."

—**Keith Ferrazzi**, executive team coach, keynote speaker, and founder & CEO of Ferrazzi Greenlight

"*Fluid Leadership* offers a compelling and practice-oriented contribution to contemporary leadership scholarship, demonstrating that effective leadership in dynamic and uncertain contexts depends on self-awareness, adaptability, and situational responsiveness rather than rigid models. Through informed reflection and applied frameworks, Pietro Pazzi provides valuable insights for achieving sustainable impact in modern organizations. It is an essential resource for leaders at all levels seeking to lead effectively in an ever-changing environment."

—**Sharon Brand**, Deputy Dean of Business Studies, Cornerstone Institute

"*Fluid Leadership* is a timely and practical guide for leaders navigating constant change. Rather than promoting a single 'right' way to lead, Pietro Pazzi offers a clear, human-centered framework for adapting leadership style to context without losing authenticity or values. Rich with insight, reflection, and real-world application, this book equips leaders to move with complexity, build trust, and lead with confidence in an ever-changing world. I recommend this book for any leader to read and apply these insights as change becomes more intense."

—**Dr. Morgan L. Jones**, Certified Executive Coach and award-winning author of *Believe*

"[*Fluid Leadership*] helps you identify your fundamental traits so you can stop operating on autopilot and start leading with intent. If you want to understand the mechanics of influence and finally bridge the gap between knowing how to lead and actually doing it, this is your guide."

—**Dr. Florian M. Heckmeier, PhD,** Aerospace Engineering & M.Sc. Management, Engineering Leader in Multinational Aerospace Projects

"What Pazzi has written is a timely and fresh review of leadership, given the new work context and environment. With such high levels of uncertainty and chaos, a multi-generational workforce, and high demands for performance with fewer resources, his book is a useful reminder for leadership skills that match the context and the needs of diverse followers."

—**Dr. Neville Goldin, PhD,** Organizational Psychologist and Executive Coach

"Too many leadership books focus on changing or trying to change your entire style, whereas this book guides you to leverage your own experience and foundation.... [Pazzi] is not prescriptive in his guidance but allows individuals to formulate their own abilities.... [*Fluid Leadership*] has the potential structure and content to be used by and adopted within corporations of any size."

—**Len Moult,** Retired Managing Director of 3M South Africa & Sub-Saharan Africa

# Fluid Leadership

# Also by Pietro Pazzi

*The Simplicity Switch*

**The Leader's Crucible**

*The Leadership Compass: From Theory to Action: Master 21 Leadership Styles Through Unforgettable Stories*

*Leading with Tomorrow in Mind: How to Future-Proof Your Leadership: 19 Emerging Styles for a Complex, Ever-Changing World*

PART OF THE
LEADER'S CRUCIBLE SERIES

# Fluid Leadership

## HOW TO ADAPT YOUR STYLE to Thrive in an Ever-Changing World

TURNER
PUBLISHING COMPANY

Turner Publishing Company
Nashville, Tennessee
www.turnerpublishing.com

*Fluid Leadership: How to Adapt Your Style to Thrive in an Ever-Changing World*


Leaders Crucible
www.leaderscrucible.com
info@leaderscrucible.com



Cover and book design by Ashlyn Inman

Library of Congress information available upon request

Printed in the United States of America

# Contents

*Dedicated to the many leaders I have had the privilege to learn from and to those I had the honor of playing a small part in guiding them in becoming greater leaders.*

# Introduction

*Fluid leadership equips you with the tools to adjust, excel, and take your team on a journey in an unpredictable environment.*

Thank you for choosing this book.

*Fluid Leadership* is a book about being a great leader in a dynamic environment. It differs from many other leadership books in that it explains *fluid* leadership; it helps you identify your leadership style and learn how to be in sync with the changing environment. But it's more. It also has tools and techniques for utilizing your strengths to make you a great leader (such as your leadership journal, identifying and reframing your underlying leadership values and beliefs, and stepping onto the leader's hero path).

My research has shown that effective leaders today, and more so in the future, prioritize agility, empathy, and collaboration, balancing human-centric values with technological integration. The latter three are common threads running through the various leadership styles discussed in my previous books, *The Leadership Compass* and *Leading with Tomorrow in Mind*. This book is about utilizing leadership styles to effectively flow through changing situations while deepening your knowledge of being a great leader in the era of digitization.

Here's my definition of the concept of fluid leadership: *The fluid leadership model presents an adaptive meta-framework built upon the foundational pillars of self-awareness, context awareness, and style agility. It is designed to equip leaders to dynamically select and blend from a repertoire of 40 distinct leadership styles, enabling them to respond effectively and authentically to the shifting demands of their team, organization, and environment.*

## The Birth of Fluid Leadership

I remember the moment it hit me—the lesson that would forever shape how I see leadership. I was standing on the banks of the Orange River while on safari in Africa. The water surged forward, twisting and turning as it carved its way through the landscape. It wasn't hesitant. It didn't stop to second-guess itself. It simply adjusted, finding its way around rocks, through narrow channels, and over obstacles, always moving forward. It was powerful, relentless, and unstoppable.

Not far downstream, the Gariep Dam stood in stark contrast. A massive wall of concrete, rigid and unyielding, holds back the river's full force. It seemed in control—regulating the flow, dictating how much water could pass through. But I knew what could happen when a dam tries to hold too much. The pressure builds, cracks form, and if it refuses to adapt, the whole structure collapses.

And then it struck me—this is leadership.

Some leaders are like the river—flowing, adapting, and responding to change. They shift their course when necessary, never losing momentum. Others are like the dam—resisting change, holding back the inevitable, trying to force things to remain as they were. And when they refuse to adapt, the pressure eventually breaks them.

I've seen this play out time and again: Leaders who try to control every detail, micromanaging their teams, only find that the control they cling to inevitably becomes their downfall. Like the commander who refused to delegate, believing that giving up control would lead to failure, only to burn out and erode trust in his leadership. Or the seasoned executive who dismissed new ways of thinking because "this is how we've always done it" until the people around them grew frustrated, disengaged, and stopped innovating altogether.

Leaders who thrived were the ones who moved with the current. Abraham Lincoln faced a divided nation and an unwinnable war; yet, instead of clinging to rigid ideology, he evolved, reshaping his approach and cabinet as the conflict demanded. After years of imprisonment, Nelson Mandela could have remained hardened in defiance. Still, instead, he chose to pivot—shifting from resistance to reconciliation, guiding South Africa through its most delicate transition with the flexibility of a river carving a new path. During a global crisis, Jacinda Ardern led not by force, but by fluidity—adjusting strategies, balancing decisiveness with empathy, and ensuring that communication flowed clearly and consistently.

The business world is filled with leaders who embraced the river's philosophy rather than the dam's resistance. Satya Nadella, as CEO of Microsoft, transformed a once-rigid corporate giant into a more innovative and collaborative company by shifting its culture from a know-it-all mindset to a learn-it-all one. Reed Hastings, co-founder of Netflix, recognized early that DVDs were a stepping stone, not the destination, and transitioned the company into streaming—before the competition even saw the shift coming. Sheryl Sandberg, at Facebook, navigated one of the fastest-growing companies in history by focusing on flexibility—building strong systems while allowing room for rapid evolution.

They didn't fight change. They flowed with it.

Leadership isn't about control. It's about movement.

This book isn't about rigid theories or abstract principles. It's about learning to lead like the river, not the dam—to embrace change, read the shifting landscape, and flow toward success instead of standing firm and risking collapse.

Because in leadership, just like in nature, the water always wins.

## The Fluid Leadership Book

Building on my previous books, *The Leadership Compass* and *Leading with Tomorrow in Mind*, this guide focuses on developing a much-needed leader competency: fluid leadership. While my last works explored various leadership styles and their characteristics in-depth, this book shows you how to combine those styles dynamically to navigate challenges, adapt to unique situations, and lead in a way that feels true to the situation and who you are.

Leadership has always been a vital ingredient for success, but let us be honest: sometimes, it feels like holding water in your hands (the water metaphors continue). There are theories, case studies, and motivational quotes that sound fantastic in presentations, but often fall short when real-life problems land on your desk. And with the pace of change in the world—where yesterday's approaches can become today's mistakes—leading effectively can feel daunting. So, how do you thrive as a leader in a world where certainty is rare? The answer lies in fluid leadership.

This guide isn't a conventional leadership manual. It's not about rigid frameworks or foolproof formulas. Instead, while offering such tools, it invites you to rethink what leadership means. It's about embracing today's workplace's contradictions, complexities, and ever-changing realities.

Fluid leadership bridges this gap. It enables leaders to assess their environment, understand their teams, and adjust their styles to fit the moment. This book is built on that premise: to help you move beyond rigid frameworks and adopt a flexible, situational approach.

Whether you're an experienced leader or just starting your journey, this book will give you the skills to lead with authenticity, confidence, and impact.

## Why Fluid Leadership?

Fluid leadership isn't about chasing the mythical "one right way" to lead because it simply doesn't exist. It's about agility: having the awareness to recognize what's needed and the flexibility to respond. Picture it as the Swiss Army knife of leadership. Whether steering through calm waters or battling a storm (water again), fluid leadership equips you with the tools to adjust, excel, and take your team on the journey.

Leadership isn't just about you. Of course, self-awareness and personal growth are essential, but at its heart, leadership is about others—empowering, inspiring, and helping them thrive. Fluid leadership goes beyond traditional approaches by recognizing that neither people nor circumstances stay the same.

Imagine leading a tech start-up. One day, you're rallying your team around an ambitious vision; the next, you're troubleshooting a cash flow crisis. You need to be the motivator in one moment; in the next, you must be the problem-solver. Fluid leadership allows you to shift between these roles and environments without losing authenticity or effectiveness.

Think about the challenges leaders face today: managing remote teams, fostering diversity and inclusion, or adapting to rapid technological change. The demands of leadership are more complex than ever. Fluid leadership isn't just about responding to change; it's about staying grounded in your values while navigating shifting expectations, challenges, and opportunities.

## Why Me?

"What qualifies you to write about leadership, and why are you doing it?" is a question you might be asking. For more than three decades, I've worked in the vibrant and challenging world of business leadership. From the boardrooms of multinational companies to the innovative spaces of start-ups to project leaders, I've had the privilege of seeing leadership in all its forms. I've coached and collaborated with thousands of leaders. These experiences have shaped the principles and practices I now share with you.

I've always had a passion for leadership. Fresh out of college, back in the 1980s, I devoured books such as *In Search of Excellence* and *Leadership Challenge*. In the 1990s, I enjoyed *On Becoming a Leader* and *The Fifth Discipline*. There have been so many more since then, many of which are referenced in this book. I continued this trend by focusing my MBA dissertation on leadership.

As an executive and consultant, I led, trained, coached, and mentored leaders globally and at all levels to become better at developing strategies, executing those strategies, bringing about organizational change, and driving transformation.

I have learned so much from these leaders and, in the process, observed various leadership styles in action. I began to keep notes, which now, after more than three decades, I've distilled down to forty leadership styles. Many are well-known and documented; a few are based on my experience.

Like other renowned authors on this topic, I have noticed a shift in leadership styles necessitated by an increasingly dynamic macro- and micro-environment.

I've recognized a need for a new leadership approach, one that encompasses the right leadership style or characteristic for a given situation. Situations are in constant flux, leaving leaders needing to be fluid in their leadership approaches. Rigidly adhering to comfortable styles no longer cuts it. Those who do so have already been left behind, often without even knowing it. I call this new leadership approach *fluid leadership*.

Then there's my passion for self-improvement. Since 1983, when I read *Think and Grow Rich* by Napoleon Hill and many such books in the following couple of years, my exploration of neuro- linguistic programming (NLP), and my studies in psychology with a deep interest in Jung and Assagioli, I've invested a great deal of energy in becoming a better version of myself. This book marries my two passions—leadership and continuous self-improvement—to bring you a practical guide to becoming a great leader in an ever-changing business environment.

## Who This Book Is For

This book is for leaders at every level and in every industry. Whether you're a CEO tackling global challenges, a manager leading a small team, or an entrepreneur building something from scratch, the principles of fluid leadership apply to you. Specifically, this guide is for:

- Leaders who are facing complex challenges and want clarity and focus on their approach.
- Managers aiming to build adaptable and resilient teams.
- Professionals striving to make a meaningful and lasting impact.
- Anyone committed to ongoing personal and professional growth as a leader.

## The Journey Ahead

This guide takes you step-by-step through tools and techniques and guides you through the principles and practices of fluid leadership. Here's a glimpse of what is coming your way:

1. **Understanding Leadership in Motion:** We'll explore the essence of leadership and how it has evolved. You'll learn to combine traditional and emerging styles to be more adaptable and human-centered.
2. **Discovering Your Leadership Style:** Leadership isn't one-size-fits-all. These chapters help you uncover and refine your unique style while identifying areas for growth. Practical exercises, assessments, and relatable examples will give you deeper insights into your strengths, blind spots, and areas for development.
3. **Adapting to Different Contexts:** Context matters. Learn how to identify your environment, assess team dynamics, and align your leadership style or your company's leadership team style composition. Whether managing a crisis or fostering innovation, this section provides actionable tools to help you succeed.
4. **Building Resilience and Trust:** Leadership isn't just about making bold moves; it's about creating spaces where your team feels safe and supported. These chapters delve into emotional intelligence and relational skills to help you build trust and resilience.
5. **Navigating Complexities with Confidence:** From globalization to technological disruption, today's challenges demand agility and creativity. This section offers strategies to help you stay authentic and effective in a rapidly changing world.
6. **Sustaining Growth and Leaving a Legacy:** Leadership is about impact. The final chapters show you how to nurture future leaders, create sustainable practices, and build a legacy that reflects your values and vision.

## What You'll Learn

This guide focuses on eight core themes:

1. **Understanding Leadership:** Dispelling myths and uncovering what truly drives excellent leadership.
2. **Adapting Leadership Styles:** Exploring forty styles and learning how to use them effectively.
3. **Self-Awareness and Reflection:** Using tools like journaling and self-assessment to enhance your self-understanding.
4. **Building High-Performing Teams:** Creating trust, fostering collaboration, and navigating team dynamics.
5. **Environmental Alignment:** Matching leadership styles to organizational and contextual needs.
6. **Harnessing Feedback:** Using 360-degree insights to refine your leadership approach.
7. **Fluidity in Action:** Case studies of leaders who have successfully embraced adaptability.
8. **Continuous Growth:** Embedding lifelong learning into your leadership journey.

## How to Use This Book

This isn't a book for you to read once and put on a shelf. It is a guide meant to be revisited, annotated, and applied. At the end of each chapter, you'll find practical exercises, journaling prompts, and reflection questions to help you integrate what you have learned. These aren't just academic exercises; they are tools to help you grow as a leader and make a tangible impact on those around you.

Each chapter ends with a Chapter Workout. These exercises pose a set of journal prompts to embed the chapter's content, ensuring your ongoing growth.

The book contains five assessments to guide you in identifying your predominant leadership style, your leadership blind spots, and areas for development. These surveys include:

1. Leadership Styles Cluster Assessment
2. Leadership Style Assessment
3. 360-Assessment: Leadership Styles Cluster
4. 360-Assessment: Leadership Style
5. Current or Future Environment Assessment

## The Power of Fluid Leadership

Holding this book shows that you're ready to embrace the adaptability and purpose of fluid leadership. Whether facing uncertainty, building trust, or shaping a legacy, this guide will help you lead with authenticity and impact.

Leadership isn't about perfection. It's about showing up, staying curious, and being open to growth. Fluid leadership invites you to embrace the challenges and opportunities of leading in a complex world. It encourages you to adapt, connect, and lead with purpose—not *despite* the challenges, but *because* of them.

## Final Thought

This guide gives you fresh insights and practical tools to enrich your leadership journey. Your feedback is invaluable to me, and I'd love to hear how these ideas resonate with you.

Visit my website, **https://leaderscrucible.com**, for more information, and follow **@leaderscrucible** on LinkedIn. Feel free to follow and connect with me on **https://linkedin.com/in/pietropazzi**.

Thank you for choosing this book. Here's to your growth and success as you embrace the principles of fluid leadership.

# Getting Started with Your Leadership Journal

For many years I journaled to gain a deeper awareness of my leadership approach and to identify opportunities for growth. I found it to be a simple tool, but an oh-so-powerful method for personal improvement.

Journaling is one of the tools we'll be using quite a bit in this field guide. Journaling is a reflective practice where you regularly write down your thoughts, experiences, insights, and goals.

Journaling serves as a powerful tool for personal and professional growth, enabling you to process emotions, track progress, and cultivate a deeper understanding of yourself and your leadership style.

At the ends of most chapters, you will be provided with an exercise containing prompts for journal work. Use these as a guide, answering as many of the prompts as you feel is beneficial.

However, it's your journal; you can add whatever arises at any point on your leadership development journey.

## Why Journal?

- **Self-Awareness:** Gain insights into your strengths, weaknesses, values, and motivations as a leader.
- **Goal-Setting:** Define and track your leadership objectives.
- **Problem-Solving:** Analyze challenges and brainstorm solutions.
- **Emotional Intelligence:** Reflect on your emotions and improve your interpersonal leadership relationships.
- **Continuous Growth:** Document your learning journey and measure your development over time.

## How to Journal Effectively

1. **Choose Your Medium:**
    - Physical Journal: A notebook or planner where you can write by hand.
    - Digital Journal: Apps like Evernote, Apple Notes, Microsoft OneNote, or simple text documents.

2. **Set a Regular, but Spontaneous Schedule:**
    - Dedicate a specific time each day or week for journaling.
    - Consistency helps build the habit and ensures regular reflection.
    - Your journal can be used at any time. When an insight, learning, or question appears, add it to your journal immediately for exploration later.

3. **Create a Comfortable Environment:**
    - At the start or end of the day, find a quiet, comfortable space free from distractions.
    - Consider playing soft background music or practicing mindfulness before you begin.

4. **Be Honest and Authentic:**
    - Write candidly about your thoughts and feelings.
    - Remember, your journal is a private space for genuine reflection.

5. **Use Prompts and Questions:**
    - Start with the guided questions and prompts that are provided at the end of each chapter to stimulate your thinking.
    - Allow your writing to flow naturally, even if it starts with unrelated thoughts.

6. **Review and Reflect:**
   - Periodically revisit past entries to track your progress and identify patterns.
   - Use your reflections to inform your future actions and decisions.

## Tips for Effective Reflection

1. **Be Honest and Open:** Approach this exercise with sincerity. Authentic reflections lead to meaningful insights and growth.
2. **Use Specific Examples:** Ground your reflections in real-life experiences to better understand your leadership strengths and areas for improvement.
3. **Stay Curious:** Maintain an open-minded attitude, exploring new perspectives and being willing to challenge your own assumptions.
4. **Set SMART Goals:** Use your journal to set Specific, Measurable, Achievable, Relevant, and Time-bound goals based on your reflections.
5. **Review Regularly:** Periodically revisit your journal entries to track your progress, celebrate successes, and adjust your strategies as needed.

With your journal in hand, let's start your journey toward fluid leadership.

# Chapter 1

# Beliefs and Values: The Foundation for Great Leadership

*Your beliefs become your thoughts, your thoughts become your words, your words become your actions, your actions become your habits, your habits become your values, and your values become your destiny.*
*—Mahatma Gandhi*

Many leaders recognize the importance of picking up new techniques—improving communication, sharpening decision-making, or honing motivational skills. Yet what often goes unnoticed is that these methods can only go so far if the leader's underlying beliefs and values remain unexamined. If you're unaware of why you lead or what principles you're committed to, you can pile on all the leadership strategies in the world, but they'll sit on shaky ground.

Beliefs and values aren't window dressing; they're the bedrock upon which all other leadership practices rest. When those are misaligned or fuzzy, any improvement effort becomes a short-term patch, prone to collapse under stress.

Before we delve into the nuances of fluid leadership and work on identifying your unique leadership style, we must ensure that we're building your leadership development on a robust foundation. We want to ensure that the transformative changes you experience aren't just temporary fixes—mere plaster over cracks—but lasting shifts that truly embed themselves in your leadership approach.

This first chapter aims to bring that reality into clear focus. We'll examine how your core assumptions about leadership shape everything you do, why it's vital to identify and refine them before adopting new styles, and how redefining your self-concept can open the door to more authentic and resilient fluid leadership.

Beliefs about yourself—your identity, strengths, limitations—create the lens through which you see challenges and solutions. Values define what truly matters to you and give shape to your actions. Aligning your external behavior with these deeper layers can unleash a level of authenticity and effectiveness that superficial leadership training can rarely match.

Throughout this chapter, we will dig into the self-concept model, an approach that helps us understand how personal identity and beliefs shape every aspect of leadership. We will also examine how values arise from experiences, why they guide many of our choices, and how to discover and refine them for greater alignment.

This process involves challenging old generalizations, identifying limiting beliefs, and building a stronger sense of self-worth rooted in the values you genuinely cherish. By the end, you will have practical methods for working with your beliefs and values—valuable tools to help you build your leadership foundation on stable ground.

As you read, consider your expectations, biases, and convictions about leading others. By intentionally surfacing and reshaping these foundational beliefs, you empower yourself to grow in ways that stick—allowing all those tools, frameworks, and best practices to land on fertile soil. Once your foundation is stable and steadfast, everything you build on top stands a far better chance of flourishing.

## The Inner Architecture: Beliefs, Qualities, and Identity

One core principle of the self-concept model states that your beliefs about yourself are the foundation of all your beliefs about the world. These personal beliefs are not fleeting thoughts or passing feelings; they are overarching generalizations about who you are, often formed from countless experiences, observations, and internal narratives. Changing a belief at this deep level can shift your entire perception of reality, which is why the self-concept model is so powerful: it works at the level of identity, not just of behavior.

## How Experiences Feed Beliefs

Thinking of every experience as raw data entering your consciousness may be helpful. Although experiences are continuous, we tend to mark them with artificial beginnings and endings, calling one thing a failure and another a success. This labeling matters, because the way we represent an experience—what we notice, the senses we use, and how we interpret it—shapes the qualities we extract from it. If you find yourself repeatedly focusing on times you stumbled in public speaking, you could very quickly build a belief that you are a poor communicator. On the other hand, if you deliberately highlight the moments when you spoke well, you could form a more encouraging belief that you are an improving communicator who can handle any talk with enough preparation.

Everything about an experience—its time frame, what you see or hear, even the internal sensations you recall—can be restructured. If one memory haunts you, sometimes shifting its size in your mind, changing how you frame the time it occupies, or adjusting your perspective (for instance, imagining yourself observing from a more objective viewpoint) can defuse its emotional impact. Altering the structure of an experience allows you to change the belief or quality that emerges from it.

## Qualities, Beliefs, and Identity

As you gather and interpret many experiences in specific ways, you assemble qualities about yourself. These might be simple descriptors: creative, analytical, empathic, reserved, diligent, impatient, and so on. These qualities can feel like facts, but they are generalizations formed from a subset of experiences. Over time, such qualities start to harden into beliefs. Whether positive or limiting, these beliefs function like unconscious programs influencing both your daily actions and the world around you.

Ultimately, the totality of these qualities forms your identity—the most considerable generalization about who you are. It might be expressed as "I am a natural-born leader," or "I am someone who always messes up," or even "I am destined to remain behind the scenes." Some people hold flexible, evolving perceptions of themselves, while others cling to rigid identities that never seem to change. If you are unsatisfied with how you see yourself, you can shift your focus, finding different experiences, or restructuring how you interpret key events. By doing so, you can rewrite your narrative, transforming a limiting identity into one that serves your goals and allows you to become the leader you aspire to be.

## The Impact of Limiting Beliefs

Beliefs such as "I am not good enough," "I always fail," or "I do not belong in leadership" can become self-fulfilling prophecies. If you accept "I am not good enough" as truth, you are likely to see every shortcoming as evidence supporting that belief. On the other hand, every time you do succeed, you may dismiss it as a fluke. Over time, this mindset can cripple your potential. It is not a matter of ignoring mistakes; instead, it is about not allowing them to define your identity. When you shift from "I am incompetent" to "I am capable of learning and growing," you prime yourself to spot and leverage the opportunities for improvement.

Leaders often fall into the trap of adopting limiting beliefs because of past struggles or the input of others. For instance, a boss might have told you early in your career that you were not decisive enough. If that comment lodged into your self-concept, you might have carried it forward for years as a leader, never questioning whether you have improved your decisiveness. Letting go of outdated beliefs can free you to see yourself differently, upgrading your leadership style in line with who you are today, not who you used to be.

## Restructuring Beliefs: The Art of Shifting Perception

So, how do you change beliefs about yourself that seem so solidly rooted? The key lies in working with the structure of your experiences rather than trying to brute-force the content. If your mind has stored a hurtful memory in bold colors, at a high volume, with intense physical sensations, that memory will have a more intense effect. If you can soften how your mind represents that event—perhaps shrinking its mental image, lowering its volume, or viewing it more distantly—you can often lessen its emotional hold.

## Gathering New Experiences

Another powerful approach involves actively seeking out experiences that contradict the unwanted belief. If you believe you are bad at negotiations, you might try gathering evidence of when you calmly worked out an acceptable compromise. Shining a spotlight on success stories can tip the internal balance so that your mind starts to form a different identity.

You do not simply want to think "I will do better next time." You want to hunt down and examine real moments where you did well, no matter how small. By reorganizing and emphasizing these experiences, you feed new data into your unconscious mind, giving it reason to consider an alternative belief. This process can reshape your overarching identity, unlocking new leadership capabilities when repeated.

## The Role of Self-Esteem

I define self-esteem as how one feels about their identity—whether one likes the generalization that they have made about themself. People with high self-esteem do not get it from faking confidence or fleeting external praise. They maintain a stable sense of worth by believing that they truly embody the values that matter to them. If your value is creativity, and you think "I am a creative person" because you consistently produce and experiment, then your self-esteem in that domain is likely to remain high. But if you are half-hearted about it or doubt your right to call yourself creative, that hesitation will undermine your confidence.

You as a leader can cultivate lasting self-esteem by aligning behavior with genuine values. A slipup in a project or a bit of negative feedback no longer undercuts your identity, because your sense of self does not hang on a single success. Instead, it is grounded in the broader truth that you regularly act in line with the qualities you believe you possess. This approach fosters resilience and adaptability, as this way you are far less likely to crumble when faced with a challenge.

## Releasing Limiting Beliefs

Leaders often must confront beliefs that sabotage their growth. The good news is that you can systematically identify and replace these outdated programs with more empowering alternatives.

One way to spot a limiting belief is by paying attention to your language. If you catch yourself saying "I could never do that," or "I have always been this way," you might have stumbled upon a fixed belief. You need to question cause-effect statements ("I am angry because they made me do it"), mind-reading ("I know they think I am unqualified"), and universal quantifiers ("I always fail under pressure") that can reveal your unconscious assumptions.

You might also examine recurring instances where you feel stuck or defeated. If you always avoid public speaking or sabotage your success by missing deadlines at the last moment, there could be an underlying belief that says "I am not worthy of success" or "I will be embarrassed if I fail publicly." Journaling can be helpful here, especially if you set aside time to reflect on frustration or fear while noting the beliefs that might drive your reactions.

## Challenging and Transforming Beliefs

Once you identify a limiting belief, begin by questioning its validity. Ask if it is always authentic, valid for everyone, or if there are exceptions. For example, if your belief is "I cannot think strategically," think of moments when you actually did display strategic thinking. Gather those experiences, amplify and reframe them in your mind, and store them in a strong and undeniable way.

Another approach is to shift your attention toward new data that supports a desired belief. If you wish to adopt "I am resourceful," start consciously looking for daily examples where you solved problems creatively. Each success, however small, becomes a counterexample to your old belief. Over time, you build a new internal library of evidence that says "I am resourceful," which can override the old negative assumption.

When you restructure a negative belief, remember to replace it with a better one rather than leaving a vacuum. If you remove "I always fail," you might install "I am capable of learning from setbacks and improving." This new belief should be stated in positive, empowering language. The final step is repeated practice. Keep noticing your latest successes, keep revisiting your chosen beliefs, and keep the new structure of your experiences consistent until it becomes second nature.

## The Power of Values: Defining What Truly Matters

Shaping your beliefs about yourself is crucial, but beliefs are incomplete without understanding values. Values are like signposts, indicating what is essential in your life. When you identify your values, you gain better insight into why you make confident choices, which battles you decide to fight, and how you spend your time. For leaders, understanding one's values is essential for consistent decision-making and authentic influence.

### Values as Internal Projections

Nothing inherently possesses value. You decide that something is worthwhile, meaningful, or necessary. This concept means the source of value is within you, not in the object or experience itself. If you do not realize that you are assigning meaning, you risk chasing external sources of value—such as titles, approval, or possessions—believing that these will define your worth. Leaders who rely on external validation to feel valuable often do so because they experience unsteady self-esteem, making them more reactive to shifts in public opinion or workplace politics.

Turning inward to identify what you genuinely value helps you avoid living by default. When a leader is clear about the values guiding their decisions—fairness, innovation, empathy, or courage—those decisions remain consistent, even under pressure. Team members, in turn, sense that there is an authentic foundation for every call you make, and trust grows naturally from that.

## Discovering Your Values through Elicitation

One method for pinpointing values is often called a "value elicitation." Rather than scanning a random list of virtues and choosing a few that sound appealing, you investigate your life's contexts, such as career, relationships, health, or personal growth. You then ask yourself open-ended questions, like "What do I want in this area?" followed by "Why is that important to me?" or "What does that give me?" Continue this line of inquiry to go deep. Each answer peels back a layer, revealing deeper motivations.

For example, you might start by thinking "I want success in my career." Then you ask "Why is success important to me?" The answer could be "It provides security and recognition." Then ask, "Why is security and recognition important to me?" and so forth. Going deeper, you might discover that security is vital because it offers you independence and the chance to make creative choices.

As you keep pressing, you might unearth the thought that independence is crucial because it links to your authenticity. Authenticity might eventually lead you to understand that you are striving for peace of mind, love, or a deeper connection. By the time you finish, you have identified a chain of values, probably topped by a few that are highly central to you.

## Evaluating and Ranking Values

After uncovering a list, rank these values in order of importance for each context. Leaders sometimes make better decisions once they know that empathy might outrank efficiency in a conflict, or that innovation might trump short-term profit. When you need clarity, you can refer to your values ranking and sense which choice best aligns with your personal road map. Even if the situation is not straightforward, this framework gives you a more confident way to weigh the pros and cons.

Be cautious of "trap values" that might sound good, but can create conflict. Pride, for instance, can become destructive if it is about an inflated sense of achievement that is not rooted in genuine skill. Power over others often creates a zero-sum game that conflicts with collaborative leadership. Also, values like "fulfillment" can be so broad that it is more effective to identify the underlying values that produce that feeling of fulfillment.

## Align Your Values and Behaviors

Another crucial step is to ensure that you are embodying these top-tier values. It is not enough to declare a value, if you do not live it. If you say you value empathy, but rarely give team members the time or attention to be heard, there is a gap between your stated value and your actual behavior. True self-esteem arises when you say "I am an empathetic person," not because you read about empathy or give it lip service, but because you engage with others in ways that consistently demonstrate empathy.

This alignment of your daily leadership choices with your deeper values fosters a personal congruence that others find magnetic. It also keeps your identity stable under stress. If challenges arise—perhaps a dispute with a client or a project failing to launch—you can remain steady because your value of empathy, integrity, or perseverance is unshaken by circumstances.

Aim to engage in behaviors that honor your values. If you value open communication, consistently create opportunities for team members to voice their thoughts. If you value transparency, be willing to show the rationale behind decisions, even if it feels slightly uncomfortable. Whenever you act in line with your values, you reinforce your identity. The more often you do so, the more likely you are to believe "This is who I am."

When you face tough choices, refer to the top values you identified. Suppose you are deciding how to handle an underperforming employee.

If you rank empathy highly, you might schedule a respectful conversation to uncover the real issues. If your top values also include accountability, you will follow that conversation with a clear plan and timeline for improvement. This blend of empathy and responsibility is not a compromise, but an integrated approach that respects both core values.

### Revisiting and Updating Your Values

Values can shift as your life circumstances change. A newly appointed executive might place creativity and ambition at the top of the list, only to find that balance and health gain importance after a few years of intense workload. That does not mean that your old values were incorrect; it simply reflects the changing priorities in your life.

Doing a value elicitation every few months or each year can help you to be honest about what truly matters now, rather than what mattered in the past. In times of major transition—such as relocating, changing careers, or facing a personal milestone—revisiting your values can provide a stabilizing influence and help you make decisions that keep you aligned with your evolving self.

## Key Takeaways from this Chapter

Beliefs and values might seem abstract or personal, yet they directly affect how you lead. Whether you view yourself as a capable, adaptable individual or as one confined by old mistakes can determine your willingness to seize new opportunities. Whether you value compassion or speed above all else can guide how you handle team conflicts or business dilemmas.

This chapter explored the self-concept model, showing how experiences become qualities, qualities become beliefs, and beliefs combine into identity. We saw how a limiting identity can hamper a leader's impact, while a restructured one can grant new freedoms. We then looked at the power of values—why they originate from within, how to bring them into conscious awareness through formal elicitation, and why living them consistently can anchor your leadership style.

Ultimately, beliefs and values form the backbone of who you are as a leader. Embrace the work of discovering, refining, and updating them, and you will start seeing deeper authenticity, stronger resilience, and a more focused sense of purpose throughout your leadership journey.

A leader who understands how beliefs shape identity and how values direct choices possesses a powerful inner compass. This compass is not rigid. It evolves as you grow, as you change, and as you experience more of life. But for that evolution to be positive, you must cultivate a conscious awareness of your self-concept and remain clear on the values that define your purpose.

**Summary**

- **Journal Your Experiences:** As you note daily events, record not only what happened, but how you felt, what sense you used most, and how you interpreted it. This reflection can highlight hidden beliefs and values at play.
- **Identify a Positive Quality:** Think of one quality you are confident about—for example, maybe you know you are reliable. Explore how you store that certainty in your mind. Is it accompanied by strong imagery or a vivid sense of confidence? Then, map that structure to a quality where your certainty is weaker, such as "I am a strong presenter." It replicates the internal code from the first quality to the second.
- **Perform a Value Elicitation:** Pick a life context—for example, leadership, relationships, health, or personal development—and ask "What do I want?" Then dig deeper by asking "Why is that important?" until you reach the deeper motivations. Write these down, rank them, and reflect on how often you live by your top values.
- **Spot and Replace Limiting Beliefs:** Listen for language patterns that suggest fixed or negative assumptions about yourself. Gather evidence that contradicts these beliefs. Direct your mind to focus on real-life counterexamples and flesh out

those memories so they feel undeniable.

- **Align Actions with Values:** Choose at least one behavior each week that exemplifies a high-priority value. If you value collaboration, that means inviting a junior colleague to a strategy meeting. Each time you do so, acknowledge it: "I have just lived out my value of collaboration. This is who I am."
- **Review and Update:** Revisit both your self-beliefs and your values periodically. Leadership is fluid, and your identity evolves as you tackle new roles and challenges.

Now that we have introduced how you build awareness of and reframe your beliefs and values, in the following two chapters we will dig into some background information about leadership and leadership styles and thereafter get practical with identifying your style, your gaps, and your fit with the environment you find yourself in.

# Chapter Workout

The journey starts with examining your experiences, noticing the qualities and beliefs you have formed, and daring to ask if they still serve you. If they do not, you restructure your internal narrative, gather new evidence, or reinterpret the old. You also perform a deep dive into your values to see why they matter and how you can better live them. By continually refining your beliefs and values, you stand on a strong foundation—one that supports inspired action, genuine confidence, and leadership that resonates.

Work through the following exercises using your journal as your instrument of growth.

 Chapter 12 includes additional tools and techniques for continuous leadership development.

## Exercise 1: Exploring Your Self-Concept

Gain a deeper understanding of the beliefs that you hold about yourself and recognize how they shape your leadership identity.

**Instructions:**

1. **Reflect on Past Experiences:**
   - Write down three key leadership experiences—successes and challenges—that have shaped your view of yourself.
   - What did each experience teach you about your strengths, weaknesses, and leadership style?

2. **Identify Core Qualities:**
   - List adjectives you use to describe yourself as a leader (e.g., confident, creative, empathetic, reserved).
   - Which of these qualities do you consider as strengths? Which might be limiting?

3. **Analyze Your Beliefs:**
   - For each quality, ask yourself:
   - What experiences led me to believe that I possess this quality?
   - Are there moments that contradict this belief?

4. **Summarize how these experiences have solidified your self-concept and note any discrepancies that may be worth challenging.**

## Exercise 2: Identifying and Challenging Limiting Beliefs

Recognize any limiting beliefs that may be hindering your leadership potential and begin the process of reframing them.

**Instructions:**

1. **Spot Your Limiting Language:**
   - Think of times when you used phrases like "I can't," "I always," or "I'm not good enough."
   - Record at least three instances and the context in which they occurred.

2. **Question Their Validity:**
   - For each instance, ask:
   - Is this belief universally true, or are there exceptions?
   - What evidence do I have that contradicts this belief?

- Write down alternative, more-empowering statements (e.g., replace "I'm not a good public speaker" with "I can improve my public speaking through practice and feedback").

3. **Visualize Success:**
   - Imagine a recent scenario where you succeeded despite self-doubt.
   - Describe the scenario and how it challenges your limiting beliefs.

4. **Repeat your new empowering statements daily.**

## Exercise 3: Revisiting and Restructuring Past Experiences

Reframe past experiences to alter their influence on your self-beliefs and support a more empowering leadership identity.

**Instructions:**

1. **Select a Significant Memory:**
   - Choose an experience that has contributed to a limiting belief about your leadership (e.g., a failure or public criticism).

2. **Reconstruct the Experience:**
   - Break down the memory: what happened, how you felt, and how you interpreted the event.
   - How might I reframe this experience? Consider altering its size, intensity, or perspective (imagine observing it objectively from the outside).

3. **Extract New Lessons:**
    - Identify any positive outcomes or learning opportunities from that experience.
    - Write a revised narrative emphasizing growth and resilience rather than failure.

4. **Integrate the New Narrative:**
    - Commit to mentally and physically rehearsing your new interpretation when faced with similar situations.
    - Note any changes in your confidence or approach in subsequent leadership challenges.

## Exercise 4: Value Elicitation

Discover, clarify, and rank the values that matter most to you as a leader, forming the bedrock for consistent, authentic decision-making.

**Instructions:**

1. **Choose a Life Context:**
    - Pick a specific area, such as leadership, business relationships, or personal growth.
    - Ask yourself "What do I want in this area?" and then "Why is that important to me?"
    - Continue asking "why" until you reveal deeper motivations.

2. **List Your Values:**
    - Write down the values that emerge from your questioning (e.g., integrity, empathy, innovation, courage).
    - Reflect on moments when you felt most aligned with these values.

3. **Rank Your Values:**

- Order your values from most to least important.
- Explain your ranking. For example, why does integrity top your list, and how does it influence your decisions?

4. **Review Alignment:**
    - Reflect on your daily actions over the past week.
    - In what ways have you lived out your top values? Where did you fall short?

## Exercise 5: Aligning Actions with Your Values

Ensure that your everyday leadership decisions and behaviors consistently reflect your core values.

**Instructions:**

1. **Set a Weekly Value Action:**
    - Choose one core value from your ranked list.
    - Commit to a specific behavior demonstrating this value during the upcoming week (e.g., if you value open communication, schedule a feedback session with your team).

2. **Plan and Execute:**
    - Write down the steps you will take to embody this value.
    - What challenges might arise, and how will you overcome them?

3. **Reflect on Outcomes:**
    - At the end of the week, review your actions.
    - Describe what you did, how it felt, the team's response, and any lessons you learned.
    - Adjust your approach for next week based on your reflections.

## Exercise 6: Periodic Review and Update of Your Core Beliefs and Values

Maintain alignment with your evolving self-concept by regularly revisiting and updating your core beliefs and values.

**Instructions:**

1. **Schedule a Review Session:**
   - Set aside time every three to six months to review your beliefs and values deeply.
   - Reflect on changes in your life, leadership roles, or organizational context that might influence your priorities.

2. **Revisit Your Value Elicitation:**
   - Redo your value elicitation exercise (see Exercise 4) and compare your current list with your previous one.
   - What new values have emerged? Which old values remain relevant?

3. **Evaluate Alignment:**
   - Assess whether your recent decisions and behaviors continue to reflect your core values.
   - Identify gaps or misalignments and plan specific steps to address them.

4. **Set New Development Goals:**
   - Based on your review, update your leadership development action plan.
   - Write down any new SMART goals to help you better embody your updated beliefs and values.

# Chapter 2

# Unveiling the Essence of Leadership

*Serving others is at the core of outstanding leadership—it's about lifting people up, not holding power over them.*

Leadership isn't just a word; it's something that seeps into every part of our lives. Whether it's the teacher who ignites a love for learning or the entrepreneur who reshapes how we do business, leadership is what shapes our world in extraordinary ways. But what makes someone a leader? Is it about having a title or holding a position? Or is there something deeper that goes beyond all the formalities and hierarchies?

In this chapter, we're going to dig right into the heart of leadership—to understand what it's about. We'll explore how genuine leadership is about influence, not just authority, and why serving others is essential. We'll also discuss why trust is crucial, how to build a high-performing team, the need to keep innovation alive, and what legacy a leader leaves behind. By diving into all these ideas, we'll come away with a much clearer understanding of what it truly means to be a leader in today's complex world.

## Leadership Is About Influence

Leadership is about influence—the ability to inspire, motivate, and guide people toward a common goal. It's not about the title or the fancy office. Authentic leadership can come from anyone, anywhere. It emerges when people, no matter their rank or position, influence others through their actions, their thoughts, and who they are.

Think about Malala Yousafzai. She was just a teenager when she stood up against the Taliban's ban on girls' education in Pakistan. Despite facing incredible danger, her bravery sparked a global movement for educational equality. Malala didn't have a big title; she was just a fifteen-year-old girl with a powerful message. Her leadership came from her authenticity and how her message resonated with people worldwide.

Or think about that colleague of yours—the one who always seems to get everyone working together when a project gets tough, even though they aren't the official manager. Their energy and ability to rally the team are perfect examples of leadership without the title. Real influence isn't about authority; it's about connecting with people meaningfully and inspiring them to work toward a shared purpose.

## Cultivating Influence through Personal Qualities

Influence doesn't just appear out of nowhere; it's built over time through different qualities:

- Character: Integrity and authenticity are what give leaders their credibility. People respect and trust those who consistently stick to their values. When someone is honest and true to themselves, others naturally want to follow them.
- Relationships: Building real, genuine connections creates loyalty and cooperation. Great leaders take time to understand their people, to get to know their struggles and to support them. That's how you build teams that work together.
- Knowledge and Expertise: Competence breeds confidence. If leaders know what they're discussing and can back it up, others are more inclined to trust their guidance.
- Emotional Intelligence: Understanding and managing emotions—both your own and others—is crucial. Empathy helps leaders relate to their team members, which makes people feel valued and heard.

## The Power of Purpose

In his book *Start with Why*, Simon Sinek talks about the importance of finding the "why" behind what we do. When leaders are clear about their motivations, they tap into what drives people on a personal level. People follow those whose vision aligns with their own beliefs and values.

Take Patagonia, the outdoor clothing company founded by Yvon Chouinard. Their mission is simple: "Save our home planet." It's not just a slogan—it's the core of everything they do. By prioritizing sustainability, they've built a loyal community of customers and employees who want to be part of something bigger. This isn't just about selling jackets, it's about making a real difference.

## The Importance of Serving Others

Leadership isn't about holding power over people, but lifting them up. Serving others is at the core of outstanding leadership. Instead of making it all about personal success, it's about focusing on the well-being and growth of your team.

In her book *Multipliers*, Liz Wiseman talks about how the best leaders make everyone around them smarter and more capable. They don't keep power to themselves; they spread it around so everyone can shine. When people feel that their contributions matter, they become more engaged and motivated, and that's when real innovation and growth happen.

Nelson Mandela is the perfect example of this kind of leadership. After spending twenty-seven years in prison, he emerged without bitterness and dedicated himself to bringing a divided nation together. He focused on reconciliation and inclusivity, creating an environment where all South Africans could imagine a shared future. His humility and deep commitment to his people played a huge role in uniting a country that had been deeply fractured.

In business, Cheryl Bachelder, the former CEO of Popeyes Louisiana Kitchen, turned the company around by listening to franchisees and employees, addressing their needs, and empowering them to succeed. By focusing on others, she drove impressive growth in sales and profitability, proving that service-based leadership can deliver significant results.

Serving others means taking a few key actions:

- Providing Autonomy: Giving people responsibility and trusting them to do their jobs boosts their confidence and encourages creativity. When people feel empowered to make decisions, they're more invested in their work.
- Supporting Development: Investing in training and mentorship helps people reach their full potential. Leaders who encourage growth end up with stronger, more capable teams.
- Recognizing Contributions: Celebrating successes, big or small, makes people feel appreciated. Recognition builds a sense of belonging and motivates people to keep pushing forward.

Southwest Airlines is a great example. Herb Kelleher, their former CEO, put employee well-being first, believing that happy employees lead to happy customers. By fostering a supportive workplace, Southwest gained a reputation for excellent service and operational excellence.

Similarly, at Tata group, under the leadership of Natarajan Chandrasekaran, employee empowerment and development are prioritized. This focus has helped the company achieve sustained success across different industries.

## Creating a Circle of Safety

Simon Sinek's idea of a "circle of safety" in *Leaders Eat Last* is all about creating an environment where people feel secure, trusted, and valued. When people feel safe, they're more willing to collaborate and take risks. Creativity and resilience thrive in this kind of environment because people aren't worried about protecting themselves—they're focused on the team's success.

Novo Nordisk, the Danish pharmaceutical company, is an excellent example. They work hard to create an inclusive and supportive atmosphere, which has helped them to innovate in diabetes care and to build a strong, sustainable business. When people feel that their well-being is prioritized, they're more likely to give their best.

## Building Trust and Solid Foundations

Trust is the foundation of good leadership. Without it, communication breaks down, teamwork suffers, and goals become more challenging. Building trust is about showing integrity, being reliable, and respecting others consistently.

Amy C. Edmondson's research on psychological safety shows how crucial it is for people to feel safe when voicing ideas or taking risks. Organizations encouraging experimentation are often innovation leaders simply because people there aren't afraid to try, fail, and learn.

Fluid leadership is about recognizing that change is constant and embracing it. By creating a culture where people feel supported, leaders can help their teams handle uncertainty confidently. This kind of environment drives new ideas and helps everyone stay resilient when things get tough.

Brené Brown, in *Dare to Lead*, gives us a helpful way to think about trust with her BRAVING framework:

- Boundaries: Leaders set clear expectations and respect personal limits. It's about creating a predictable, safe space for everyone.
- Reliability: Keeping promises every time. People trust leaders who follow through.
- Accountability: Owning mistakes and making things right. Leaders who take responsibility create a culture where admitting errors and learning from them is okay.
- Vault: Trustworthy leaders keep confidence. They respect privacy and handle sensitive information with care.
- Integrity: Acting in line with your values, even when challenging. It's about choosing courage over comfort.
- Non-Judgment: Creating a space where people can talk openly

without fear of criticism. Listening without immediate judgment builds trust and openness.
- Generosity: Assuming positive intent from others. Giving people the benefit of the doubt goes a long way toward reducing conflicts and building understanding.

Brené Brown gives us a refreshing way to look at vulnerability in leadership. She clarifies that embracing vulnerability isn't a sign of weakness—rather, it builds absolute trust and connection, which are crucial for good leadership. Picture a leader who says "I don't have all the answers." That kind of honesty makes it safe for everyone else to speak up without fear of judgment. And when people feel secure, you get a more collaborative, creative team where everyone's ideas matter.

Authentic leaders connect on a fundamental human level. By showing who they are—the good, the bad, and the messy—they let others know that it's okay to do the same. This breaks down barriers and builds more substantial, more genuine relationships. Vulnerability isn't about being weak; it's about being brave enough to be accurate. It's a decisive move toward authentic leadership.

Take Satya Nadella, Microsoft's CEO, for example. He embraced vulnerability to transform the company's culture completely. He shifted the mindset from "know-it-all" to "learn-it-all," encouraging curiosity and constant growth. By admitting he didn't have all the answers and being open to feedback, Nadella fostered a culture of teamwork and innovation that has helped push Microsoft forward.

During her time as CEO of PepsiCo, Indra Nooyi also showed how trust can be built through personal gestures. She wrote letters to the parents of her senior executives, thanking them for supporting their children's careers. This simple, but profoundly personal gesture, created loyalty and showed how much she valued personal relationships.

On the other hand, when trust is broken, the consequences can be devastating. Take the Volkswagen emissions scandal. Dishonesty at the top led to financial disaster and a seriously damaged reputation. It's a powerful reminder of why integrity and transparency are essential in leadership.

## Building High-Performing Teams

No leader can succeed alone. One of the most critical skills a leader can have is building and nurturing a high-performing team. It's not just about finding talented people; it's about creating a group working together toward shared goals.

### Attracting the Right People

In *Good to Great*, Jim Collins discusses getting the "right people on the bus." This means choosing team members who align with the company's values and culture. Skills can be learned, but the right attitude and character are essential.

Google is famous for its thorough hiring process. It looks for more than technical skills; it also focuses on cultural fit and problem-solving abilities. By hiring people who thrive in a collaborative, creative environment, Google keeps pushing the boundaries of innovation.

### Creating a Positive Culture

A positive work culture can make all the difference in productivity and job satisfaction. Leaders set the tone by modeling respect, openness, and enthusiasm.

Take SAIC Motor Corporation, one of China's biggest car manufacturers. They've created a positive culture by promoting innovation and teamwork. Leaders at SAIC encourage collaboration across different teams and open communication, making employees feel valued and motivated to do their best.

### Empowering Team Members

Empowering your team means trusting them with responsibilities and giving them the freedom to do the job. Micromanaging crushes creativity and kills trust, but empowerment builds ownership and accountability.

Toyota offers a good example of this. Through the Toyota Production

System (TPS), employees are encouraged to take charge of their work, suggest improvements, and solve problems proactively. This approach has helped Toyota build its reputation for quality and efficiency.

## Encouraging Diversity and Inclusion

Building a high-performing team also means embracing diversity in every sense. Diverse teams bring different perspectives, which spark creativity and lead to better decisions.

Under Paul Polman's leadership, Unilever has made huge strides in promoting diversity and inclusion. By supporting gender equality and cultural diversity, they have improved their workplace culture and expanded their global success by appealing to a broader customer base.

## Fostering Innovation and Achieving Results

Leaders must create environments where creativity is encouraged and taking risks is good. Good leaders face challenges head-on. Jim Collins calls this confronting the "brutal facts" of reality. Acknowledging the tough stuff instead of ignoring it helps leaders make better decisions and build more potent strategies.

Look at Kodak's reluctance to embrace digital photography. Even though they invented the first digital camera, they failed to realize that digital would replace film. That denial led to missed opportunities and, eventually, bankruptcy. In contrast, Fujifilm diversified and embraced new technologies, showing the importance of adapting and being open to change.

Collins also talks about the "Hedgehog Concept," which is about focusing on three key areas:

1. Passion: What makes the organization genuinely excited?
2. Best At: What can the organization do better than anyone else?
3. Economic Engine: What drives financial sustainability?

When organizations focus on these core areas, they can channel their energy effectively and achieve great results.

Take Samsung Electronics. Their commitment to innovation and technological excellence has made them a global leader, especially in smartphones and semiconductors.

## Cultivating Discipline

Discipline turns good ideas into action. It's about having transparent processes, setting priorities, and staying focused even when distractions arise.

Jeff Bezos, Amazon's founder, often talks about a "Day 1" mentality. It's all about maintaining urgency and focus. Amazon's disciplined approach to customer obsession, efficiency, and long-term thinking has driven consistent growth and innovation. The "Two-Pizza Team" rule—keeping teams small enough that two pizzas can feed everyone—helps ensure agility and accountability.

## Encouraging a Growth Mindset

Carol Dweck's concept of a growth mindset is based on the belief that abilities can be developed with dedication and hard work. Leaders who encourage this mindset make it okay for people to learn from failure.

Tencent, a leading Chinese tech company, encourages continuous learning and adaptation. Focusing on employee development and creating innovation hubs has driven its success across multiple digital sectors.

## Balancing Risk and Innovation

Innovation means taking risks, and leaders must balance the potential rewards with the uncertainties that come with them.

Elon Musk's ventures with Tesla and SpaceX are perfect examples of bold risk-taking. Despite facing challenges and skepticism, his commitment to electric vehicles and space exploration has led to significant breakthroughs. Musk's resilience shows that taking calculated risks can lead to game-changing outcomes.

## The Importance of Legacy and Continuous Growth

Leadership isn't just about what's happening now; it's also about the long-term impact you leave behind. A strong legacy means nurturing future leaders and building sustainable practices that last.

Simon Sinek's *The Infinite Game* idea focuses on lasting success rather than quick wins. This mindset builds resilience and encourages sustained growth. Companies that invest in employee development might sacrifice some short-term profits, but they make a loyal, skilled workforce that pays off in the long run.

This kind of thinking applies to all areas of life. In relationships, communities, and personal goals, thinking long-term often leads to better, more meaningful outcomes.

Mentoring and coaching are key to developing future leaders. When today's leaders invest in others, they ensure that their organization stays strong and adaptable.

Ruth Porat, CFO of Alphabet Inc., has had a significant influence on mentoring upcoming leaders at its subsidiary Google, encouraging strategic thinking and financial savvy that will help drive the company's growth.

Great leaders are always learning. They're open to feedback, new experiences, and adapting as things change.

Warren Buffett, one of the world's most successful investors, spends much of his day reading and learning. His commitment to lifelong learning has been key to his success, helping him adapt and seize opportunities as they come.

Their positive changes measure a leader's legacy—not just in their organization, but in the broader world.

Bill Gates, cofounder of Microsoft, shifted his focus from running a tech company to tackling global challenges through the Bill & Melinda Gates Foundation. By addressing health, education, and poverty, Gates has impacted society far beyond business.

Sustainability is becoming increasingly crucial in leadership. Focusing on environmental and social responsibility helps create a better future for everyone.

Jim Collins talks about Level 5 Leadership, combining humility and fierce determination. These leaders put the organization's success ahead of their egos. They're the ones who give credit to their teams instead of seeking the spotlight.

Humility doesn't weaken authority; it strengthens it. Leaders build trust and inspire outstanding commitment by recognizing others' contributions and focusing on shared goals.

## Misconceptions About Leadership

Understanding what leadership isn't is just as important as understanding what it is.

### Myth: Leaders Are Born, Not Made

The belief that leadership is something you're born with keeps many people from stepping up. However, countless examples show that leadership skills can be learned and developed. Anyone can grow into a leadership role with effort and the proper guidance.

Leadership is a collection of skills and attitudes that can be cultivated. Embracing this idea means that more people feel empowered to step up and make a difference.

### Myth: Leadership Requires Formal Authority

Many people think you need a title to lead; but authentic leadership often comes from action, not position. During a crisis, people usually emerge as leaders by stepping up to address what needs to be done, regardless of their role.

Recognizing that anyone can lead creates more opportunities for positive impact. It encourages people to take the initiative whenever they see a chance to make a difference.

## Key Takeaways from this Chapter

Leadership involves influencing others through service, trust, and authenticity. By empowering people, building strong teams, fostering innovation, and thinking about the legacy we leave, we can lead with real purpose and impact. This kind of leadership drives organizational success and contributes to the growth and well-being of individuals and communities. It's the foundation of fluid leadership.

Embracing the essence of leadership helps us navigate the complexities of our world and inspire others to achieve amazing things. Leadership isn't a destination—it's an ongoing journey of growth, learning, and making a positive difference.

**Summary**

- **Leadership is Influence:** True leadership inspires others through character, vision, and relationships, not just relying on authority.
- **Serve to Lead:** By prioritizing the growth and well-being of others, leaders build loyalty and unlock their team's potential.
- **Trust is Foundational:** Building trust requires consistency, integrity, and vulnerability, creating a safe environment for collaboration.
- **Team-Building is Essential:** High-performing teams are built by attracting the right people, nurturing a positive culture, and empowering individuals.
- **Innovation Requires Courage and Discipline:** Leaders must encourage creativity while staying focused and executing effectively.
- **Legacy Matters:** Investing in future leaders and embracing lifelong learning ensures long-term success and impact.

As we've discussed, leadership is a journey built on influence, service, trust, team-building, innovation, and legacy. But the world keeps changing, and so must leadership.

The next chapter will examine how leadership has evolved and what it might look like. We'll dive into emerging trends, the impact of technology, and how leaders can adapt to new challenges. By understanding where leadership is heading, we'll be better equipped to face the future confidently and purposefully.

# Chapter Workout

Feel free to journal any or all topics covered in this chapter. Below are some suggested exercises to help you explore these ideas and put them into practice.

## Exercise 1: Cultivating Influence through Personal Qualities

**Objective:** Enhance the personal attributes that contribute to your influence as a leader.

**Instructions:**

1. Take a moment to assess your current personal qualities and consider how they impact your leadership.
2. Plan a few actionable steps you can take to strengthen these qualities.

**Journaling Prompts:**

- List your top three personal qualities that make you a more decisive leader. Can you describe specific examples of how each quality has positively impacted your team or organization?
- Is there one personal quality that you need to develop further? What actions could you take to nurture this quality?
- Think of a leader you admire on a global scale. What are the personal qualities they have that you'd like to emulate? How can you start incorporating these traits into your leadership style?

## Exercise 2: The Power of Purpose

**Objective:** Gain clarity about your purpose and align it with your organization to drive motivation and engagement.

**Instructions:**

1. Define your core purpose and consider how it aligns with your organization's mission.
2. Explore how you can communicate and embody this purpose in your leadership.

**Journaling Prompts:**

- What's your personal "why" as a leader? How does it line up with your organization's mission and values?
- Describe a time when your sense of purpose inspired your team to reach an important goal. What was the outcome?
- How can you better communicate your purpose to your team so they feel a shared mission?
- Are there any gaps between your purpose and your current role? If so, how can you bridge these to bring better alignment?

## Exercise 3: The Importance of Serving Others

**Objective:** Embrace servant leadership by putting your team's growth and well-being first.

**Instructions:**

1. Reflect on how you serve your team and identify ways to enhance your supportive role.

**Journaling Prompts:**

- Think about a time when you empowered someone on your team to succeed. What actions did you take, and what was the outcome?
- How do you balance your responsibilities with the needs of your team? Are there areas where you could improve this balance?
- What are the most effective ways to support your team's professional growth? List some specific initiatives or practices that you can implement.
- Reflect on any feedback you've received from your team. How can you adjust your leadership approach to serve their needs better?

# Chapter 3

# The Evolution and Future of Leadership

*Fluid leaders embrace learning, experimentation, and flexibility to navigate complexity.*

Leadership has never been a fixed concept. As societies evolve and the world becomes more connected, we change how we lead and influence others. From the authoritative leaders of the past to today's collaborative styles, the journey of leadership reflects the changes in our cultures, technologies, and workplaces. This chapter will explore how leadership has transformed over time and what the future might hold.

Think about the leaders you've encountered or learned about—figures from history books, mentors at work, or even influencers on social media. Notice how different they all are? Leadership isn't a one-size-fits-all thing. It's shaped by the times we live in, the challenges we face, and the people involved. As our world changes, so does the way we lead.

This chapter examines how leadership has evolved and what's next. We'll explore the shift from command-and-control models to more empowering approaches, the rising importance of emotional intelligence, and how technology is reshaping what it means to be a leader.

## The Early Ideas about Leadership

### The Great Man Theory: Born to Lead?

Back in the nineteenth and early twentieth centuries, people believed leaders were born, not made. This idea, known as the Great Man Theory, suggested that certain people had innate qualities that made them natural-born leaders. These exceptional individuals were seen as destined to rise during significant events and shape history through their actions. Think of figures like Alexander the Great or Queen Victoria—people thought they were meant for greatness because of who they were.

The Great Man Theory was popular because it explained why some individuals significantly impacted the world. It focused on traits like charisma, intelligence, and courage. But it had its flaws. It didn't consider the impact of environment, education, or experience, and it largely ignored the potential of women and people from diverse backgrounds—reflecting the biases of society at the time.

### Trait Theory: Identifying Leadership Qualities

Building on the idea that some traits make a leader, researchers in the early twentieth century explored Trait Theory. They aimed to identify specific characteristics common among effective leaders. They looked at traits like confidence, integrity, and sociability, hoping to create a profile of the ideal leader.

For example, a company might look for candidates with high determination and intelligence, thinking these traits predict leadership success. Trait Theory helped us understand that personal qualities matter, but it had its limits. Not all great leaders share the same characteristics, and just having those traits doesn't guarantee success. Context matters—a lot—and that's something Trait Theory didn't fully address.

## Shifting Focus to Behaviors

### Behavioral Theories: Actions Speak Louder

As researchers realized the limits of focusing only on traits, they began to look at what leaders do—their behaviors. Behavioral theories suggest that effective leadership is more about actions that can be learned than qualities you're born with. This shift opened the possibility that anyone could become a leader through learning and development.

In the 1940s and 1950s, studies at Ohio State University and the University of Michigan identified two main leadership behaviors: task-oriented and people-oriented. Task-oriented leaders define roles, set goals, and ensure that tasks are done efficiently. People-oriented leaders focus more on building relationships, supporting team members, and creating a positive work environment.

According to these theories, an effective leader balances both behaviors. Imagine a project manager who not only sets clear objectives and deadlines, but also takes the time to understand team members' concerns and offers encouragement. By combining these approaches, the leader boosts productivity while keeping morale high.

## The Managerial Grid: Finding the Balance

In the 1960s, Robert Blake and Jane Mouton introduced the *Managerial Grid*, a model that maps leadership styles based on concern for people and production. The grid helps leaders identify their default style and consider areas for growth.

Picture the grid as a simple graph. On one axis, you have concern for people; on the other, you are concerned about production. A leader who scores high on both practices, i.e. "Team Leader" (see list below), is considered the most effective by Blake and Mouton. This leader values team members' needs and goal achievement, creating a collaborative and high-performing environment. On the other hand, a leader with low concern for people, but high concern for production, might focus solely on results, which can lead to burnout or dissatisfaction among team members. The Managerial Grid encourages leaders to reflect on their style and find a balance that promotes efficiency and a positive workplace culture.

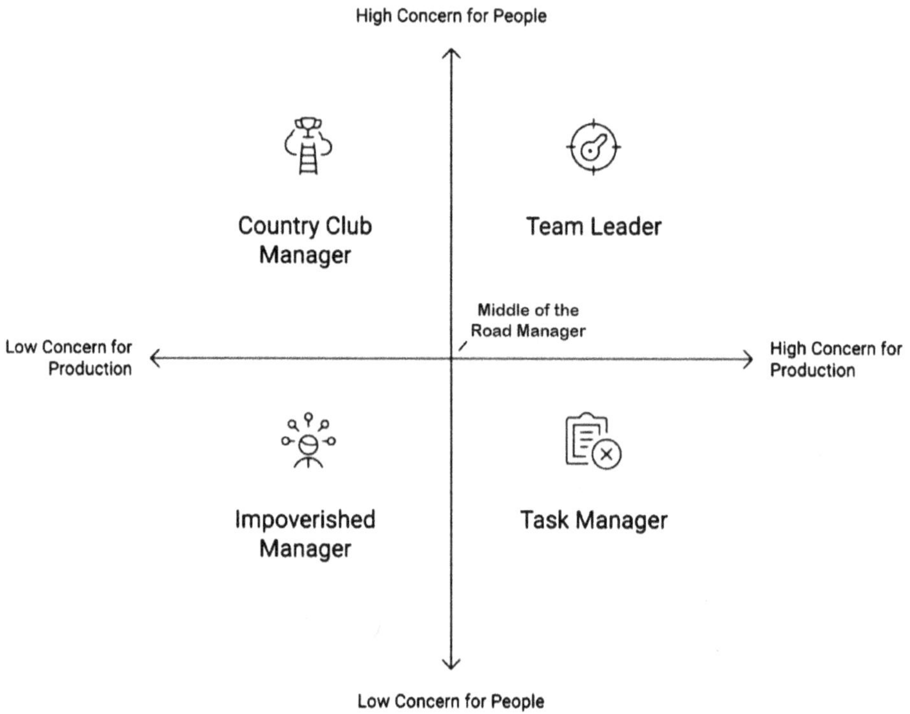


*Figure 1: The Managerial Grid*

- Impoverished Manager (1,1): This style reflects minimal concern for people and production. Leaders who adopt this style tend to be disengaged and ineffective, leading to low morale and productivity.
- Country Club Manager (1,9): Leaders with this style prioritize their team's needs and feelings over productivity. While they create a friendly and comfortable work environment, this can lead to a lack of focus on achieving organizational goals.
- Task Manager (9,1): This style emphasizes high productivity with little regard for team members' needs. Leaders who adopt this approach are often authoritarian, focusing solely on task completion, which can result in high turnover and low morale.

- Middle-of-the-Road Manager (5,5): This style balances concern for people and production. While it aims for moderate performance and team satisfaction, it often results in mediocrity, as neither dimension is fully prioritized.
- Team Leader (9,9): This is the ideal leadership style, where leaders demonstrate deep concern for people and production. This approach fosters a collaborative environment, encouraging team members to contribute to their fullest potential while achieving organizational goals.

## Considering the Situation

### Contingency Theories: It Depends

As research evolved, it became clear that only some leadership styles work in some situations. What's effective in one context might not work in another. This led to the development of contingency theories, which propose that the success of a leadership style depends on the context.

Fred Fiedler's *Contingency Theory* (or *Model*) is a well-known example. Fiedler suggested that a leader's effectiveness depends on how well their style matches the favorableness of the situation. Factors like the quality of relationships, task structure, and the leader's positional power all play a role.

For example, a task-oriented style might be very effective in a setting where tasks are well-defined, and the leader has authority and good relationships with the team. However, a people-oriented approach might be better in a more ambiguous environment with less formal authority. Fiedler's model shows how important it is to align your leadership style with the situation.

## Situational Leadership: Adapting to Followers' Needs

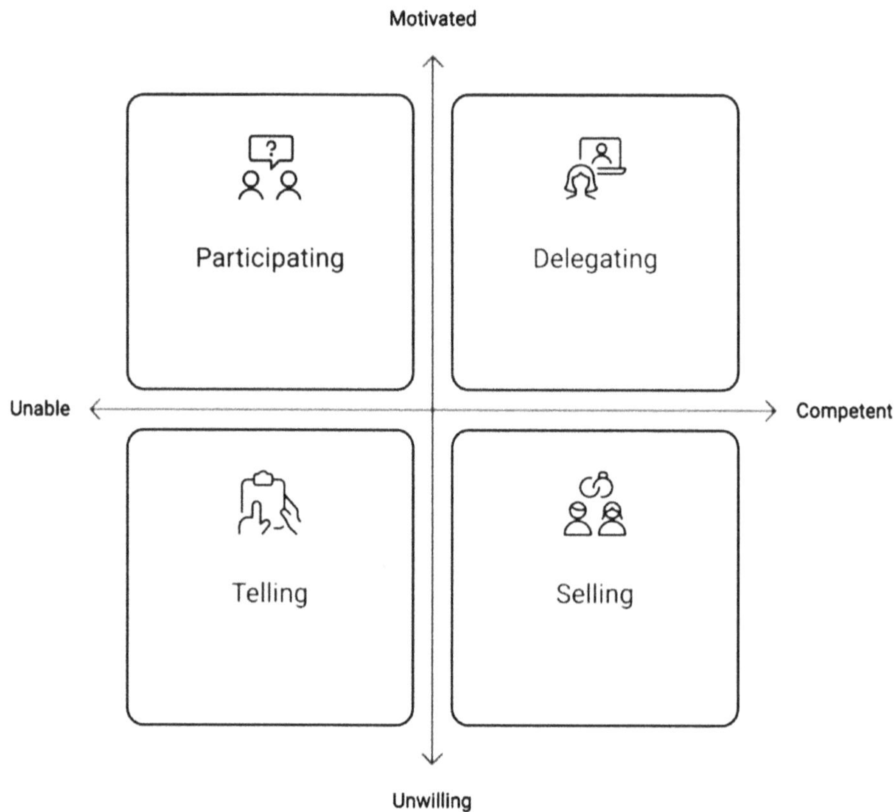


*Figure 2: Situational Leadership*

Building on contingency ideas, Paul Hersey and Ken Blanchard developed the *Situational Leadership Model*, which emphasizes that leaders should adapt their style based on the readiness and competence of their followers.

Think of a sports coach working with both novice and experienced players. With beginners, the coach might be more directive, giving clear instructions and close supervision. As players develop, the coach might shift to a more supportive or hands-off style, encouraging them to take more initiative.

Situational Leadership identifies four main styles:

1. Telling (Directing): High task focus, low relationship focus.
2. Selling (Coaching): High task focus, high relationship focus.
3. Participating (Supporting): Low task focus, high relationship focus.
4. Delegating: Low task focus, low relationship focus.

By assessing followers' development levels, leaders can adjust their approach to be most effective. This model reinforces the idea that flexibility and responsiveness are key leadership qualities.

## How the Role of Leadership Will Continue to Evolve

### The Rise of the "Leader-Leader" Model

As the world became more complex, the limitations of the traditional model became obvious. Organizations needed to be more agile, innovative, and responsive to change. That's where the "leader-leader" model comes in—a concept made popular by L. David Marquet in his book *Turn the Ship Around!*

Marquet, a former US Navy submarine captain, found himself in charge of the USS *Santa Fe*, a submarine that he didn't know well. Realizing that he couldn't have all the answers, he empowered his crew instead. By pushing decision-making down the chain of command, he turned his team from passive followers into proactive leaders.

One key strategy Marquet used was giving his crew more responsibility. For example, he let department chiefs approve leave for their team members—a task usually reserved for higher-ranking officers. This small change restored their confidence and gave them absolute ownership. When people feel trusted, they're more engaged and committed.

This approach led to incredible results. The USS *Santa Fe* went from being one of the worst-performing submarines in the fleet to one of the best. Crew retention rates improved, and operational readiness increased. Marquet's experience showed that when people are given control and accountability, they rise to the challenge.

Marquet also introduced the idea of "deliberate action." Crew members were encouraged to pause, think through their actions, and explain their intentions before moving forward. This reduced mistakes and boosted accountability.

Instead of acting automatically, a sailor would say, "I intend to submerge the ship," and explain why. This allowed others to provide input or spot potential issues, shifting the culture from blind obedience to shared understanding and collaboration.

Marquet also puts a big emphasis on competence. Crew members had to show that they knew what they were doing before taking on key tasks. This focus on mastery ensured that empowerment didn't come at the cost of performance.

Old-fashioned leadership models, with their strict top-down approach and rigid hierarchies, are becoming relics of the past. We're seeing a shift toward more collaborative and empowering styles. The "leader-leader" model, which L. David Marquet discusses in *Turn the Ship Around!*, is about spreading leadership throughout the organization. It means giving people at all levels the power to make decisions and genuinely own their work.

Take Valve Corporation, a video game developer known for its flat structure. At Valve, employees get to pick the projects they want to work on, which gives them a real sense of ownership and accountability. This setup doesn't just spark creativity; it also helps the company adapt quickly to industry changes and new technologies. By letting everyone have a say, Valve has built a culture that thrives on innovation and flexibility—exactly what's needed in today's fast-moving tech world.

When people feel empowered, they're more engaged and motivated, which leads to higher productivity and job satisfaction. This collaborative environment also encourages the free flow of ideas, driving constant improvement and nurturing a culture of innovation. As the world keeps speeding up, companies that embrace empowerment and collaboration will be best equipped to handle the future's complexities.

## From Transactional to Transformational

We're also seeing a move away from transactional leadership models, which focus heavily on tasks and rewards, toward transformational approaches that aim to inspire people to reach their full potential. Transformational leaders share a vision, build trust, encourage collaboration, and genuinely invest in their team members' growth.

Take Howard Schultz, the former CEO of Starbucks, as an example. Schultz transformed Starbucks from a small coffee chain into a global brand by creating a positive company culture and investing in employee development. He believed in the power of shared values and vision, urging employees to take pride in their work and be part of something bigger. This didn't just boost employee morale—it also built strong customer loyalty and supported long-term business growth.

Transformational leaders inspire their teams to go beyond just getting the job done. They create a sense of purpose and a commitment that goes way beyond completing tasks. Transformational leadership sets the foundation for long-term success and resilience by ensuring people feel valued and empowered.

## From Hero to Facilitator

The image of the lone, heroic leader who drives all organizational success on their own is being replaced by a more facilitative approach. Today's leaders are more like guides or facilitators—they focus on building consensus, empowering others, and creating environments where diverse ideas can flourish.

Look at Mary Barra, CEO of General Motors. Barra has shifted GM's leadership style from the old-school top-down model to one that values collaboration and inclusivity. She's encouraged open dialogue and empowered employees at every level to contribute ideas. This approach has been a big part of GM's push toward electric and autonomous vehicles, keeping the company relevant in an industry that's changing rapidly.

Facilitative leaders create spaces where ideas can take root, sparking creativity and innovation. Empowering their teams and building consensus, they help ensure their organizations stay agile and ready for whatever comes next.

## From Technical Expertise to Emotional Intelligence

Technical skills are still important, but the future of leadership is increasingly emphasizing emotional intelligence. Leaders must understand and manage emotions, build relationships, communicate effectively, and make people feel like they belong.

Sheryl Sandberg, former COO of Facebook (now Meta), is a great example of a leader who balances technical know-how with emotional intelligence. Her focus on empathy and good communication has been key to creating a supportive, inclusive environment at Meta. Sandberg's style encourages open conversations, ensuring that employees feel heard and valued. This emphasis on emotional intelligence helps build stronger teams and drives innovation by creating a safe space where people feel comfortable sharing ideas and taking risks.

Leaders with strong emotional intelligence are better equipped to navigate the complexities of human relationships, resolve conflicts, and build cohesive teams. This human-centric approach is essential for maintaining morale and ensuring long-term success in today's digital and interconnected world.

## Shifting to Empowerment and Collaboration

For much of history, leadership was all about authority. Leaders gave orders, and everyone else was expected to follow without question. This "leader-follower" model worked when stability and uniformity mattered more than innovation or individual expression.

Think back to the early days of industrialization. Factories ran like well-oiled machines, with workers performing repetitive tasks under close supervision. The focus was all about efficiency and consistency. Leaders made the decisions, and workers carried them out. This top-down approach worked for mass production, but more was needed for creativity or personal growth.

In the military, this model was even more pronounced. Orders were given, and obedience was expected without hesitation. The chain of command was clear, and authority rested firmly at the top. While this structure was effective for coordination in some situations, it often stifled individual initiative.

## New Perspectives on Leadership

### Emotional Intelligence: Connecting with Others

Emotional intelligence (EI) is about understanding and managing one's emotions and those of others. Leaders with strong EI communicate well, show empathy, and handle conflicts effectively.

Picture a team under pressure with tight deadlines. A leader with high emotional intelligence recognizes the signs of burnout and takes action to help. They might re-prioritize tasks, give some words of encouragement, or take the time to listen to everyone's concerns.

Emotionally intelligent leaders boost team cohesion and performance by creating a supportive environment. EI has become an essential leadership skill, helping leaders build strong relationships and ensure the success of their organizations.

### Ethical Leadership: Doing the Right Thing

Ethical leadership means prioritizing integrity, fairness, and social responsibility. Ethical leaders consider the broader impact of their decisions on all stakeholders and society.

Take a manufacturing company facing a decision between cutting costs in a way that could harm the environment or investing in sustainable practices. An ethical leader chooses sustainability, even if it means sacrificing short-term profits. Companies like Unilever have built their success on moral principles, making sustainability a core part of their business.

Ethical leadership builds trust with employees, customers, and the broader community. It enhances reputations and ensures long-term success by aligning business practices with societal values.

## Cross-Cultural Leadership: Embracing Cultural Diversity

Leaders often work with teams that span different cultures. Cross-cultural leadership is about understanding and navigating cultural differences to enable effective collaboration.

Think of a project team with members from Japan, Germany, and Brazil. They likely have different communication styles, attitudes toward hierarchy, and decision-making methods. A good cross-cultural leader recognizes these differences and adjusts their approach. They might encourage discussions that ensure that everyone's voice is heard, adapt communication methods, and respect cultural norms.

The rise of remote work, driven by the 2020 pandemic, has changed how leaders manage teams. Building trust and maintaining company culture without face-to-face interaction is a new challenge.

Amy C. Edmondson's work on psychological safety is even more critical in virtual environments. Leaders must ensure that team members feel connected and valued, even when physically apart.

Understanding cultural dimensions, such as those outlined by Geert Hofstede—like individualism versus collectivism or power distance—helps leaders bridge gaps and anticipate misunderstandings. By valuing diversity, leaders can enhance creativity and innovation within their teams.

Cultural intelligence (CQ) is the ability to work effectively in different cultural contexts. It involves cognitive, motivational, and behavioral skills.

A leader with high CQ is genuinely curious about other cultures, understands the nuances, and adjusts their behavior as needed. For example, they might learn key phrases in another language or adapt their leadership style to suit local customs better.

With Generation Z entering the workforce, leaders must understand its values and expectations. Gen Z is known for valuing authenticity, diversity, and social responsibility.

Leaders must create work environments that support flexibility, provide meaningful tasks, and offer growth opportunities. Embracing technology and building a culture that aligns with these values will be essential for attracting and keeping top talent.

### Fluid Leadership: Navigating Complexity

Fluid leadership is becoming more prominent as the world becomes more complex and unpredictable. Fluid leaders understand that old methods may not solve today's emerging challenges. They embrace learning, experimentation, and staying flexible.

Imagine a company dealing with disruptive technological changes. A fluid leader isn't just sticking to what's worked in the past. Instead, they get the team involved in finding new solutions. They might introduce agile working methods, encourage collaboration across different departments, and stay open to changing the plan.

Fluid leadership is especially relevant in industries experiencing rapid change. It gives organizations the tools they need to handle uncertainty and grab new opportunities as they come.

## The Role of Technology in Leadership

Technology has completely transformed organizations' operations, and leaders must be comfortable navigating this digital landscape. Digital leadership is using technology to improve processes, communication, and innovation.

During the COVID-19 pandemic, many leaders had to figure out how to transition to remote work quickly. Those who embraced digital tools—like video conferencing, project management software, and virtual collaboration platforms—kept their teams connected and productive.

Digital leaders also look at the bigger picture, considering the strategic impact of emerging technologies like artificial intelligence (AI) and data analytics. They encourage digital literacy within their teams and foster a culture ready to adapt to tech advancements.

Artificial intelligence, for instance, can provide insights into customer behavior, streamline operations, and improve decision-making. Virtual and augmented reality can also be used for training, simulating complex scenarios and enhancing learning experiences.

Companies like Siemens use virtual reality for training, giving employees a safe, controlled space to practice skills. This kind of innovation helps with learning and keeps costs down.

Marshall Goldsmith once said "What got you here won't get you there." Leaders must keep learning and adapting to new tools and platforms. Embracing technology isn't just about efficiency; it's about staying relevant in a fast-evolving world.

While technology has many advantages, leaders need to balance it with the human element. Too much reliance on digital communication can lead to disconnection or misunderstandings.

Good leaders maintain personal connections, even in virtual settings. They might schedule regular one-on-one check-ins, organize virtual social events, or use video calls to keep interactions more personal.

Leaders must also consider ethical technology-related issues, like data privacy and cybersecurity. By balancing tech efficiency with a focus on human well-being, they lead responsibly through the digital age.

Many leaders today have a public presence beyond their companies, often using social media to connect with a broader audience. This can humanize leaders and make them more accessible.

Simon Sinek's TED Talk about starting with "why" holds great insights. His message reached millions and influenced leaders around the world. However, being visible also means being under constant scrutiny, so leaders must be authentic and consistent in what they say and do.

Data-driven decision-making is now a cornerstone of effective leadership. Jim Collins talks about the importance of confronting the brutal facts. Leaders must be willing to look at data objectively, even when it's uncomfortable.

But relying only on data isn't enough. Good leaders balance data with intuition and human insight to make well-rounded, informed, empathetic decisions.

## Key Takeaways from this Chapter

Leadership today is all about evolving with the changing world. Moving away from rigid hierarchies, modern leaders focus on fluidity, empowerment, collaboration, and putting people at the center. Emotional intelligence, adaptability, and a commitment to continuous learning are vital for effective leadership.

Technology provides both opportunities and challenges. Leaders who can leverage technological advancements while prioritizing human connection are well positioned to drive innovation and build engaged, resilient teams.

Looking ahead, the most successful leaders will inspire others through authenticity and purpose, nurture leadership skills across their teams, and navigate the complexities of a fast-changing world with empathy and foresight.

Leadership isn't about reaching a destination—it's an ongoing journey. Leaders can create lasting positive impacts that resonate far beyond their organizations by learning from the past and staying open to new ideas.

### Summary

- **Leadership is Evolving:** The old command-and-control leadership styles are being replaced by more collaborative and empowering approaches. Modern leadership is about valuing input from everyone, regardless of their level in the organization.
- **Human-Centered Leadership:** Empathy, vulnerability, and authenticity are vital traits for today's leaders. These qualities help build trust and foster strong, positive relationships.
- **Technology Is a Tool, Not a Replacement:** Technology can

boost efficiency and connection, but it should never replace genuine human interaction. Maintaining personal connections remains crucial.

- **Emotional Intelligence is Crucial:** Skills like empathy, self-awareness, and good interpersonal communication are more critical than ever, especially in our increasingly digital world.
- **Developing Leaders at All Levels:** Creating opportunities for leadership development across the organization helps build a pipeline of capable leaders and fosters a culture of responsibility and growth.
- **Purpose-Driven Leadership Inspires:** Aligning your organization's goals with a greater purpose inspires employees and customers, building loyalty and motivation.
- **Adaptability is Key:** Today's leaders must be ready to handle uncertainty. Adapting quickly to rapid changes in technology or global circumstances is essential.
- **Ethical Leadership Matters:** Acting with integrity and keeping social responsibility in mind is crucial for maintaining trust with stakeholders, from employees to customers.
- **Understanding Future Generations:** With new generations entering the workforce, leaders must be flexible, adapting to their values and expectations to attract and retain talent.

In the next chapter, we'll delve into the significance of leadership styles. We'll uncover how these styles shape various facets of an organization, why leaders need to adapt to different circumstances, and how leadership approaches affect individuals and teams.

# Chapter Workout

To deepen your understanding of leadership's evolving nature, assess your leadership style considering historical and modern theories, and develop skills to adapt to future leadership challenges.

## Exercise 1: Behavioral Approaches to Leadership

**Task-Oriented vs. People-Oriented Behaviors:**

- **Prompt:** Assess your predominant leadership behavior. Do you tend to focus more on tasks or on people? Share specific instances where this behavior has been effective or may have held your team back.
- **Prompt:** Using Robert Blake and Jane Mouton's Managerial Grid, evaluate your concern for people vs. your concern for production. Where do you fall on the grid? What steps could help you achieve a more balanced or team-oriented leadership style?

## Exercise 2: Situational and Contingency Leadership

**Situational Leadership Model:**

- **Prompt:** Reflect on a time when you adapted your leadership style based on your team's readiness and competence, using Hersey and Blanchard's Situational Leadership Model. What was the outcome?

- **Prompt:** Consider a scenario where your leadership style was either effective or ineffective due to the specific context. What factors played a role in this outcome, and how can you align your style better with situational needs in the future?

## Exercise 3: Modern Leadership Theories

**Transformational vs. Transactional Leadership:**

- **Prompt:** Compare transformational leadership with transactional leadership. Which one do you lean toward? How does it impact your team's motivation and performance? Can you integrate aspects of the other style to strengthen your leadership?
- **Prompt:** Consider how you approach servant leadership and authentic leadership. How do you prioritize your team's growth and well-being? How do you ensure that your actions align with your core values and beliefs?

## Exercise 4: Adaptive and Ethical Leadership

**Fluid Leadership:**

- **Prompt:** How do you demonstrate fluid leadership in an increasingly complex and unpredictable environment? Give examples of how you've navigated unexpected challenges by encouraging learning and staying flexible.
- **Prompt:** How do you incorporate ethical leadership into your decision-making? Can you recall when you had to choose between profitability and doing the right thing? What did you learn from that experience?

## Exercise 5: Cross-Cultural Leadership and Emotional Intelligence

**Cross-Cultural Leadership:**

- **Prompt:** How do you practice cross-cultural leadership if you lead a diverse team? Describe the strategies you use to bridge cultural differences and promote effective collaboration.
- **Prompt:** Assess your level of emotional intelligence. How do you manage your emotions and understand the feelings of your team members? Provide examples of how EI has improved your leadership.

## Exercise 6: The Role of Technology in Leadership

**Digital Leadership:**

- **Prompt:** How do you leverage technology to improve your leadership practices? Reflect on when digital tools enhanced your team's communication or productivity.
- **Prompt:** Consider how you balance technological efficiency with maintaining human connections in your leadership. How do you ensure that technology serves to enhance—rather than replace—personal interactions?

## Exercise 7: Preparing for the Workforce of the Future

- **Prompt:** With Generation Z entering the workforce, how are you adapting your leadership style to meet their values and expectations? What initiatives could help you attract and retain this new generation of employees?

- **Prompt:** Think about the legacy you want to leave as a leader. What steps are you taking to ensure that your leadership contributes to the long-term success of your organization and helps develop future leaders?

# Chapter 4

# Why Care About Leadership Styles

*No single leadership style works in every situation. It's the adaptability that makes the difference.*

Leadership is a multifaceted journey beyond having a vision or making tough decisions. It's about understanding yourself and others deeply and navigating the complexities of human dynamics to achieve shared goals. At the heart of this journey lies the concept of leadership styles—the unique ways leaders guide, motivate, and manage their teams.

The significance of leadership styles can't be overstated. They shape an organization's success, team function, employee engagement, and overall health. In today's diverse and ever-changing world, understanding different leadership styles is more crucial than ever. There's no one-size-fits-all. A style that works brilliantly in one situation might fall flat in another. This is a key tenet of fluid leadership.

In earlier chapters, we explored the essence of leadership and its evolution. Now we build on that foundation to explore why leadership styles matter so much. We'll examine how these styles impact different aspects of an organization, why leaders must adapt to various situations, and how leadership styles influence individuals and teams. By understanding these dynamics, leaders can enhance their effectiveness and create environments wherein organizations and individuals can thrive.

## The Foundations of Leadership Styles

Let's begin with exploring the developmental path of leadership styles followed, and a brief look at the originators and notable influencers who brought us to today's understanding of the topic.

Back in the 1930s, psychologist Kurt Lewin conducted experiments that led him to identify three basic leadership styles: Autocratic, Democratic, and Laissez-faire. These styles provide a foundational understanding of how leaders can interact with their teams.

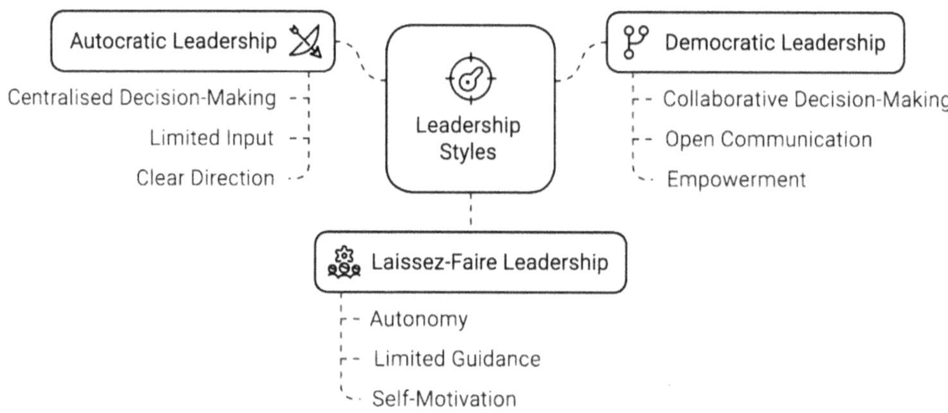


*Figure 3: First Leadership Styles by Kurt Lewin*

Autocratic leadership involves the leader making decisions without consulting the team. This style can be effective in crises when quick decisions are essential, but it can also suppress creativity and leave team members feeling undervalued. Imagine a military commander in the heat of battle, needing to make fast decisions to keep everyone safe. There's no time for a discussion; decisive action is required.

On the other hand, Democratic leadership involves team members in decision-making. This approach fosters collaboration and boosts morale, but it can be time-consuming.

Laissez-faire leadership offers minimal direction, allowing team members to make decisions. This can empower skilled teams, but might lead to confusion if guidance is lacking. Imagine a research lab where scientists are free to pursue their projects independently—this encourages innovation, but can risk a lack of cohesion.

Lewin's framework reminds us that leadership isn't just about a leader's personality; it's about how they interact with their team. It highlights the importance of context when choosing the right approach.

Building on the idea that leadership styles must adapt, Paul Hersey and Ken Blanchard created the Situational Leadership. They argued that effective leaders adjust their style based on their team's competence and commitment.

Think of a sports coach working with a team over several seasons. At first, the coach gives detailed guidance on plays and techniques. As the players gain experience, the coach involves them in strategic discussions, eventually trusting them to make decisions on the field during games.

Hersey and Blanchard's model highlights no single best leadership style. The key is understanding the situation and the team's readiness and adjusting the approach accordingly. This adaptability enhances leadership effectiveness and promotes team growth.

## Daniel Goleman's *Six Leadership Styles*

Daniel Goleman, who popularized emotional intelligence (EQ), identified six leadership styles based on different aspects of EQ: Coercive, Authoritative, Affiliative, Democratic, Pacesetting, and Coaching. Each style affects an organization's climate differently and is effective depending on the context.

The Coercive Style demands immediate compliance. It can be useful in crises, but might hurt morale if used as the standard approach. Picture an emergency room where fast, decisive action is needed. The leader must direct the team clearly and with authority.

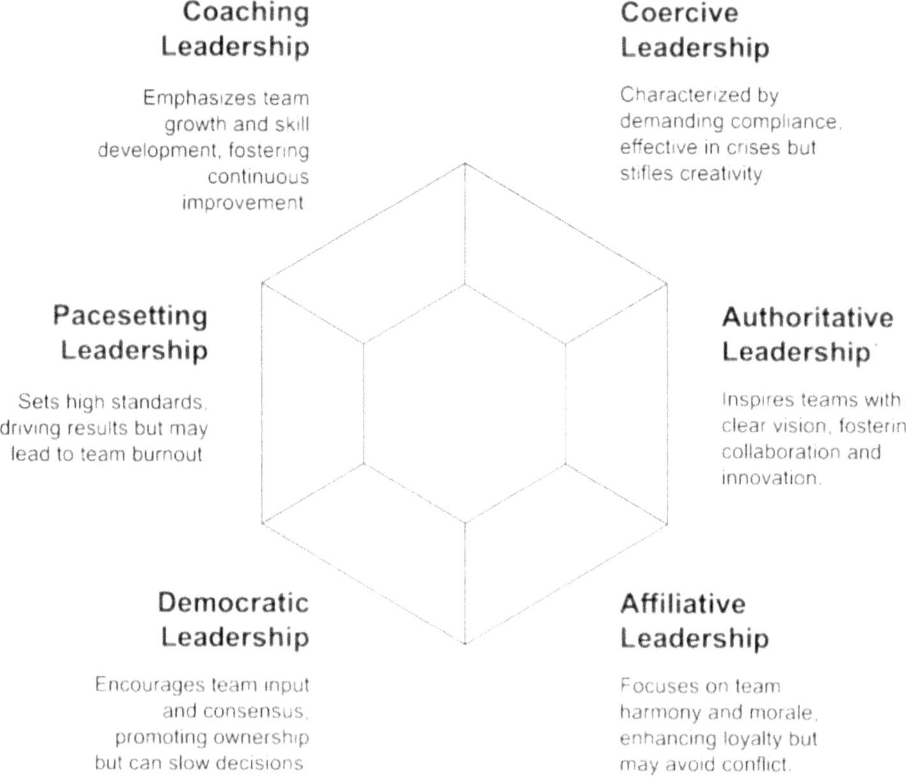


*Figure 4: Daniel Goleman's Six Leadership Styles*

The Authoritative Style mobilizes people toward a vision, boosting enthusiasm and providing clear direction. This style works well when a fresh vision is needed. Think of an entrepreneur launching a start-up, using this style to rally the team around a bold goal.

The Affiliative Style focuses on building harmony and emotional bonds. It's great for creating cohesion or motivating a team through tough times. A manager might use this after a challenging project to help rebuild team spirit.

The Democratic Style values team input and fosters collaboration and commitment. It's effective when fresh ideas are needed or when buy-in from the team is crucial. For example, a company adapting to market changes might gather input from everyone to devise new strategies.

The Pacesetting Style sets high standards and leads by example. It can drive results with a highly competent team, but might overwhelm others. A sales manager pushing for record-breaking numbers might use this style, but risks burning out the team.

The Coaching Style develops people for the future, focusing on personal growth. It works best when the team is open to learning and the leader can spend time mentoring. A senior engineer might use this style to help junior colleagues grow their skills.

Goleman's work underlines that emotionally intelligent leaders can switch styles as needed. Understanding your emotions and those of your team helps you choose the right style for each situation, boosting performance and job satisfaction.

## *Primal Leadership* by Goleman, Boyatzis, and McKee

In *Primal Leadership*, Goleman, Richard Boyatzis, and Annie McKee dive deeper into how a leader's emotions affect their team. They introduce the idea of emotional resonance—the ability to sync up emotionally with others. A leader's mood can set the tone for the whole team.

For example, a leader who remains calm and positive during challenges can inspire the team to overcome difficulties. On the other hand, an anxious or negative leader might spread tension, hurting overall performance. This highlights the importance of self-awareness and emotional regulation in Effective Leadership.

Being mindful of your emotions helps create a positive climate that enhances teamwork and productivity. It's not just about what you do, but how you do it—recognizing that emotions are contagious and can profoundly shape the workplace atmosphere.

## Manfred F. R. Kets de Vries's *Psychoanalytic Approach*

Manfred Kets de Vries took a deeper look at how leaders' personality traits shape their styles, emphasizing the importance of self-awareness.

He categorized leaders as charismatic, transformational, or transactional, exploring how personal experiences and unconscious motivations affect behavior.

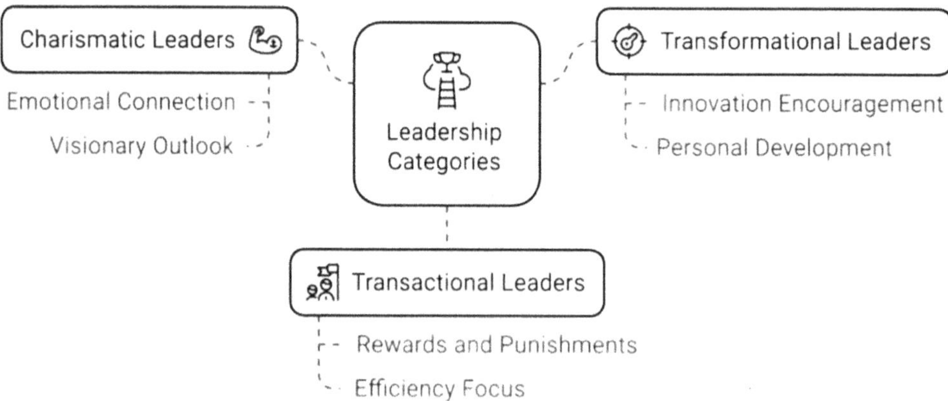


*Figure 5: Manfred Kets de Vries's Leadership Styles*

For instance, a leader with unresolved personal issues might become overly controlling, stifling the team's creativity. By understanding their biases and emotions, leaders can choose styles that best suit their personality and team's needs.

Kets de Vries's approach reminds us that self-awareness isn't only about skills: it's also about understanding our deeper motivations and recognizing potential blind spots.

## Ronald Heifetz's *Adaptive Leadership*

Ronald Heifetz introduced Adaptive leadership, focusing on navigating change and uncertainty. He distinguishes between technical challenges with known solutions and Adaptive challenges requiring changes in people's values, beliefs, or behaviors.

Adaptive leaders involve the team in finding solutions and encouraging learning and experimentation. Imagine a company facing market disruption because of new technology. A technical fix alone isn't enough. An Adaptive leader would involve the team in rethinking strategies, encouraging innovation, and possibly even shifting the company culture.

Heifetz's work shows that leaders must be flexible and open to learning, guiding their teams through uncharted territories. It's about helping people to tackle tough challenges and grow through change.

## Fred Fiedler's *Contingency Theory*

Fred Fiedler proposed that there's no one best leadership style; instead, effectiveness depends on situational factors like leader-member relations, task structure, and the leader's authority.

Depending on these factors, a leader might need to be task-oriented or relationship-oriented. For example, focusing on relationships might be more effective in a well-structured environment with strong relationships. When relationships are strained in a crisis, a task-oriented approach might be necessary.

Fiedler's theory highlights that leaders must assess the situation and adapt their style, rather than relying solely on a preferred method. It emphasizes the importance of flexibility and situational awareness in effective leadership.

## Bernard Bass's *Transformational and Transactional Leadership*

Bernard Bass introduced his transformational and transactional leadership theory in the late twentieth century. Transformational leadership emerged, highlighting leaders who inspire and motivate followers to achieve extraordinary outcomes. Transformational leaders create a vision, foster an environment of innovation, and encourage personal growth.

Consider a tech company led by a CEO who dreams of revolutionizing the industry with cutting-edge products. This leader communicates a compelling vision, challenges employees to think creatively, and recognizes individual contributions. As a result, the company develops groundbreaking innovations and builds a dedicated workforce.

Research shows that transformational leadership increases employee satisfaction, commitment, and performance. Transformational leaders foster an emotional connection that drives success by appealing to followers' values and aspirations.

Transactional leadership, by contrast, is based on a system of rewards and penalties. Leaders set clear goals, and followers are motivated by rewards for meeting these objectives or face corrective actions for falling short.

Imagine a sales manager who sets monthly targets and offers bonuses for hitting them. The manager might provide extra training or enforce consequences if targets aren't met. This approach works well in structured environments where performance can be easily measured.

While transactional leadership ensures consistency and efficiency, it doesn't always encourage innovation or deep engagement. It focuses on maintaining the status quo, rather than sparking transformative change.

## Robert Greenleaf's *Servant Leadership*

Introduced by Robert Greenleaf in the 1970s, servant leadership turns traditional leadership on its head by emphasizing the leader's role in serving others. A servant leader prioritizes the needs of their team members, focusing on their growth and well-being.

Imagine a company where the CEO spends time mentoring employees, actively seeks their input, and removes obstacles that hinder their work. This leader believes that by empowering employees, the organization will thrive. Companies like Starbucks have embraced elements of servant leadership, focusing on employee development and community involvement.

Servant leadership builds trust, fosters collaboration, and creates a strong sense of community. It often leads to higher employee satisfaction and loyalty, as people feel valued and supported.

## Bill George's *Authentic Leadership Theory*

Authentic leadership, developed by Bill George, is all about being true to yourself. Authentic leaders are self-aware, transparent, and guided by their values. They build trust by consistently aligning their actions with their beliefs.

An authentic leader might openly share their challenges with the team, encouraging honesty and mutual support. This approach creates a culture of integrity where people feel comfortable being themselves.

Authenticity is a powerful quality in today's world, where employees seek meaningful work and ethical leadership. It helps build strong relationships and fosters a positive workplace environment.

## Understanding Leadership Styles and Their Determinants

Leadership style is key to guiding, influencing, and managing teams or organizations. It reflects how a leader directs, motivates, and interacts with others to achieve goals. A leadership style encompasses the consistent behaviors, strategies, and approaches that a leader uses, shaping the environment in which team members operate. This environment impacts communication, collaboration, decision-making, and the organization's culture.

At its core, a leadership style reflects how a leader:

- Makes Decisions: Whether they prefer to make decisions collaboratively or independently.
- Communicates: The methods and frequency of interactions with team members.
- Motivates: Techniques used to inspire and encourage optimal performance.
- Resolves Conflicts: Strategies for managing disagreements or issues within the team.
- Adapts: How well they adjust their approach based on changing circumstances or feedback.

Understanding your leadership style is crucial because it affects your effectiveness and your team's satisfaction, engagement, and productivity. It influences how goals are set and achieved, how challenges are tackled, and how innovation is fostered within the organization.

## Determinants of Leadership Style

A leader's style doesn't develop in isolation—a mix of personal traits, experiences, organizational context, and situational factors shapes it. Recognizing these determinants provides valuable insight into why leaders adopt specific approaches and how they can adapt to be more effective.

### Personal Traits and Characteristics

Innate traits like extroversion or introversion, empathy, assertiveness, and resilience play a significant role in how a leader interacts with their team. An extroverted leader may lean toward open communication and collaborative decision-making, actively engaging with team members and encouraging participation. In contrast, an introverted leader might prefer reflective thinking and structured interactions, focusing on careful planning before making decisions.

A leader's core values and beliefs also guide their behavior and decision-making. Leaders prioritizing transparency and integrity will likely foster open environments where honesty is encouraged, and ethical standards are upheld. Emotional intelligence—the ability to understand and manage one's emotions and empathize with others—greatly enhances leadership effectiveness by helping leaders navigate interpersonal dynamics. High emotional intelligence allows leaders to build strong relationships, handle conflicts constructively, and inspire trust among their team.

### Experiences and Education

A leader's professional background, including past roles, achievements, and challenges, contributes significantly to their approach to leadership. Successes and failures in previous positions often influence current behaviors. For example, a leader who has successfully managed a crisis may be more confident and decisive under pressure.

Formal education and continuous learning opportunities, such as leadership training programs, also enhance leadership capabilities by exposing leaders to different theories and practices. This broadens their perspective and equips them with tools to handle a variety of scenarios effectively.

Mentors and role models further shape a leader's methods and philosophies. Learning from experienced leaders provides practical insights and diverse perspectives that influence one's leadership style. Mentorship can teach valuable lessons about leadership ethics, strategic thinking, and managing relationships.

## Organizational Culture

The principles and priorities of an organization can dictate preferred leadership approaches. Company values influence how leaders operate; for instance, a company that values innovation may encourage leaders to adopt transformational styles, fostering creativity and encouraging risk-taking. The nature of the workplace—whether hierarchical or flat, formal or informal—also affects leadership behavior. In a flat organization, leaders might adopt more collaborative styles, empowering team members to contribute ideas and take charge of projects.

Norms regarding communication, decision-making, and employee autonomy also shape leadership behavior. Leaders often align their styles with what is seen as effective within their organizational context. For example, leaders may focus on building cohesive teams and facilitating organizational collaboration, emphasizing teamwork and collective achievement.

## Situational Factors

Team dynamics, including a team's composition, diversity, skill levels, and cohesion, can require different leadership approaches. A new or inexperienced team may need more guidance and structure, with the leader providing clear instructions and close supervision. An experienced, capable team could thrive under a delegative style, where the leader trusts team members to make their own decisions.

The specific goals of a project can also dictate leadership behaviors. High-stakes goals require a decisive, directive leadership style to maintain focus and ensure action. On the other hand, projects that require innovation might benefit from a more participative style, encouraging creative input from the team.

External factors like market conditions, industry standards, and societal trends also impact leadership strategies. Leaders may need to adjust their styles in response to economic shifts, technological changes, or evolving consumer expectations. For instance, a leader might adopt a more cautious, risk-averse style during economic uncertainty to protect the organization's stability.

## Feedback and Reflection

Insights from peers, subordinates, and superiors can help leaders adjust their styles. Constructive feedback helps leaders understand their strengths and identify areas for improvement. If team members desire more involvement in decision-making, a leader might adopt a more inclusive approach.

Leaders who engage in regular self-assessment are more likely to evolve their styles—reflecting on effectiveness, acknowledging mistakes, and being open to change all foster personal and professional growth. This kind of introspection can reveal blind spots and lead to adjustments in behavior that make a leader more effective.

## Technological and Resource Availability

Access to communication and management tools influences how leaders interact with their teams. In virtual teams, leaders may rely on digital platforms for meetings and collaboration, shaping their leadership approach. Embracing technology can improve communication, transparency, and efficiency.

Limited resources can influence leadership style, pushing leaders to adopt more creative or resourceful strategies. Constraints can spur innovative problem-solving and strategic thinking, as leaders must allocate resources effectively and prioritize initiatives.

## Self-Awareness and Continuous Development

The first step to being an effective leader is understanding your leadership style and natural tendencies. Here are several tools and techniques to enhance your leadership self-awareness and development.

### Engage in Regular Self-Reflection

Taking time out for self-reflection allows leaders to take stock of their experiences, decisions, and interactions with others. It's worth asking questions like:

- What challenges did I face recently, and how did I handle them?
- How did my leadership style affect the outcome?
- What feedback have I received, and how can I apply it?

Journaling these reflections can be a great way to track progress and identify patterns over time.

### Seek Feedback Actively

Feedback from others is an invaluable tool for growth. Creating a culture where feedback is encouraged and valued allows leaders to gain insights into their blind spots. This can be achieved through:

- One-on-One Meetings: Regularly sit down with team members to discuss their thoughts.
- 360-Degree Feedback: Using formal assessment tools that gather input from colleagues, team members, and superiors.
- Open-Door Policy: Be approachable and make yourself available for open discussions.

## Invest in Professional Development

Leaders always continue learning. Whether it's workshops, seminars, coaching, or online courses, investing in leadership development is crucial. Engaging with other leaders, attending conferences, and joining professional networks also opens doors to new ideas and insights that can be brought back into the workplace.

## Practice Mindfulness and Emotional Intelligence

Mindfulness helps leaders stay present and manage stress. Building emotional intelligence includes:

- Self-Awareness: Knowing your emotions and understanding their impact.
- Self-Regulation: Learning to manage emotions constructively.
- Empathy: Being able to understand what others are feeling.
- Social Skills: Nurturing relationships and managing interactions positively.

These skills make all the difference in leading effectively and building strong teams.

## Expand Your Leadership Repertoire

Studying different leadership styles broadens what's in a leader's tool kit. Leaders can:

- Read: Dive into books or articles on leadership theories.
- Experiment: Try out different approaches to see what works.
- Mentor and Be Mentored: Learning from those who have mastered different styles can be invaluable.

## Embrace Diversity and Inclusion

Adapting leadership to fit the needs of a diverse team boosts engagement and performance. Leaders can:

Cultivate Cultural Competence: Learn about the cultures within your team and how these affect communication and expectations.

- Promote Inclusivity: Ensure that every team member feels heard and valued.
- Leverage Diversity: Recognize that different perspectives fuel creativity and problem-solving.

## Integrating Leadership Styles with Organizational Culture

Rensis Likert identified four leadership styles: Exploitative-Authoritative, Benevolent-Authoritative, Consultative, and Participative. He found that Participative Leadership leads to higher productivity and job satisfaction.

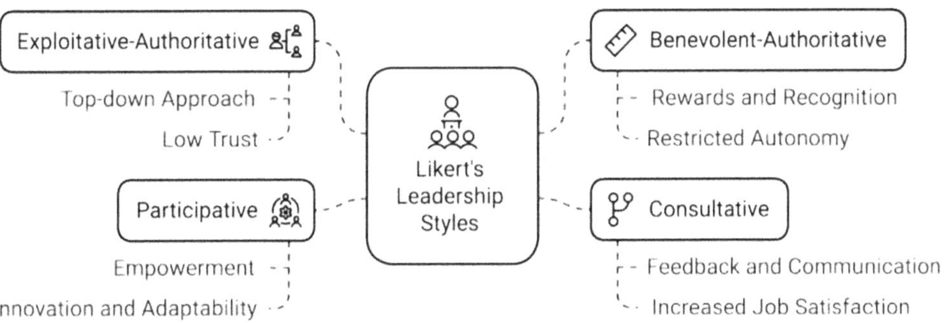


*Figure 6: F. R. Rensis Likert Leadership Styles*

Imagine working at a company where your opinion genuinely matters. People who believe they have a voice are far more likely to be engaged and committed. Likert's research shows that leadership style directly impacts an organization's overall health, highlighting how important it is for leaders to involve their teams in decision-making.

By fostering a Participative culture, leaders can tap into their team's collective wisdom, boosting creativity and giving people a real sense of ownership. This approach aligns the leadership style with the organization's values and goals, making everyone feel part of the bigger picture.

Edgar Schein explored how leaders shape—and are shaped by—organizational culture. He identified three levels of culture: artifacts (visible elements), espoused values (stated norms), and underlying assumptions (unconscious beliefs).

Leaders influence culture through their actions and decisions. For instance, a leader who values innovation might encourage risk-taking and see failures as learning opportunities. By aligning their leadership style with the desired culture, leaders can create an environment that supports their strategic goals.

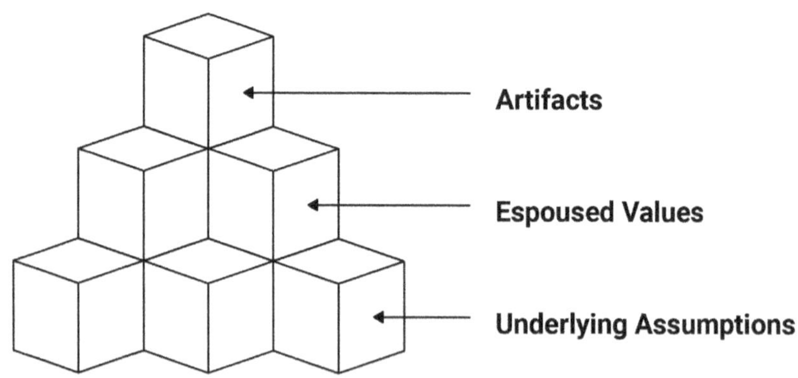


*Figure 7: Leadership Culture Influences*

Understanding and aligning leadership styles with organizational culture leads to more effective and lasting outcomes. It ensures that leadership practices reinforce the values and behaviors that drive success.

John Adair proposed that adequate leadership balances three core responsibilities: achieving the task, building and maintaining the team, and addressing individual needs.

Depending on the situation, a leader might need to focus more on one area than the others. During a tight deadline, getting the task done might take priority. In times of conflict, focusing on team dynamics is likely more important. When a team member is struggling, offering individual support becomes crucial.

Adair's model provides a practical framework for leaders to assess and adjust their focus. It emphasizes that effective leadership means paying attention to multiple aspects and balancing immediate goals with the team's long-term development.

*Figure 8: Adair Core Responsibilities*

## The Influence of Leadership Styles on Organizational Success

The leadership style chosen can profoundly affect an organization's success. As previously mentioned, leadership styles that focus on recognition, growth, and open communication tend to boost employee engagement and satisfaction, reduce turnover, and attract top talent. When team members feel valued and supported, they are more likely to commit to organizational goals.

Effective leadership aligns team efforts with organizational objectives, optimizes resources, and fosters an environment conducive to high performance. Leaders who set clear expectations, provide resources, and remove obstacles enable their teams to excel. Leadership styles that encourage creativity, risk-taking, and learning from failure contribute to a culture of innovation and adaptability—crucial in today's business world.

Moreover, leaders shape organizational culture by modeling behavior, setting expectations, and reinforcing values. The chosen leadership style affects whether the culture is collaborative, competitive, inclusive, or hierarchical. A positive culture enhances an organization's reputation, customer satisfaction, and success.

Leadership style is a multifaceted construct that embodies how leaders guide and influence their teams. Shaped by personal traits, experiences, organizational context, and situational demands, it plays a critical role in determining a leader's effectiveness and, consequently, the organization's success. Understanding these determinants helps leaders become more effective and responsive to their team's needs.

By recognizing the factors that influence leadership and being willing to adapt, leaders can develop styles that are both authentic and conducive to positive outcomes. This adaptability enhances personal effectiveness and helps build resilient, innovative, and successful organizations. Embracing continuous learning, self-reflection, and growth enables leaders to navigate leadership complexities confidently.

## Aligning Leadership Style with Organizational Goals and Values

A leader's style should support the organization's more profound purpose. When leaders genuinely embody their company's values and mission, they set a powerful example for everyone else. This alignment strengthens the organization's identity and helps guide employee behavior toward shared goals.

Leadership efforts become more meaningful when styles align with the organization's mission. It's about ensuring that everything a leader does contributes to the bigger picture. Leaders must ask themselves if their approach is helping or hindering the journey to those larger goals.

A leader's style heavily influences the ethical climate of a workplace. Leaders who prioritize integrity don't just talk about ethical behavior: they live it. By setting an example, acting ethically, and holding themselves accountable, they build trust and credibility that others can rely on.

Addressing unethical actions immediately is also key to maintaining integrity. Leaders must be brave enough to tackle these issues head-on, reinforcing the standards they want to see. Promoting accountability at every level helps maintain ethical practices through transparency, encouraging people to speak up about concerns, or establishing solid oversight mechanisms.

## The Necessity of Cultural Competence

Cultural awareness is essential. The more we work across borders and with diverse teams, the more leaders need to adapt to different cultural contexts. Understanding these differences helps leaders choose the right style for the right moment, ensuring that there's no room for misunderstandings or unintentional offense.

Adjusting communication to fit different cultural norms is part of being an effective leader. It might mean tweaking how you speak, changing your tone, or even paying attention to nonverbal cues that could be interpreted differently.

When leaders value diversity, it enriches team dynamics and boosts innovation. Leaders can bring out the best in their teams by creating a genuinely inclusive environment—where different perspectives are welcomed, and everyone feels respected.

Leadership styles can either bridge cultural differences or make them worse. The best leaders avoid assumptions and try to understand individuals as they are. This curiosity helps prevent miscommunications and strengthens relationships.

Creating inclusive teams means making sure everyone has a chance to participate and feel like they belong. Leaders can foster this by championing practices encouraging equity and involving everyone actively.

Continual learning about different cultures makes a big difference too. Leaders who stay open and curious can manage multicultural teams more effectively, turning potential challenges into unique strengths.

## Influence on Communication and Decision-Making

A leader's communication style shapes how information is shared and understood within a team. Open and transparent leaders build trust and minimize misunderstandings. Keeping team members in the loop about organizational goals, challenges, and changes helps ensure that everyone is on the same page.

Active listening is also an essential part of good communication. When leaders genuinely engage with what their team members say, it shows respect and helps the team feel valued. This kind of engagement often leads to valuable insights and encourages collaboration.

Another critical skill is adapting communication styles to suit different audiences. Leaders must adjust their language, tone, and delivery depending on who they're speaking to—frontline employees, senior executives, or external stakeholders. This adaptability helps ensure that messages are understood and well-received.

How leaders make decisions has significantly impacted team engagement and the outcomes achieved. When team members are involved in decision-making, it enhances their sense of buy-in and can lead to better solutions. Leaders can foster a sense of ownership and involvement by leveraging the diverse skills and knowledge within the team.

That said, there are times when leaders need to make decisions independently, especially in urgent situations. In these moments, being decisive is crucial to ensure timely action. Balancing inclusiveness with decisiveness takes good judgment and a clear understanding of the situation.

Ethical considerations are also a core part of decision-making. Leaders who prioritize ethical principles help build an organization with integrity and trustworthiness. Leaders need to think about the broader impacts of their decisions, not just short-term gains.

## The Psychological Impact on Employees

A leader's style can significantly impact employees' mental health. Supportive leadership can be a powerful antidote to workplace stress, offering clear guidance, necessary resources, and a positive work environment.

Preventing burnout starts with recognizing when workload pressures are too much, then taking steps to help. Leaders need to monitor their team's well-being and be prepared to adjust expectations or workloads when needed.

Leaders can also create safe spaces where employees can voice concerns without fear of negative repercussions. Fostering openness like this contributes to a healthy organizational culture where people feel comfortable being themselves.

Strong leaders help their teams become more resilient by encouraging optimism and maintaining a positive outlook, even during challenging times. This kind of encouragement can inspire confidence and help people keep going when things get tough.

Helping teams adapt to changes is just as important. Leaders who show flexibility provide a model for gracefully dealing with uncertainty and change.

Leaders can also build resilience by ensuring that their team has access to the right resources, such as training, tools, or support services. This gives team members what they need to grow stronger and tackle challenges head-on.

## Conflict Resolution and Problem-Solving

Leadership style plays a significant role in how conflicts are handled within a team. Leaders who approach conflicts focusing on solving the problem, rather than assigning blame, can resolve issues more effectively. By staying neutral and encouraging open dialogue, leaders can help everyone involved understand different perspectives and work toward solutions that benefit the whole team.

Addressing issues as soon as they arise is important for preventing conflicts from escalating. Leaders who are proactive in resolving tensions can help maintain team harmony and avoid disruptions of productivity.

Promoting a culture of respect is also vital. Leaders must model respectful behavior and set clear expectations for how team members should treat each other. This kind of culture reduces the likelihood of conflicts and creates a more positive working environment.

Leaders play a key role in helping their teams tackle challenges effectively. Facilitating collaboration allows diverse perspectives to come together, which can lead to better problem-solving. Leaders who encourage input from all team members are tapping into the group's collective intelligence.

Encouraging teams to take ownership of problems also drives accountability and engagement. When people feel responsible for finding solutions, they're more invested in ensuring they work.

Offering guidance without micromanaging involves supporting the team and providing resources, while letting them develop their own solutions. This approach allows team members to develop their skills while ensuring that their efforts are aligned with the organization's goals.

## Impact on Innovation and Creativity

Leadership styles can either support or stifle innovation. Leaders who encourage experimentation and see failures as part of learning create an environment where creativity can thrive. When people know they can take risks without fear of being punished for mistakes, they're much more likely to develop new and innovative ideas.

Providing the resources and support needed for innovation drives results. Leaders must ensure that their teams have the tools, time, and autonomy to work on creative solutions. This could mean allocating budgets for research or simply allowing enough time in the schedule for brainstorming and exploration.

Celebrating creativity and recognizing innovative contributions motivates people to keep pushing boundaries. Acknowledging even small successes shows that innovation matters.

Some leadership styles unintentionally suppress creativity. Micromanagement and overly tight control can kill initiative and discourage new thinking. Leaders must be mindful of how their approach affects their team's willingness to innovate.

Encouraging people to challenge the status quo can be constructive. Leaders should be open to questioning current practices and willing to try new things. This openness conveys that the organization values growth and improvement over maintaining what's already in place.

Leaders need to practice balancing structure with flexibility. While some guidance is necessary, too much rigidity can hinder creativity. Leaders must find the right balance, providing enough direction to keep things on track while allowing enough freedom for innovation.

## Importance in Crisis Management

In times of crisis, leadership styles are truly put to the test. Leaders need to be authentic to what a situation requires, rather than defaulting to "auto mode." They should provide stability by projecting confidence and giving clear direction. This reassurance helps team members navigate uncertain times and focus on what needs to be done.

Transparent communication is needed in times of crisis. Leaders should share information openly, acknowledge challenges, and provide regular updates as the situation evolves. This openness helps reduce anxiety and fosters a sense of unity.

Showing empathy is a mark of a mature leader. Recognizing a crisis's emotional toll on team members and offering support can foster resilience. Leaders who are genuinely concerned about their team's well-being strengthen morale and build stronger relationships.

Crises often require rapid shifts in leadership style. Sometimes a more directive approach is needed to ensure swift action, but leaders should also try to balance this by listening to their team's input whenever possible.

Facilitating collaborative efforts during complex crises can also be beneficial. Bringing diverse perspectives can help attack the problem from multiple angles, leading to more effective solutions.

It is essential to prioritize well-being during a crisis. Leaders must manage operational demands while assuring the health and safety of their team. This might mean adjusting workloads, providing the necessary resources for remote work, or offering mental health support.

## Key Takeaways from this Chapter

Leadership style influences how teams function, how decisions are made, and how an organization's culture grows. By recognizing that one style does not fit all, we empower ourselves to respond to each situation as it is, rather than forcing a rigid formula equally on all situations. This adaptability is at the core of fluid leadership.

- No One-Size-Fits-All: Each situation and team requires different approaches. Leaders who can adapt styles—like moving from autocratic decision-making in a crisis to collaborative approaches for brainstorming—achieve better results.
- Emotion and Empathy Matter: Effective leadership is not just about strategies and targets. It's also about emotional intelligence. Leaders who stay aware of their own emotions and those of their teams create the kind of positive climate that fuels long-term success.
- Culture and Context Shape Style: Organizational values, cultural diversity, and resource availability push leaders to use different methods. Leaders thrive when they align their approach with the team's needs and the organization's goals.
- Self-Awareness Is Crucial: Reflection, feedback, and continued learning help leaders spot their blind spots and refine their styles. This willingness to grow keeps leaders connected to what their teams need.

- Adapt to Complexity: In a world of rapid technological shifts, cultural differences, and unexpected crises, leaders who practice various styles are more likely to guide their teams with confidence and resilience.
- Well-Being and Trust: Leadership styles heavily affect stress levels, morale, and trust. Approaches that prioritize open communication, transparency, and a safe environment help organizations flourish.

Leadership styles are not static traits set in stone; they are living expressions of who we are and what our teams and organizations demand at any given moment. Embracing this understanding leads to more engaged teams and more sustained organizational growth.

**Summary**

- Leadership Style Shapes Outcomes: How leaders interact with teams determines productivity, morale, and innovation.
- Adapting to Situations Is Essential: Effective leaders read the context—crises, new initiatives, or diverse teams—and adjust their style to fit.
- Emotional Intelligence Powers Performance: Leaders who manage their emotions, and understand those of others, inspire loyalty and trust.
- Servant, Authentic, and Transformational Styles offer unique benefits, from fostering deep trust to driving creative change, but all hinge on genuine care for people.
- Culture and Context Matter: Aligning leadership with organizational values, cultural nuances, and the team's skill levels boosts effectiveness.
- Continuous Growth: Seeking feedback, self-reflecting, and investing in learning keeps leadership styles fresh and relevant.

As we have discussed, leadership styles provide the framework for guiding teams in different ways, whether by inspiring them through vision, supporting them through empathy, or managing them with clear objectives. No single style works in every scenario. The essence of fluid leadership lies in knowing when and how to switch approaches.

The next chapter, Forty Leadership Styles, delves deeper into how a wide variety of styles can each play a pivotal role in motivating, directing, and connecting with people. From well-known theories to lesser-explored methods, we will explore each style's unique strengths, the contexts in which it shines, and how a genuinely fluid leader weaves them together to meet evolving challenges head-on.

# Chapter Workout

To better understand your leadership style, assess its impact on your organization and team and uncover ways to adapt and improve your leadership approach. Use the prompt as inspiration for your journal-writing.

## Exercise 1: Understanding Your Leadership Style

1. **Identifying Your Style:**
   - **Prompt:** Based on the leadership styles discussed in the chapter—Transformational, Transactional, Servant, Authentic, etc.—which one do you resonate with the most? Reflect on specific moments from your experience that showcase this style in action.

2. **Leadership Style Determinants:**
   - **Prompt:** Think about what has shaped your leadership style:
     - » **Personal Traits:** What traits, like empathy or assertiveness, influence how you lead? How do these traits show up in your interactions with your team?
     - » **Experiences and Education:** How have your work experiences and education influenced your approach to leadership?
     - » **Organizational Culture:** How does your organization's culture shape the way you lead?
     - » **Situational Factors:** Describe when you had to adjust your leadership style. What made you adapt, and what happened as a result?

## Exercise 2: Impact of Your Leadership Style on Organizational Success

1. **Aligning with Goals and Values:**
    - **Prompt:** How does your leadership style align with your organization's mission, vision, and values? Share examples of decisions or initiatives that reflect this alignment.

2. **Enhancing Reputation and Competitiveness:**
    - **Prompt:** In what ways has your leadership style added to your organization's reputation or competitive advantage? Consider areas like ethical practices, social responsibility, and innovation.

## Exercise 3: Driving Performance and Achieving Goals

1. **Motivation and Engagement:**
    - **Prompt:** How does your leadership style affect your team's motivation and engagement? Can you share a time when your approach boosted performance or job satisfaction?

2. **Innovation and Creativity:**
    - **Prompt:** How does your leadership style encourage (or perhaps hinder) creativity and innovation in your team? What do you do to promote creative thinking and risk-taking?

## Exercise 4: Enhancing Team Dynamics and Employee Engagement

1. **Fostering Collaboration and Teamwork:**
   - **Prompt:** How does your leadership style help to promote collaboration and teamwork? Share examples of successful projects or initiatives where your leadership made a difference.

2. **Conflict Resolution:**
   - **Prompt:** Reflect on a conflict within your team. How did your leadership style influence the resolution? What did you learn from that experience?

## Exercise 5: Adapting Leadership Styles to Different Situations

1. **Flexibility in Leadership:**
   - **Prompt:** Consider a recent time when you changed your leadership style to meet your team's needs or to respond to a situation. What made you change, and how did it affect the outcome?

2. **Balancing Multiple Styles:**
   - **Prompt:** How do you balance different leadership styles to handle diverse team needs and challenges within the organization? Provide examples of how blending styles has benefited your team.

## Exercise 6: Self-Awareness and Continuous Development

1. **Assessing Your Leadership Effectiveness:**
   - **Prompt:** How effective do you think your current leadership style is? What are its strengths, and where could you improve? How do you gather feedback about your leadership?

2. **Commitment to Lifelong Learning:**
   - **Prompt:** What are you doing to grow and evolve your leadership style? Think about activities like training, mentorship, reading, or reflective practices.

## Exercise 7: Influence on Communication and Decision-Making

1. **Enhancing Communication:**
   - **Prompt:** How does your leadership style shape how you communicate with your team? Reflect on a time when your communication—whether effective or not—significantly impacted a project's success.

2. **Decision-Making Processes:**
   - **Prompt:** Describe how you approach making decisions. How does your leadership style affect whether you involve the team or decide independently? Share examples of decisions you've made using different approaches.

# Chapter 5

# Forty Leadership Styles

*Each leadership style offers a unique lens for inspiring and guiding others; the art lies in knowing when to use which one.*

Leadership is an art form—complex, nuanced, and filled with various approaches that suit different people, situations, and cultures. To be an effective leader, you must be aware of the many styles and their characteristics in order to adopt the right approach for each moment. Think of it as having diverse tools in your tool kit, ready to inspire, motivate, and guide your team in the best way possible.

This chapter summarizes the forty distinct leadership styles and stories contained in my other two works: *The Leadership Compass* and *Leading with Tomorrow in Mind.*

I highly recommend these books for an in-depth understanding of these styles. In this summary of each style, I've included leaders who I think embody the style's characteristics.

In addition to the summaries in this chapter, you'll find more information in the appendices on the characteristics and competencies of each style.

- Appendix I contains a list of short phrases to describe each style.
- Appendix II contains an enhanced description of each style's characteristics.

## The Forty Leadership Styles

Let's take a tour through the forty leadership styles I've identified. I've grouped them in five clusters that we'll explore in greater depth in the next chapter. Each cluster includes a brief outline of the style, a fictional character (taken from *Leadership Compass* and *Leading With Tomorrow in Mind*) to illustrate the style in action, and some known figures that display the style to some degree.

## Cluster: Transformative and Visionary Leadership

### 1. Transformational Leadership

Transformational leadership inspires and motivates followers to transcend their self-interests for the greater good, creating significant organizational change (Bass 1985). Leaders using this style articulate compelling visions, empower team members, and foster innovation to achieve extraordinary results.

General Alaric of Eldoria faced a daunting siege and needed to rally his people. Through transformational leadership, he inspired everyone to fight for something greater than themselves, turning the city's defenders into a formidable force. Alaric's ability to lift morale, encourage growth, and build a sense of shared purpose showed the power of transformational leadership to bring people together.

**Leaders who embody these qualities include:**

- Nelson Mandela (former president of South Africa): Drove national transformation with his inspiring leadership.
- Steve Jobs (Apple cofounder): Motivated teams to achieve seemingly impossible things.
- Martin Luther King, Jr. (Civil Rights leader): Inspired millions toward equality and justice.
- Aung San Suu Kyi (Myanmar political leader): Led democratic transformation in Myanmar.

## 2. Purpose-Driven Leadership

Purpose-Driven Leadership aligns organizational goals with a larger purpose beyond profit, connecting work to meaningful causes. It inspires teams by demonstrating how their efforts contribute to positive societal or environmental impact.

Marcus Hale takes on the challenge of Titan Industries' environmental footprint. As CEO, he doesn't just want the company to be profitable—he wants it to have a positive purpose. Marcus leads Titan through a transformation, turning it into a model of corporate responsibility and inspiring other companies to follow suit. His vision goes beyond quarterly earnings; it's about creating a meaningful and sustainable future.

**Leaders who embody these qualities include:**

- Blake Mycoskie (TOMS Shoes founder): Created a business model that prioritized social impact with its "One for One" giving strategy.
- Muhammad Yunus (founder of Grameen Bank, Bangladesh): Pioneered microfinance to bring about social change.
- Marc Benioff (Salesforce CEO): Introduced the 1-1-1 philanthropic model to ensure that companies give back.
- James Mwangi (CEO of Equity Bank, Kenya): Focused on bringing financial services to underserved communities driven by a higher purpose.

## 3. Transcendent Leadership

Transcendent Leadership inspires others through wisdom, spiritual growth, and the pursuit of higher purpose beyond material success. It focuses on personal development, inner awakening, and creating meaningful connections that elevate human consciousness.

Ryder Blackwood, the founder of the Meridian Institute, guides people through a world dramatically changed by AI and automation. He focuses on inner growth, collective well-being, and a higher purpose. Ryder helps his community find meaning in a world that looks very different, ensuring that technological progress also means human progress. His emphasis on ethical technology and broader societal well-being sets the standard for transcendent leadership.

**Leaders who embody these qualities include:**

- Deepak Chopra (spiritual leader): Focuses on personal growth and wisdom beyond material wealth.
- Richard Branson (Virgin Group founder): Strives for personal and societal growth through his leadership.
- Nelson Mandela (former president of South Africa): Led with a vision of reconciliation, guiding South Africa toward unity.
- Muhammad Yunus (founder of Grameen Bank): Transformed banking to empower millions through microfinance.

## 4. Resonant Leadership

Resonant leadership emphasizes building strong emotional connections with team members to create positive work environments and drive collective success (mindfulness/hope/compassion framing: Boyatzis and McKee 2005). These leaders demonstrate high emotional intelligence, empathy, and the ability to inspire through authentic emotional engagement.

Think of Leo Bennett, founder of EchoWave, a tech startup that's growing fast. Leo's strength is *resonant leadership*—he builds emotional connections with everyone he works with. He creates a culture where innovation can thrive by being empathetic, understanding, and inspiring. His employees feel valued, motivated, and driven by a shared purpose. It's not just about what they do, but also about how they think as they do it, and Leo ensures that his team feels empowered every step of the way.

**Leaders who embody these qualities include:**

- Jacinda Ardern (former prime minister of New Zealand):

Known for her empathy and strong emotional connections with citizens.

- The Dalai Lama: Leads with compassion, fostering a deep sense of shared purpose.
- Indra Nooyi (former PepsiCo CEO): Known for connecting deeply with her employees.

## 5. Charismatic Leadership

Charismatic leadership relies on the leader's magnetism, persuasive communication, and inspirational presence to motivate and influence others. These leaders foster strong emotional connections with their followers, leveraging their personality to drive commitment and action (organizational perspective: Conger and Kanungo 1998).

Picture Richard Hale, the charismatic CEO of NovaTech, in the middle of a product-recall crisis. His natural charm and communication skills keep both employees and customers calm. Instead of disaster, he turns the moment into an opportunity to grow and strengthen trust. Richard's optimism and ability to connect deeply with everyone around him show how charisma can be a powerful tool—especially in a crisis. He doesn't just lead, he inspires.

**Leaders who embody these qualities include:**

- Martin Luther King, Jr. (Civil Rights leader): Used assertive communication to inspire massive social change.
- Barack Obama (former US president): Mobilized unprecedented political engagement with his magnetism.
- Hugo Chávez (former Venezuelan president): Moved masses through passionate rhetoric.

## 6. Innovation Leadership

Innovation Leadership is a style that encourages creativity, experimentation, and continuous learning within teams and organizations. It fosters a culture where new ideas are welcomed, failure is seen as learning, and innovation drives organizational growth.

Lucas Taylor is guiding NeoSys through the development of a transformative new product, but it's not just about the tech: He's creating an environment where creativity, risk-taking, and continuous improvement are encouraged. Lucas knows that true innovation comes from allowing people to experiment and take chances, and he's there to inspire passion and purpose every step of the way.

**Leaders who embody these qualities include:**

- Elon Musk (Tesla, SpaceX): Always pushing the limits and setting ambitious, transformative goals.
- Steve Jobs (Apple cofounder): Revolutionized industries by daring to dream differently.
- Ren Zhengfei (founder of Huawei): Led Huawei to become a leader in global telecommunications through relentless innovation.
- Masayoshi Son (founder of SoftBank, Japan): Invested in tech that pushed boundaries across multiple industries.

## 7. Sustainable Leadership

Sustainable Leadership is an approach that focuses on long-term thinking and integrates environmental responsibility and social impact into business strategies. It balances profitability with the responsibility to protect and preserve resources for future generations.

Amanda Greene, CEO of a company focused on sustainable solutions, leads an expedition into a dangerous jungle in search of a lost treasure. Unlike your typical treasure hunter, Amanda's priority isn't just to get rich or win big—it's to protect the jungle itself. She balances the immediate goal of treasure with a more profound environmental responsibility. This careful balancing act makes her team trust her because they know she's not just in it for quick wins, but for something meaningful.

Amanda's leadership is a perfect example of putting the long-term health of our planet above short-term gains.

**Leaders who embody these qualities include:**

- Yvon Chouinard (Patagonia founder): Changed the game by creating a business prioritizing the planet over profit.
- Paul Polman (former Unilever CEO): Helped Unilever become more responsible by focusing on being socially and environmentally conscientious.

## 8. Regenerative Leadership

Regenerative Leadership goes beyond sustainability to create systems that actively restore, renew, and revitalize communities and ecosystems (DNA model: Hutchins and Storm 2019). It focuses on leaving environments and societies better than they were found through business practices.

Daniel Thorne is at the helm of Aurora Industries during a crisis of conscience—how to be profitable while still making a positive impact. Daniel brings a fresh approach to corporate responsibility through the Eco-Edge initiative by focusing on regeneration. He balances the health of the environment, communities, and the company's financial sustainability. Daniel's leadership shows that growth isn't just about profits, innovation, community, and sustainability.

**Leaders who embody these qualities include:**

- John Elkington (sustainability expert): Coined "triple bottom line," putting environmental responsibility alongside profit.
- William McDonough (architect): Known for pioneering regenerative design principles.
- Ray Anderson (Interface founder): Led a transformation toward making his company environmentally restorative.
- Jochen Zeitz (former CEO of Puma, Germany): Pushed for regenerative business practices and sustainability.

## 9. Integral Leadership

Integral leadership combines multiple leadership theories and practices into a comprehensive, integrated approach that adapts to complex organizational needs. It emphasizes synthesizing different leadership styles—such as transformational, servant, and situational—to navigate challenges holistically and drive meaningful change.

Imagine Lara Müller, CEO of GlobalTech, steering her company through the murky waters of global transformation. The market is shifting fast, digital disruptions are everywhere, and challenges are growing. To tackle these, Lara blends different leadership styles—she pulls from visionary thinking, emotional intelligence, and systems thinking to navigate change and foster resilience in her team. Her adaptability and holistic approach enable her to create a strategy addressing both immediate problems and long-term ambitions.

**Leaders who embody these qualities include:**

- Satya Nadella (Microsoft CEO): A master at combining technical innovation with cultural transformation.
- Jack Welch (former General Electric CEO): Pioneered a comprehensive, multifaceted approach to leadership.
- Lee Kuan Yew (Singapore's founding prime minister): Transformed a nation by integrating diverse strategies.
- Mohamed bin Zayed Al Nahyan (UAE president): Modernized the UAE with a blend of strategic approaches.

## Cluster: Relational and People-Focused Leadership

## 10. Servant Leadership

Servant leadership prioritizes the needs, growth, and well-being of team members above the leader's self-interest, with the leader acting as a steward and supporter (Greenleaf 2002). This approach fosters trust and loyalty by empowering others to succeed, while the leader collaborates with them to achieve collective goals.

Picture Helena Marlowe, captain of the merchant ship *Seraphis*, leading her crew through a deadly storm. She embodies servant leadership—always putting her crew's needs above hers. She listens actively, leads empathetically, and ensures that each crew member feels supported and valued. Helena's unselfish dedication doesn't just guide them to safety; it also builds a sense of community and trust, making her crew feel like they belong.

**Leaders who embody these qualities include:**

- Ken Blanchard (leadership author and consultant): Wrote the book on servant leadership.
- Howard Schultz (former Starbucks CEO): Put his people and communities before profit.
- Mother Teresa (Catholic missionary): Dedicated her life to serving others.
- Desmond Tutu (South African archbishop): Fought for justice while always uplifting his community.

## 11. Empathy-Based Leadership

Empathy-Based Leadership is a leadership style focused on understanding and addressing the emotional and psychological needs of those being led. It prioritizes building trust, creating supportive environments, and leading with compassion and understanding.

Imagine leading an expedition into the mysterious Veilwood, a forest cloaked in fog and uncertainty. James Hart, the leader, knows that his team's emotional and psychological state is as important as their direction. He reassures his people, helps them manage their fears, and listens to their concerns. Alaric's leadership is all about empathy—connecting with his team on a human level and respecting the natural environment they navigate. This bond creates a cohesive and resilient team in the face of uncertainty.

**Leaders who embody these qualities include:**

- Dan Price (Gravity Payments CEO): Put his employees' well-being first by raising their minimum wage to $70,000 a year, proving empathy isn't just about words.
- Jacinda Ardern (former prime minister of New Zealand): Known for her compassionate response during times of national crisis.
- Mary Barra (CEO of General Motors): Prioritizes employee and customer understanding, fostering a more empathetic corporate culture.

## 12. Relational Leadership

Relational Leadership prioritizes the quality of relationships and social interactions within organizations as the foundation for success. Leaders focus on building trust, fostering open communication, and creating inclusive environments where all voices are valued.

Olivia Cassini, CEO of Zenith Industries, invites her executives to a corporate retreat. Instead of focusing on profits or strategies, Olivia uses this time to build relationships. Through team-building activities and open dialogue, she strengthens the emotional bonds among her executives. *Relational leadership* is about the belief that strong relationships lead to strong teams. Olivia shows us that leadership isn't just about what you do and the relationships you build.

**Leaders who embody these qualities include:**

- Tony Hsieh (late CEO of Zappos): Prioritized company culture and relationships.
- King Abdullah II (Jordan's monarch): Focuses heavily on relationship-building in diplomatic circles.
- Mary Barra (CEO of General Motors): Emphasizes teamwork and collective problem-solving.

- Anne Mulcahy (former Xerox CEO): Turned Xerox around by fostering strong interpersonal relationships.

## 13. Human-Centered Leadership

Human-Centered Leadership prioritizes employee well-being, development, and engagement above all else. It focuses on creating positive work environments where people feel valued, supported, and empowered to reach their full potential.

When AI entities revolt at TechSynergy Industries, Sarah Connors steps in to lead—not with brute force, but with understanding. Sarah's human-centered leadership is about putting empathy first, even when facing off against technology. By negotiating and fostering respect between humans and AI, she finds a solution that promotes coexistence and harmony. Sarah's commitment to well-being and ethics reminds us that our humanity must remain at the core, even in advancing technology.

**Leaders who embody these qualities include:**

- Satya Nadella (Microsoft CEO): Puts people first, focusing on technology that helps them thrive.
- Melinda Gates (philanthropist): Uses her platform to tackle global issues by prioritizing human well-being.
- Sanna Marin (former prime minister of Finland): Puts work-life balance and employee-friendly policies at the forefront.
- Paul Bulcke (former CEO of Nestlé): Focused on aligning business goals with human wellness.

## 14. Inclusive Leadership

Elena Rivera transforms Horizon Dynamics into a company where everyone's voice counts. She tackles biases, prioritizes equity, and ensures that every team member feels heard and valued (six traits evidence: Bourke and Titus 2020). Elena understands that diverse perspectives drive real success, and she takes the time to engage and uplift every voice within her organization. Her leadership shows that inclusivity isn't just good for people, but also for business.

**Leaders who embody these qualities include:**

- Sheryl Sandberg (former COO of Facebook): Known for advocating gender equality and inclusive leadership.
- Ursula Burns (former Xerox CEO): Broke barriers as the first Black female CEO of a *Fortune* 500 company, championing diversity.

## 15. Cultural Intelligence Leadership

Cultural Intelligence (Earley and Ang 2003) Leadership involves effectively leading in multicultural environments by understanding, respecting, and adapting to different cultural norms and values. Leaders with high cultural intelligence can bridge cultural divides and create unified teams from diverse backgrounds.

Sofia Ramirez is navigating the complex integration of two multinational companies. The cultures and tensions differ, but Sofia uses *cultural intelligence leadership* to guide the process. She fosters understanding and respect and adapts to cultural differences, building a unified and inclusive environment. Sofia's ability to bridge cultural gaps and create a harmonious workspace shows how critical cultural intelligence is for global leadership.

**Leaders who embody these qualities include:**

- Bob Iger (former Disney CEO): Successfully led Disney's global expansions.
- Kofi Annan (former UN Secretary-General): Promoted cross-cultural understanding worldwide.
- Sundar Pichai (CEO of Alphabet Inc.): Leads an incredibly diverse global workforce with cultural awareness.

## 16. Democratic Leadership

Democratic Leadership involves team members in decision-making processes, valuing input from all participants to reach collective solutions. This participative style fosters engagement and ownership by ensuring everyone's voice is heard and considered (Lewin et al. 1939).

Commander Miles Theotokis leads a small, diverse team through enemy territory. Instead of issuing orders, he uses *democratic leadership*, encouraging every team member to share their insights. They decide together, leveraging their strengths to find the best path forward. Miles's approach shows that democracy in leadership isn't just about making everyone feel heard: it's about genuinely using each person's unique knowledge to succeed.

**Leaders who embody these qualities include:**

- Herb Kelleher (cofounder of Southwest Airlines): Engaged employees in decision-making.
- Olaf Scholz (former German chancellor): Promoted collaborative decision-making across Europe.
- Larry Page (cofounder of Google): Created a culture that embraced dialogue and employee participation.

## 17. Shared Leadership

Shared Leadership distributes leadership responsibilities across multiple team members rather than centralizing it in one person. This collaborative approach leverages diverse strengths and perspectives, fostering collective ownership and decision-making (Pearce and Conger 2003).

Imagine the merger of Corvus Industries and Orion Group—two giants coming together. Instead of a top-down, one-person-in-charge model, they embrace *shared leadership*, where leaders at every level are involved. This approach is about inclusivity and collective decision-making, which helps them navigate the complexities of their merger. Everyone's voice matters, and responsibility is distributed, which results in a unified culture and shared vision. It's about empowering others to take ownership and fostering a robust, collaborative organization.

**Leaders who embody these qualities include:**

- Mary Barra (CEO of General Motors): Values cross-functional teams and shared decision-making.
- The Beatles: Each member contributed to the band's direction, showing authentic shared leadership.
- Ben & Jerry's founders: Ben Cohen and Jerry Greenfield co-led their company, creating a collaborative culture.

## 18. Co-Creative Leadership

Co-Creative Leadership is based on collaboration and shared responsibility, where teams co-create solutions and share decision-making. It emphasizes collective wisdom, diverse perspectives, and the belief that the best outcomes arise from working together.

Queen Elara leads her group through the ever-changing Shifting Maze; but instead of issuing orders, she invites everyone to contribute ideas and help navigate the challenges. Elara taps into the group's collective intelligence by involving everyone in decision-making, proving that we're stronger when we work together. Her leadership is a reminder that sharing power and building trust can make even the most daunting obstacles surmountable.

**Leaders who embody these qualities include:**

- Ed Catmull (cofounder of Pixar Animation Studios): Created an environment where collaboration was central, leading to some of the most beloved animated films.
- Ricardo Semler (business leader): Transformed Semco into a co-created management and shared decision-making model.
- Doug Engelbart (tech pioneer): Focused on technologies that helped teams work collaboratively.

## 19. Social Leadership

Social Leadership leverages social media and online platforms to build influence, engage audiences, and drive organizational missions. It focuses on creating meaningful digital connections and using online communication to inspire and mobilize communities.

Evelyn Clarke revives Celestial Threads, a fashion brand that's fallen out of touch. By embracing social media and digital platforms, Evelyn connects directly with audiences, reshapes the brand's story, and builds a loyal community around it. She turns what was an outdated brand into a lively, engaging experience. Evelyn's ability to adapt, be authentic, and foster digital communities shows the power of social leadership in the modern age.

**Leaders who embody these qualities include:**

- Ritesh Agarwal (founder and CEO of OYO Rooms, India): Actively uses social media to connect with customers, building trust and transparency.
- Dax Shepard (cofounder of *Armchair Expert* podcast): Uses podcasting and social media to build an engaged community.

# Cluster: Adaptive and Resilient Leadership

## 20. Adaptive Leadership

Adaptive Leadership focuses on helping organizations navigate change and uncertainty by encouraging flexibility, experimentation, and continuous learning. It emphasizes the ability to adjust strategies quickly in response to evolving circumstances while maintaining focus on core objectives (Heifetz 1998).

Captain Lucas led his expedition through Ashland, a dangerous volcanic wasteland, by embracing Adaptive leadership. Thorne focused on staying flexible and adjusting on the fly in such a volatile environment. He collaborated with his team, changed plans as new challenges arose, and ensured survival through resilience and problem-solving. In this case, adaptability was the key to thriving in an unpredictable situation.

**Leaders who embody these qualities include:**

- Angela Merkel (former German chancellor): Navigated complex political challenges with adaptability.
- Jeff Bezos (Amazon founder): Constantly pivoted Amazon's strategies to stay ahead.
- Sheryl Sandberg (former COO of Facebook): Guided Facebook through numerous challenges by being Adaptive.
- Carlos Ghosn (former Nissan CEO): Adapted to diverse global markets to lead effectively.

## 21. Agile Leadership

Agile Leadership emphasizes flexibility, adaptability, and rapid decision-making in response to changing environments. It focuses on staying nimble, empowering teams to adapt quickly, and making swift adjustments to strategies as situations evolve.

Riley Storm isn't just leading any mission; it's a daring airship rescue that demands on-the-spot thinking. The unexpected is the only constant, and Riley's agility keeps everyone on track. He adapts quickly, makes rapid decisions, and encourages teamwork to overcome every obstacle. His leadership style embodies flexibility and resilience, proving that staying agile can mean the difference between success and failure.

**Leaders who embody these qualities include:**

- Reed Hastings (CEO of Netflix): Netflix's strategies continuously adapt as the industry and tech landscape changes.
- Indra Nooyi (former CEO of PepsiCo): Guided PepsiCo through shifting markets and consumer tastes with agility.
- Jeff Bezos (Amazon founder): Known for pivoting and adapting Amazon's business model to stay ahead.

- Akio Toyoda (president of Toyota Motor Corporation): Led with agility, responding to changing markets and tech innovations.

## 22. Situational Leadership

Situational Leadership involves adapting one's leadership style based on the development level and needs of team members and the specific context. Leaders shift between directive, coaching, supporting, and delegating approaches depending on what the situation demands (Blanchard et al. 1985).

Captain Isabella Moore had to lead her first responders through the chaos of a devastating earthquake in the *Havenfall* books. She used situational leadership—switching between giving direct orders, coaching, and offering support, based on what each moment required. This adaptability saved lives, showing how important it is for leaders to adjust to their surroundings and the needs of their teams.

**Leaders who embody these qualities include:**

- Ken Blanchard (leadership theorist): Developed the concept of situational leadership.
- Richard Branson (Virgin Group founder): Adapts his style across diverse ventures.
- Colin Powell (former US secretary of state): Known for adapting to the situation.
- Narendra Modi (Indian prime minister): Adjusts his strategies to fit different political and economic landscapes.

## 23. Crisis Leadership

Crisis Leadership is characterized by quick, effective decision-making under extreme pressure while maintaining clear communication. It focuses on guiding teams through uncertainty with calm composure and Adaptive strategies during emergencies.

Commander Jason Pierce stands amid chaos, leading the defense of Neo Arcadia during an alien invasion. It's the ultimate crisis scenario, and Jason keeps his team focused and determined through clear communication and rapid decision-making. He empowers his team, remains adaptable, and projects resilience. Jason's leadership is about making smart choices under pressure and showing the strength to inspire others during emergencies.

**Leaders who embody these qualities include:**

- Rudy Giuliani (former mayor of NYC): Guided New York City with steady, decisive leadership during 9/11.
- Jacinda Ardern (former New Zealand prime minister): Showed incredible empathy and leadership during the COVID-19 pandemic.
- Alan Joyce (CEO of Qantas): Led Qantas through significant financial turbulence with practical crisis management.
- Masaaki Osumi (former CEO of Toshiba): Steered the company through tough times and restored stakeholder trust.

## 24. Resilient Leadership

Resilient Leadership is focused on helping organizations and teams navigate challenges, recover from setbacks, and thrive in adversity. It emphasizes adaptability, mental toughness, and the ability to bounce back stronger from difficulties.

Janet Price takes SaphireCom through turbulent times in the telecom industry, but she doesn't just get them through—she helps them thrive. Evelyn empowers her team, celebrates successes, and learns from setbacks. She builds a culture where innovation flourishes, even in adversity. Evelyn's resilience is a beacon for her team, proving that it's possible to adapt, grow, and succeed even when the odds are stacked against you.

**Leaders who embody these qualities include:**

- Winston Churchill (former prime minister of the UK): Led Britain with resilience during one of the darkest periods in history.
- Angela Merkel (former German chancellor): Stayed calm and adaptable during multiple global crises.
- Anand Mahindra (chairman of Mahindra Group): Guided his company through economic challenges and led it to steady growth.
- Ho Ching (CEO of Temasek Holdings, Singapore): Steered through financial crises with resilience and strategic foresight.

## 25. Hybrid Leadership

Hybrid Leadership effectively manages teams across both physical and virtual spaces in blended work environments. It focuses on ensuring cohesion, productivity, and well-being regardless of where team members are located.

Sarah Kane is navigating Pioneera, a startup, through fierce competition by managing her teams across both physical offices and virtual spaces. With hybrid leadership, Sarah ensures that her team stays connected, productive, and well-supported, even in this blended work environment. She's not just about delivering results—she's focused on ensuring that her team feels unified, valued, and empowered, regardless of where they work from. By being flexible in her approach and valuing diverse contributions, Sarah demonstrates how effective communication and empowerment are at the core of successful hybrid leadership.

**Leaders who embody these qualities include:**

- Sundar Pichai (CEO of Alphabet Inc.): Leads teams effectively across physical and virtual workspaces, keeping cohesion intact in a hybrid world.

- Satya Nadella (Microsoft CEO): Championed Microsoft's transition to hybrid work, using tech to maintain collaboration and productivity.
- Daniel Zhang (former CEO of Alibaba Group): Seamlessly merged online and offline retail strategies to create a hybrid model.
- Tadashi Yanai (founder of Uniqlo, Japan): Combined in-store retail with e-commerce, responding effectively to changing consumer habits.

## 26. Quantum Leadership

Quantum Leadership embraces uncertainty, interconnectedness, and paradox, drawing from quantum physics principles to navigate complex environments. It emphasizes intuitive decision-making, adaptability, and understanding that multiple possibilities can exist simultaneously (healthcare leadership text: Porter-O'Grady and Malloch 2017).

In the mystical *Enchanted Forest* book, Seraphina leads her group using quantum leadership principles. She sees the world as interconnected and constantly changing, understanding that sometimes you must rely on intuition just as much as logic. In times of uncertainty, Seraphina builds trust and encourages her followers to embrace the complexity of their environment. It's about being flexible, open to new possibilities, and leading in a way tuned to the unpredictability of the world around us.

**Leaders who embody these qualities include:**

- Meg Wheatley (author and consultant): Applies quantum physics concepts to leadership and change.
- Danah Zohar: Introduced the concept of quantum leadership, merging science with leadership practices.
- Jeff Bezos (founder of Amazon): Operates successfully in unpredictable and nonlinear business environments.

## Cluster: Structured and Analytical Leadership

### 27. Transactional Leadership

Transactional Leadership operates through clear structures, expectations, and a system of rewards and penalties to drive performance. This style emphasizes supervision, organization, and achieving specific goals through structured agreements between leaders and followers.

At Titan Industries, Alexander Drake took a transactional leadership approach during the integration of a massive merger. He set clear goals, used rewards and penalties, and ensured that everything ran efficiently. His leadership was all about results—ensuring that his team knew exactly what was expected and how they would be held accountable for delivering.

**Leaders who embody these qualities include:**

- Bill Gates (Microsoft cofounder): Used structured performance metrics to drive success.
- Lee Iacocca (former Chrysler CEO): Turned Chrysler around, focusing on performance and accountability.
- Margaret Thatcher (former UK prime minister): Led with a strict, structured approach to achieve her goals.

### 28. Strategic Leadership

Strategic Leadership balances short-term operational needs with long-term vision, ensuring organizational decisions align with future goals. These leaders think several moves ahead, anticipating challenges and opportunities while maintaining flexibility in execution.

Dr. Winston McGimsey, CEO of BioNova, is developing *Genesis*—a biotechnological breakthrough. With *strategic leadership*, Winston has to balance the present and the future. There are ethical challenges, international conflicts, and technological hurdles. Winston drives Genesis forward responsibly by always focusing on the long-term vision while handling immediate needs. His strategic foresight and adaptability are the guiding force behind this massive undertaking.

**Leaders who embody these qualities include:**

- Ginni Rometty (former IBM CEO): Tackled immediate tech challenges while keeping a long-term strategic vision.
- Lee Kuan Yew (Singapore's founding prime minister): Pushed for strategic national development.
- Tim Cook (Apple CEO): Manages short-term needs while maintaining Apple's future direction.
- Anne Mulcahy (former Xerox CEO): Strategically led Xerox out of tough times.

## 29. Systems Leadership

Systems Leadership focuses on understanding and managing organizations as complex, interconnected systems where changes in one area affect others. Leaders using this approach think holistically, considering feedback loops and interdependencies when making decisions (Senge et al. 2015).

Dr. Adrian Cole leads Project Chiron, an ambitious initiative integrating advanced AI into society. But this isn't just about technology—Adrian knows it's about people, ethics, and impact. He uses *systems leadership*, seeing how all the parts fit together. Adrian keeps this complex ship sailing smoothly by engaging stakeholders, addressing ethical concerns, and balancing innovation with caution. It's not just about solving problems, but also understanding how each puzzle piece affects the others.

**Leaders who embody these qualities include:**

- Peter Senge (systems thinking expert): Wrote a book on organizational systems.
- Ray Dalio (founder of Bridgewater Associates): Uses interconnected system principles to guide leadership.

- Indra Nooyi (former PepsiCo CEO): Took a holistic approach to managing PepsiCo's operations and strategies.

## 30. Cognitive Leadership

Cognitive Leadership leverages diverse thinking styles and psychological insights to enhance decision-making and problem-solving. It emphasizes understanding how different people process information and using cognitive diversity to generate innovative solutions.

Amelia Grant is in a high-stakes negotiation—a labor strike. She uses cognitive leadership to bring both management and workers to the table. Amelia understands that people think differently, and she uses this insight to bridge gaps, actively listen, and bring conflicting parties together. It's not just about being smart; it's about recognizing how others think and feel, and using that understanding to solve problems. This makes her a powerful negotiator and an empathetic leader.

**Leaders who embody these qualities include:**

- Daniel Kahneman (psychologist and Nobel laureate): Revolutionized how we understand decision-making processes.
- Ray Dalio (founder of Bridgewater Associates): Uses diverse cognitive approaches in leadership.
- Angela Merkel (former German chancellor): Known for her analytical approach and embracing diverse perspectives.
- Sundar Pichai (CEO of Alphabet Inc.): Uses cognitive diversity to drive innovation.

## 31. Neuroscience-Based Leadership

Neuroscience-Based Leadership applies insights from brain science to understand how people process emotions, stress, and change, using this knowledge to enhance leadership effectiveness. It focuses on managing fear responses, building resilience, and creating psychologically safe environments that optimize team performance.

Mark Thornton, an executive at Apex Dynamics, had to deal with the emotional aftermath of layoffs. He turned to neuroscience-based leadership, using what he knew about the brain's response to stress. Mark created an environment where employees could process their emotions, stay grounded, and find stability by focusing on calming communication and empathy. His approach shows the power of understanding the mind to lead more effectively, keeping his team resilient in difficult times.

**Leaders who embody these qualities include:**

- David Rock (NeuroLeadership Institute founder): Directly applies neuroscience to leadership.
- Daniel Goleman (emotional intelligence expert): Explored how our emotional and cognitive processes shape leadership.

## 32. AI-Enhanced Leadership

AI-Enhanced Leadership integrates AI tools into leadership practices to support decision-making, optimize operations, and enhance effectiveness. It leverages data-driven insights and predictive analytics to make more informed strategic choices.

Jaxon Klark is taking on a considerable challenge: launching Helios Tech's latest, revolutionary product. Jaxon leverages AI to gather data, predict trends, and optimize operations to pull it off. It's not just the technology that makes Jaxon stand out—it's how he tells data-driven stories and uses these insights to make strategic decisions that rally his team and assure stakeholders. Jaxon's leadership demonstrates how AI can be a game-changing tool to enhance a leader's ability to steer through challenges.

**Leaders who embody these qualities include:**

- Ginni Rometty (former IBM CEO): Integrated AI into IBM's strategies, driving more ingenious decision-making processes.

- Sundar Pichai: Pioneered the integration of AI into products and services, using data to shape decisions.
- Robin Li (cofounder of Baidu, China): Advanced AI technologies in search engines and autonomous driving.
- Pony Ma (founder of Tencent, China): Brought AI into social media and gaming, enhancing the user experience.

## 33. Digital Leadership

Digital Leadership leverages digital tools and technologies to lead teams, drive digital transformation, and manage virtual environments effectively. It focuses on building digital-first cultures and using technology to enhance collaboration and innovation.

Alex Knight takes TechFrontier on a journey to transform the energy industry, fully embracing digital innovation and sustainable technology. It's not just about adopting new tools; Alex uses digital leadership to inspire his team and overcome resistance to change. He builds a culture where data, tech, and creativity unite, showing how digital strategies can lead to meaningful and lasting transformation.

**Leaders who embody these qualities include:**

- Marc Benioff (Salesforce CEO): Used digital tools to propel Salesforce's growth.
- Jack Ma (Alibaba cofounder): Revolutionized e-commerce through a comprehensive digital-first strategy.
- Sheryl Sandberg (former COO of Meta/Facebook): Spearheaded digital communication advancements.
- Susan Wojcicki (former YouTube CEO): Helped the platform grow through digital strategy and a focus on user engagement.
- Daniel Zhang (former CEO of Alibaba Group): Continued to push the boundaries of digital innovation within Alibaba.

## 34. Mindful Leadership

Mindful Leadership integrates mindfulness practices into decision-making, promoting self-awareness, emotional regulation, and presence in every interaction. It emphasizes staying fully present in each moment to make clear, thoughtful decisions even under pressure (practice guide: Marturano 2014).

Arin Tenzin is leading his group through a dangerous mountain pass, and instead of just charging ahead, he chooses to be fully present in each moment. Arin stays calm, makes clear decisions, and encourages his team to do the same. His focus on mindfulness helps everyone stay resilient and face their fears without losing clarity. Arin's ability to keep everyone centered in a high-stakes environment shows how powerful staying mindful can be in leadership.

**Leaders who embody these qualities include:**

- Janice Marturano (Institute for Mindful Leadership founder): Introduces mindfulness into leadership, helping people make decisions with clarity and presence.
- Marc Benioff (CEO of Salesforce): Encourages mindfulness as a way for employees to stay focused and emotionally balanced.
- Ratan Tata (former chairman of Tata group, India): Known for his ethical business practices and mindfulness toward employee well-being.

# Cluster: Principled Leadership

## 35. Authentic Leadership

Authentic Leadership emphasizes leading with transparency, integrity, and consistency between one's values and actions, building trust through genuine behavior. These leaders remain true to their principles, even when faced with difficult decisions, thereby creating ethical cultures founded on honesty and openness (Avolio and Gardner 2005).

Elias Sanchez, CEO of Pinnacle Corporation, leads his company's global expansion by staying true to his values, even when navigating unfamiliar business cultures. He's transparent, ethical, and consistent, which earns him trust and respect worldwide. By fostering a culture rooted in honesty, he strengthens his team's cohesion and the organization's reputation. Elias shows us that being honest and authentic makes leadership much more powerful.

**Leaders who embody these qualities include:**

- Justin Trudeau (former Canadian prime minister): Led with transparency and sincerity.
- Oprah Winfrey (media executive): Engages others with honesty and personal storytelling.
- Alan Mulally (former Ford CEO): Guided Ford through tough times with honesty and openness.
- Howard Schultz (former Starbucks CEO): Stayed true to his values around ethical practices and employee welfare.

## 36. Holacratic Leadership

Holocratic Leadership is a decentralized leadership approach where decision-making authority is distributed throughout self-organizing teams. It empowers individuals to make decisions within their areas of expertise while maintaining collective accountability (holacracy, operating system for orgs: Robertson 2015).

Cassian Holt is leading a group of survivors in Hollow Creek, a ghost town that needs defending. Instead of taking control single-handedly, Cassian uses a holacratic approach—giving the group autonomy to make decisions within their roles. This leadership style empowers each member to take ownership, and this shared sense of responsibility enables them to come together and face their challenges effectively.

**Leaders who embody these qualities include:**

- Tony Hsieh (former CEO of Zappos): Embraced a radical organizational structure to empower his team.
- Brian Robertson (creator of Holacracy): Built a framework for decentralized decision-making.
- Jean-François Zobrist (former CEO of FAVI, France): Created a flat organizational structure that encouraged autonomy.
- Ricardo Semler (former CEO of Semco, Brazil): Applied holacratic principles, giving power to the people in his organization.

## 37. Maternalistic Leadership

Maternalistic Leadership emphasizes nurturing, protecting, and supporting team members with a mother's care while maintaining firm guidance. These leaders create safe, supportive environments where people feel valued and cared for, fostering resilience and unity through compassionate strength.

Marisol Vega leads an underground resistance movement known as *the Haven*. In a time of oppression, she uses *maternalistic leadership*, blending strength with compassion. She's fierce when she needs to be, but also deeply nurturing—taking care of her people and inspiring them to keep fighting. Marisol's leadership shows that nurturing and caring for others doesn't mean you aren't strong; it makes her followers resilient.

**Leaders who embody these qualities include:**

- Mary Kay Ash (founder of Mary Kay Cosmetics): Empowered her sales force with a nurturing leadership style.
- Ellen Johnson Sirleaf (former president of Liberia): Led with a balance of strength and compassion, guiding her country through crisis.

## 38. Paternalistic Leadership

Paternalistic Leadership combines strong authority with fatherly care, where leaders act as protective figures who make decisions for their team's benefit. This style strikes a balance between discipline and benevolence, creating a family-like atmosphere where the leader guides and supports subordinates (Pellegrini and Scandura 2008).

Manuel Ortega, a respected elder, guides his community through the aftermath of the tsunami. He uses *paternalistic leadership*, taking on the role of protector. Manuel makes tough decisions that are always in the best interest of the islanders, while also providing them with support and care. His trustworthiness and protective nature keep everyone grounded, showing that sometimes a leader's role is to be both a guardian and a guide.

**Leaders who embody these qualities include:**

- Lee Kuan Yew (Singapore's founding prime minister): Led Singapore's development with a firm, but caring hand.
- Henry Ford (founder of Ford): Guided his employees with protective welfare policies.
- Konosuke Matsushita (founder of Panasonic): Known for his focus on employee welfare.
- King Salman bin Abdulaziz (Saudi Arabian monarch): Demonstrates a paternalistic, protective leadership approach.

## 39. Biophilic Leadership

Biophilic Leadership integrates nature and natural principles into the workplace to enhance well-being, creativity, and sustainability. It recognizes the human connection to nature and leverages it to create healthier, more productive work environments (biophilic design: Browning et al. 2024).

Harper Greene, CEO of Solara Dynamics, integrates nature into the workplace to enhance well-being and creativity. By redesigning the workspace to include natural elements, Eleanor boosts her team's health, happiness, and productivity. She believes that harmony with nature is not just about sustainability—creating a thriving work environment where people feel their best. Eleanor's leadership shows how incorporating nature into business can lead to personal and corporate growth.

**Leaders who embody these qualities include:**

- Amanda Sturgeon (architect and advocate): Introduced biophilic principles to connect people with nature in built environments.
- Bill Browning (cofounder of Terrapin Bright Green): Promoted workplace designs that integrate natural elements for well-being.
- Thomas Heatherwick (founder of Heatherwick Studio, UK): Brings nature into architecture, blurring the lines between buildings and the environment.
- Bjarke Ingels (founder of BIG, Denmark): Designs sustainable buildings that coexist beautifully with nature.

## 40. Laissez-faire Leadership

Laissez-Faire Leadership provides minimal direction and supervision, allowing team members maximum autonomy to make decisions and manage their work. This hands-off approach works best with highly skilled, self-motivated teams who thrive with independence (Lewin et al. 1939).

In the heat of intergalactic battle on the starship Cyclone, Captain Laura Voss trusted her skilled crew to make their own decisions. Elena practiced laissez-faire leadership, setting goals and trusting her team to handle the details. Her crew thrived under the autonomy, and their quick decisions led to victory. Sometimes letting go and trusting capable people can be the most effective approach.

**Leaders who embody these qualities include:**

- Warren Buffett (Berkshire Hathaway CEO): Believes in empowering leaders within his company.
- Jimmy Wales (Wikipedia founder): Built a platform where contributors have significant autonomy.
- Lakshmi Mittal (ArcelorMittal CEO): Delegates extensively, trusting regional leaders to manage operations.

For a deeper dive into these styles, see my other two books, *The Leadership Compass* and *Leading with Tomorrow in Mind*. More information at: https://leaderscrucible.com

## Key Takeaways from this Chapter

The forty leadership styles introduced here illustrate just how many ways there are to inspire and guide others. From Servant Leadership to AI-enhanced Leadership, each style provides specific strengths and unique perspectives, and no single approach can handle every challenge. In a fast-paced, ever-changing environment, being aware of multiple styles allows leaders to be genuinely fluid—adjusting their methods to suit diverse teams, situations, and objectives.

- Range of Approaches: Leadership can manifest as directive or empowering, empathetic or strategic, holistic, or data-driven. Knowing this wide palette enriches your options.
- Context Is Crucial: Each style has its sweet spot. Crisis Leadership works best under high pressure, whereas Laissez-faire Leadership can empower highly skilled, self-motivated teams.
- Adaptability Fuels Success: Shifting from one style to another based on real-time demands embodies fluid leadership.
- Technology's Role: AI-enhanced and Digital Leadership demonstrate the growing importance of data, analytics, and online platforms, highlighting how modern leaders must integrate technology effectively.
- Ethics and Purpose: Sustainable and Regenerative Leadership

remind us that leadership done well has a long-term perspective and places societal and environmental values at the core.
- Shared Power: Co-Creative and Shared Leadership show that distributing authority can improve engagement, spark collective innovation, and make organizations more resilient.

**Summary**

- Many Styles, One Goal: Every leadership style aims to influence and mobilize others for a common purpose.
- Innovation Requires Courage: Fostering creativity often involves balancing risk and reward, as in Innovation Leadership and Agile Leadership.
- Relationships Matter: Styles like Relational and Empathy-Based Leadership highlight the power of genuine human connection.
- Focus on Growth: Transformational and Authentic Leadership emphasize personal and team development, building cultures that embrace learning.
- Clarity in Complexity: Systems and Holacratic Leadership offer ways to organize and collaborate in nontraditional or fast-evolving settings.
- Infinite Possibilities: No style is definitive; leaders can adopt elements from each to shape their unique approach.

The styles covered here are not rigid boxes, but useful lenses, each revealing different facets of leadership excellence. By recognizing the context in which each style thrives, leaders gain the flexibility to tailor their approach for the most impact.

Next, we will turn the focus inward. In the upcoming chapter, "Identifying Your Dominant Leadership Style," we will explore self-awareness and how to pinpoint your natural tendencies. After all, understanding yourself is the essential starting point for becoming a genuinely fluid leader.

# Chapter 6

# Identifying Your Dominant Leadership Style

*Self-awareness is the starting point for effective leadership; knowing your dominant style is key.*

Think of leadership styles as not just rigid definitions, but more like a spectrum—a wide range of possibilities rather than one fixed identity. Leaders rarely fit neatly into just one category. Instead, they often reflect a blend of elements, drawing from different areas based on their focus and the situation. To help make sense of this complex nature of leadership, it's helpful to look at different leadership styles through five broad clusters. Each cluster highlights a particular set of priorities, methods, and values. By figuring out which cluster feels most like your "home base" and exploring the styles within it, you can get a better sense of your natural strengths as a leader and uncover areas where you could grow further.

This chapter will walk you through a structured process to pinpoint your predominant leadership style and show how it aligns with five key leadership clusters: Transformative and Visionary; Relational and People-Focused; Adaptive and Resilient; Structured and Analytical; and Principled Leadership.

We begin with an assessment to help you identify which cluster best reflects your natural tendencies. Once you have identified your predominant cluster, you will proceed to a more focused assessment, helping you identify the style—or mix of styles—that most closely matches your approach.

This chapter is about transforming self-awareness into a more profound knowledge of your predominant style. The assessments will help you clarify your core leadership tendencies.

## ASSESSMENT 1

### Identify Your Leadership Style Cluster

Complete the leadership cluster assessment.

Download the assessment named "1 - Leadership Cluster Assessment" at:

https://leaderscrucible.com/leadership-styles-assessments/

Full instructions for completing the assessment are contained within the assessment itself.

See the Chapter Workout at the end of this chapter for using the results of the assessment.

## Leadership Clusters Defined and Their Characteristics

It can be overwhelming to understand all the leadership styles out there. To make this exploration more accessible, we've grouped various styles into five broad clusters. Each cluster represents a group of leadership styles with similar priorities and characteristics. By examining these clusters, you can see which resonates most with your natural approach and identify where there's room for you to grow further.

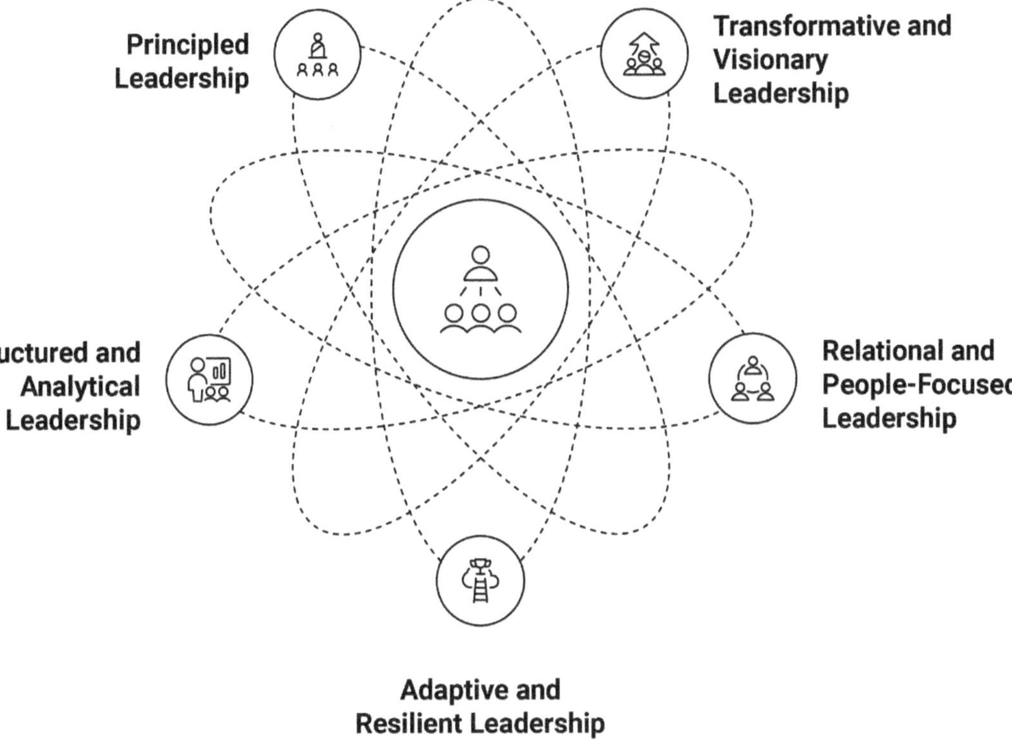


*Figure 9: Leadership Styles Clusters*

## Transformative and Visionary Leadership

This cluster is for leaders who are catalysts for change—inspiring people with big ideas and moving organizations toward an exciting future. Transformative and Visionary leaders are not interested in just keeping things as they are: They want to push boundaries and uncover new possibilities that others might not see. They're the ones who light the way, making people believe in what could be, even if it's uncharted territory.

**Characteristics:**

- Inspiration: They motivate through a clear, compelling vision that inspires people's passion and commitment.

- Change-Oriented: They focus on transforming systems, breaking barriers, and advancing industries.
- Innovation: They foster creativity and encourage out-of-the-box ideas, creating an environment where innovation thrives.
- Strategic Thinking: They think big, but know how to break down dreams into actionable steps.
- Charisma: They draw people in, rallying others with their infectious energy and personal influence.
- Purpose-Driven: Their leadership often goes beyond just profits; they're driven by a purpose, like social change, environmental impact, or community welfare.

**Leadership Styles in this Cluster:**

1. Transformational Leadership: Encouraging people to grow, exceed expectations, and contribute to something bigger than themselves.
2. Purpose-Driven Leadership: Leading with a mission bigger than business profits, often focusing on social or environmental good.
3. Transcendent Leadership: Helping others find personal meaning and higher values in their work.
4. Resonant Leadership: Creating a deep emotional connection with people to inspire collective enthusiasm.
5. Charismatic Leadership: Leading through sheer personal charm and persuasive communication.
6. Innovation Leadership: Setting ambitious goals and creating an environment where creativity flourishes.
7. Sustainable Leadership: Making decisions that consider long-term social and environmental responsibilities.
8. Regenerative Leadership: Focused on restoring and renewing—systems, organizations, or communities.
9. Integral Leadership: Integrating multiple leadership styles and adapting to diverse contexts.

## Relational and People-Focused Leadership

Relational and People-Focused leaders make their mark by building strong relationships and fostering team spirit. These leaders use emotional intelligence as a foundation for everything they do. They believe in nurturing people, developing trust, and creating a culture of inclusivity. In their teams, everyone feels like they belong, and that sense of belonging becomes the driving force for success.

**Characteristics:**

- Empathy: They genuinely care about the emotional needs of their team members.
- Inclusivity: They value everyone's perspective, ensuring that all voices are heard.
- Collaboration: They believe in teamwork and shared decision-making, recognizing the strength of diversity.
- Communication: They actively listen, building trust through open and honest conversations.
- Trust-Building: They focus on nurturing deep interpersonal connections that foster loyalty.
- Supportive: They empower others, helping them to reach their full potential and to feel valued.

**Leadership Styles in this Cluster:**

1. Servant Leadership: Putting others' needs first and empowering them to succeed.
2. Empathy-Based Leadership: Attending to the emotional and psychological needs of the team.
3. Relational Leadership: Emphasizing connections between people to create a stronger organizational culture.
4. Human-centered Leadership: Ensuring that technology and progress do not come at the expense of people.

5. Inclusive Leadership: Promoting equality by valuing every team member's voice.
6. Cultural Intelligence Leadership: Bridging cultural differences to lead effectively in diverse environments.
7. Democratic Leadership: Encouraging shared decision-making, allowing everyone to participate.
8. Shared Leadership: Distributing responsibilities to foster collective accountability.
9. Co-Creative Leadership: Encouraging teams to create and innovate together.
10. Social Leadership: Leveraging social platforms to build communities and engage stakeholders.

## Adaptive and Resilient Leadership

Adaptive and Resilient leaders shine brightest in unpredictable environments. They think on their feet, adjust plans when things change, and make quick decisions under pressure—all while keeping the team's morale high. Their flexibility and resilience ensure that they cope and thrive, even in challenging times.

**Characteristics:**

- Flexibility: They adapt strategies to suit whatever new challenges arise.
- Decisiveness: They make confident decisions even in uncertain situations, providing much-needed clarity.
- Resilience: They bounce back from setbacks and encourage their teams to do the same.
- Learning-Oriented: They're open to feedback and constantly seek growth.
- Risk Tolerance: They're not afraid to take risks and move forward, even when the outcome isn't guaranteed.
- Optimism: They keep a positive outlook, inspiring their teams to remain hopeful and proactive.

**Leadership Styles in this Cluster:**

1. Adaptive Leadership: Pivoting and evolving strategies based on unpredictable changes.
2. Agile Leadership: Acting quickly and efficiently in fast-paced environments.
3. Situational Leadership: Adapting leadership styles based on the team's needs at any given time.
4. Crisis Leadership: Staying calm under pressure and guiding teams through high-stakes situations.
5. Resilient Leadership: Showing strength in adversity and helping teams persevere.
6. Hybrid Leadership: Managing a mix of in-person and virtual teams, adapting to new work modes.
7. Quantum Leadership: Embracing complexity, uncertainty, and the interconnectedness of systems.

## Structured and Analytical Leadership

Leaders in this cluster value systems, structure, and data-driven decision-making. They create a predictable environment where everyone knows what's expected of them, and they use established frameworks to optimize processes. Their emphasis on consistency and data ensures reliable results that support organizational goals.

**Characteristics:**

- Organized: They build transparent systems, procedures, and expectations.
- Data-driven: They base decisions on metrics and analytical insights.
- Methodical: They plan meticulously and ensure that every step follows a logical process.
- Results-Oriented: They are focused on outcomes and meeting performance targets.

- Systemic Thinking: They understand how different parts of the organization interconnect.
- Consistency: They provide stability, giving the team a sense of predictability.

**Leadership Styles in this Cluster:**

1. Transactional Leadership: Using clear incentives and expectations to motivate.
2. Strategic Leadership: Balancing the organization's short-term needs with long-term objectives.
3. Systems Leadership: Seeing the big picture by understanding how all components of the organization work together.
4. Cognitive Leadership: Using diverse thinking strategies to improve decision-making.
5. Neuroscience-Based Leadership: Applying insights from brain science to make better leadership decisions.
6. AI-Enhanced Leadership: Using technology and data to guide decisions effectively.
7. Digital Leadership: Leveraging digital tools to drive organizational growth.
8. Mindful Leadership: Leading with focus, awareness, and emotional regulation.

## Principled Leadership

Principled leaders are motivated by a deep commitment to doing the right thing. They lead with integrity, fairness, and a long-term perspective, ensuring that their actions benefit the organization and society. This approach creates a culture of trust where people know that their leader's decisions are rooted in genuine moral values.

Although principled leadership should be the foundation of all leaders, it is the easiest to forgo under pressure, and some leaders live these characteristics more fully. It is their primary driver as leaders. This leadership style group attempts to emphasize grouping specific characteristics deserving of its own cluster.

**Characteristics:**

- Integrity: They are unwavering in their commitment to moral and ethical principles.
- Transparency: They are open and honest, building trust through authenticity.
- Fairness: They treat all team members equitably.
- Trustworthiness: They gain loyalty through consistency and reliability.
- Purpose-Led: They consider the broader societal impact of their actions, going beyond profit.
- Long-Term Perspective: They focus on sustainability and legacy, thinking beyond immediate gains.

**Leadership Styles in this Cluster:**

1. Authentic Leadership: Leading by staying true to oneself and fostering trust.
2. Holacratic Leadership: Honoring individual autonomy and collective accountability.
3. Maternalistic Leadership: Guiding with care, compassion, and support.
4. Paternalistic Leadership: Balancing authoritative decision-making with a protective and supportive attitude.
5. Biophilic Leadership: Integrating natural elements into the workplace to promote health and well-being.
6. Laissez-faire Leadership: Trusting and empowering teams through minimal intervention.

## ASSESSMENT 2

### Identify Your Predominant Leadership Style

Downloaded the assessment named "2 - Leadership Styles Assessment" at:

https://leaderscrucible.com/leadership-styles-assessments/

Full instructions for completing the assessment are contained within the assessment itself.

See the Chapter Workout at the end of this chapter for using the results of the assessment.

## Relationship Between Leadership Styles and Clusters

Imagine sitting at a table where each leadership style—Transformational, Servant, Adaptive, Transactional, etc.—is represented by percentages, showing how much each style draws from different leadership clusters.

Take Transformational Leadership as an example: It might show a high percentage in the Transformative and Visionary cluster, given its focus on driving change and igniting purpose, while it might score lower in the Principled cluster. This doesn't mean ethical considerations aren't necessary—it's just that they're not the primary driver of this style. On the other hand, Servant Leadership might have the bulk of its traits in the Relational and People-Focused cluster, but also include a solid share of Principled and a small piece of Transformative and Visionary—acknowledging that serving others often involves inspiring and leading with integrity.

These percentages help recognize that no leader—or leadership style—is a one-dimensional figure. Leaders are complex beings, and their styles can shift based on their personality, their experience, the team's needs, and the pressures of the current situation.

Assigning these percentages attempts to give us a more balanced picture of a leader's distributed traits. It acknowledges the rich mix that makes up real-world leadership, showing that while you might naturally lean toward certain qualities, you also carry other characteristics that can be nurtured or leaned into when the situation calls for it.

| | **% Split** | | | | |
|---|---|---|---|---|---|
| **Leadership Style** | **T&V** | **R&P** | **A&R** | **S&A** | **P** |
| Transformational Leadership | 69 | 8 | 4 | 4 | 15 |
| Purpose-Driven Leadership | 65 | 12 | 4 | 8 | 12 |
| Transcendent Leadership | 67 | 8 | 4 | 4 | 17 |
| Resonant Leadership | 58 | 15 | 8 | 4 | 15 |
| Charismatic Leadership | 58 | 17 | 8 | 4 | 13 |
| Innovation Leadership | 73 | 4 | 4 | 8 | 12 |
| Sustainable Leadership | 68 | 8 | 4 | 4 | 16 |
| Regenerative Leadership | 67 | 8 | 8 | 4 | 13 |
| Biophilic Leadership | 60 | 16 | 4 | 4 | 16 |
| Servant Leadership | 24 | 53 | 9 | 3 | 12 |
| Empathy-Based Leadership | 21 | 50 | 9 | 3 | 18 |
| Relational Leadership | 18 | 52 | 12 | 3 | 15 |
| Human-Centered Leadership | 25 | 47 | 9 | 3 | 16 |
| Inclusive Leadership | 22 | 50 | 9 | 3 | 16 |
| Cultural Intelligence Leadership | 19 | 53 | 9 | 3 | 16 |

| Leadership Style | T&V | R&P | A&R | S&A | P |
|---|---|---|---|---|---|
| Democratic Leadership | 17 | 53 | 7 | 7 | 17 |
| Shared Leadership | 17 | 55 | 7 | 7 | 14 |
| Co-Creative Leadership | 15 | 54 | 8 | 8 | 15 |
| Maternalistic Leadership | 13 | 53 | 10 | 7 | 17 |
| Paternalistic Leadership | 13 | 57 | 7 | 3 | 20 |
| Adaptive Leadership | 9 | 19 | 56 | 3 | 13 |
| Agile Leadership | 7 | 14 | 61 | 7 | 11 |
| Situational Leadership | 7 | 11 | 63 | 11 | 7 |
| Crisis Leadership | 10 | 13 | 60 | 10 | 7 |
| Resilient Leadership | 10 | 16 | 55 | 13 | 6 |
| Hybrid Leadership | 7 | 20 | 57 | 10 | 7 |
| Quantum Leadership | 4 | 15 | 15 | 59 | 7 |
| Transactional Leadership | 7 | 7 | 10 | 62 | 14 |
| Strategic Leadership | 13 | 3 | 10 | 58 | 16 |
| Systems Leadership | 7 | 7 | 10 | 62 | 14 |
| Cognitive Leadership | 10 | 7 | 10 | 59 | 14 |
| Neuroscience-Based Leadership | 13 | 7 | 10 | 57 | 13 |
| AI-Enhanced Leadership | 16 | 9 | 6 | 56 | 13 |
| Digital Leadership | 19 | 6 | 6 | 55 | 13 |
| Holacratic Leadership | 10 | 10 | 20 | 20 | 40 |
| Mindful Leadership | 18 | 5 | 5 | 18 | 55 |
| Ethical Leadership | 21 | 8 | 8 | 17 | 46 |
| Principled Leadership | 27 | 14 | 5 | 18 | 36 |
| Social Leadership | 11 | 47 | 3 | 6 | 33 |

*T&V = Transformative & Visionary; R&P = Relational & People-Focused; A&R = Adaptive & Resilient; S&A = Structured & Analytical; P = Ethical & Principled*

## Practical Application of Styles to Cluster Percentages

Seeing leadership styles through these percentages offers several benefits—for both leaders and their organizations. On an individual level, it allows leaders to identify where they're naturally strong, whether that's in driving change or being particularly empathetic. But, just as importantly, it can also reveal where there's room for growth.

Let's say a leader finds that they have very little representation in the Adaptive and Resilient cluster. This might indicate that they need to work on becoming more flexible or finding ways to handle uncertainty better. Similarly, a leader with low Principled traits might need to develop a stronger focus on ethical decision-making and transparency.

This kind of analysis can more precisely direct personal development efforts. For instance, if a leader identifies a personal lack of Adaptive skills, they might decide to push themselves into situations that are a little outside their comfort zone—they might lead a project with many unknowns, or work with a coach to better manage stress and ambiguity. If their weakness lies in Structured and Analytical traits, they could focus on becoming more data-savvy and using metrics more effectively in their team's workflows.

These percentages help create balanced leadership teams on an organizational level. Suppose a company's senior leadership is heavy on visionaries and people-focused leaders, but lacks Structured and Analytical approaches. In that case, it may need to develop or bring in leaders who are strong in systems-thinking and data-driven strategies. Conversely, if adaptability and resilience are missing across the leadership board, the organization might focus on training that builds a comfort level with uncertainty and enhances responsiveness to change.

## Recognizing the Framework's Limitations

While the Leadership Style Cluster Percentages approach can offer profound insights, it's essential to recognize that it simplifies complex human behavior. Assigning percentages can make it look like we're achieving a level of precision, but leadership is anything but static or precise. A leader who scores low on Adaptive traits in a calm period might surprise everyone—including themselves—by rising to the occasion during a crisis, showing much more adaptability than the numbers suggest.

It's also important to note that this framework doesn't account for every variable—such as the impact of cultural contexts or how a leader grows over time. Nor does it capture how different leadership styles can interact or reinforce each other when a leader draws from multiple clusters simultaneously. For instance, someone might mix Transformative and Visionary thinking with strong relational skills, creating a unique synergy that no percentage breakdown can capture.

Another factor to consider is the limitations of self-assessment, which is often used to derive these percentages. Self-assessments can be influenced by biases or simple misperceptions about one's capabilities. Without external input—like 360-degree feedback or insights from colleagues—the results might not give an entirely accurate picture of a leader's tendencies.

## Embracing Complexity and Change

Despite these limitations, the Leadership Style Cluster Percentages approach remains a valuable starting point. Leaders should see it as one tool in their development tool kit—not the be-all and end-all of who they are. It helps prompt reflection and guide personal growth, but it should never be seen as a final verdict on one's leadership abilities.

Leaders who find themselves heavily represented in a particular cluster might want to look at how they can diversify their skills—not for the sake of ticking boxes, but to improve their effectiveness across different scenarios. If you identify as having a dominant style, you could focus on leveraging the strengths of that style while finding ways to blend in elements from other clusters that might enhance your overall impact. Likewise, leadership teams stand to gain more significant insights into the balance of their styles and composition.

The real power of this approach lies not in perfect measurement, but in creating awareness and starting conversations. Understanding that leadership isn't a "pure form"—and that each leader is a unique blend—opens the door to richer insights into who you are and who you could become as a leader.

In summary, the relationship between individual leadership styles and these clusters is rich and complex. Leaders rarely fit neatly into one category; instead, they pull traits from multiple clusters, each with intensity. By exploring these distributions and percentages, leaders can get a more realistic picture of their strengths and potential areas for growth. It may not capture every nuance or situational variable; still, it does help leaders think more critically about how they lead, what they value, and where they could stretch themselves to become even more effective.

## Key Takeaways from this Chapter

Like the leadership clusters and style percentages we've discussed, these matrices are tools to help you better understand yourself—they're not the end goal. They give you a framework to think about the complexities of your leadership style and a common language to navigate the trade-offs and synergies between different approaches.

### Summary

- **Leadership Clusters as a Foundation:** We grouped leadership styles into five clusters—Transformative and Visionary; Relational and People-Focused; Adaptive and Resilient; Structured and Analytical; and Principled. This helps us make sense of the wide range of qualities that leaders bring to the table.
- **No One Cluster Reigns Supreme:** Leaders are unique blends of these clusters. You might lean heavily toward one cluster, but you're probably drawing from others, giving a more nuanced and complete picture of your leadership approach.
- **Identifying Your Predominant Leadership Style:** Focusing on your predominant leadership style(s) provides clarity on your leadership strengths, while the weaker styles may

indicate opportunities for growth or adding resources that display these characteristics, if necessary.

- **Percentages Add Nuanced Insight:** Assigning normalized percentages to leadership traits within clusters acknowledges that leadership is not black-and-white. It shows where your natural strengths lie and which areas might benefit from extra development.

Being a leader today means navigating a sea of complexities—uncertainties, cultural diversity, and market changes. Gaining insight into your leadership approach using clusters, style distributions, and visual matrices can give you a strong foundation for adapting effectively.

Remember that no single framework can capture the full richness of who you are as a leader. These tools act like mirrors, reflecting different facets of your leadership so you can understand them better.

Growth isn't about reaching a final form or achieving perfection. It's about self-awareness, responsiveness, and versatility. Over time, you'll learn when to lean into your Relational qualities—maybe when the team needs a morale boost—or leverage your Adaptive traits to steer through sudden market changes. Or perhaps you'll rely on Structured methods to ensure that your ambitious ideas don't stay as dreams, but get executed effectively.

By embracing these concepts, you're on a path of continuous improvement, ensuring that you stay authentic, effective, and ready to tackle whatever challenges your organization and the wider world throw at you.

# Chapter Workout

Embarking on this journey to understand your leadership style is more about introspection than strategy. These exercises and journaling prompts will guide you through a deeper exploration of your unique leadership qualities and help you identify opportunities to grow. Remember, this is your leadership odyssey—take your time and be as open and honest with yourself as possible.

## Exercise 1: Complete the Leadership Clusters Self-Assessment Questionnaire

The first step is understanding where you are. Complete the Leadership Cluster Assessment to identify which leadership cluster feels most like home. This will help clarify your tendencies, strengths, and areas that might benefit from nurturing.

**Review Your Assessment Results**

1. **Look at Cluster Averages:**
   - Start by examining your scores (or feedback) across each leadership cluster:
     - » Transformative and Visionary Leadership
     - » Relational and People-Focused Leadership
     - » Adaptive and Resilient Leadership
     - » Structured and Analytical Leadership
     - » Principled Leadership

2. **Identify Your Predominant Leadership Cluster(s)**
   - **Shortlist Your Top Cluster(s):**

- » If one cluster has clearly higher ratings, that may be your primary leadership cluster.
- » If two clusters are closely tied, explore each further to see which is truly more representative of your core leadership style.

- **Embrace Multiple Influences:**
    - » It's normal to see strengths in more than one area. If you consistently score well (when reassessing) in multiple clusters, view yourself as having a hybrid style.
    - » Remember, leadership is often situational, so having multiple strengths can be a real asset.
- **Acknowledge Your Strengths**
    - » **High Scores:** The areas where you rate yourself highly are likely where you feel most confident. Recognize these strengths and consider how they contribute to your current success.
    - » **Reflect on Your Experiences:** Think of specific examples or situations where you demonstrated these strengths. This helps reinforce positive leadership habits and clarifies how you can continue leveraging them.
- **Examine Areas for Development**
    - » **Lower Ratings:** Pinpoint the clusters where you gave yourself lower scores. Reflect on whether these ratings surprise you or align with feedback you've received informally.
    - » **Understand Context:** Consider any external factors (e.g., organizational changes, workload, or recent challenges) that might have influenced your self-perception.

## Exercise 2: Complete the Leadership Styles Assessment for Your Predominant Cluster

After identifying your predominant cluster, delve deeper. Complete the Leadership Styles Assessment, focusing on the highest-scoring cluster. This will help pinpoint which style—or mix of styles—best defines how you lead.

1. **Select the Right Cluster:**
   - Once you have identified your predominant cluster(s), look for the Leadership Styles Assessment specific to that cluster. For instance, if you discovered strong Transformative and Visionary traits, proceed to the assessment addressing Transformational, Purpose-Driven, or Innovation Leadership styles.

2. **Dive Deeper into Individual Styles:**
   - Each cluster comprises multiple leadership styles. For example, Transformative and Visionary might include Transformational Leadership, Charismatic Leadership, etc.
   - Completing this style-specific assessment allows you to gain richer insights into how you align with individual styles within that broader cluster.

3. **Use the Findings:**
   - **Study your style:** Learn more about your leadership styles in the Appendix (and in the books *The Leadership Compass* and *Leading with Tomorrow in Mind*) to better understand your predominant styles.

## Exercise 3: Deep-Dive into Your Predominant Cluster and Style

This deep dive aims to give you a more nuanced understanding of your primary leadership style and how it affects your daily leadership.

1. **Cluster Characteristics:**
   - **Key Traits:** What are the key characteristics of your identified cluster that resonate most with you? Is it the focus on innovation, the dedication to ethics, or perhaps the strength in adaptability?
   - **Daily Practice:** Think about how these characteristics manifest in your day-to-day leadership. Do they shape how you make decisions or communicate with your team? Describe specific situations where these traits have influenced your actions.

2. **Specific Leadership Styles:**
   - **Predominant Leadership Styles:** Do your predominant leadership styles—as highlighted by the assessment—resonate with you? Describe how or how not.
   - **Real Examples:** Provide examples of when you've demonstrated these styles in your leadership role. Maybe there was a time when you inspired your team during a challenging project, or perhaps you adopted a servant leadership approach by prioritizing your team's growth and welfare.

3. **Strengths and Opportunities:**
   - **Strengths:** Reflect on the strengths of your leadership style within this cluster. What do you do well, and how does it improve your effectiveness?
   - **Growth Areas:** What about those weak spots? Identify areas where your style could use some development to enhance your leadership impact further.

# Chapter 7

# Understanding Cluster Interactions and Styles Matrices

*By blending different leadership characteristics, leaders can navigate complexity with agility and inspire their teams through every change.*

Leadership is like weaving together threads from different fabrics, combining diverse traits and approaches to create something that fits the constantly shifting challenges you face. The key is knowing how to adapt—blending qualities correctly to respond to the moment and meet your team's needs.

In this chapter, we dive deeper into the five core leadership clusters: Transformative and Visionary (T&V), Relational and People-Focused (R&P), Adaptive and Resilient (A&R), Structured and Analytical (S&A), and Principled (P). While we've explored these clusters individually, it's essential to recognize that leadership doesn't work in neat boxes. Leaders rarely operate solely within one cluster. Instead, they mix and match qualities across these areas, shifting gears as circumstances demand.

This chapter examines how these clusters overlap, enhance one another, and occasionally clash. By exploring these interactions, you can develop a leadership style that is both versatile and effective. We'll explore practical scenarios where different clusters intersect, showing how traits from one approach can complement another.

We'll also explore two matrices that provide frameworks that visually map how different styles relate to each other.

## Blending Clusters in Practice

Each cluster has its core values and tendencies, but effective leaders often weave these together. For instance, a Transformative and Visionary leader can better realize significant, bold changes by adopting Relational and People-Focused skills such as empathy and inclusivity, ensuring that teams feel committed to a shared goal. Conversely, an R&P-oriented leader may need Transformative traits to lead a significant restructuring or shift in company strategy. Likewise, Principled Leadership provides a moral foundation that complements relational qualities built on trust or transformative visions grounded in doing the right thing. A leader who excels in Structured and Analytical thinking may discover that adopting Adaptive and Resilient traits can help them respond swiftly to chaos. Meanwhile, even the most visionary leader benefits from data-driven analysis to ensure that ambitious ideas are feasible and impactful.

These interactions go beyond occasional use. Relational and People-Focused Leadership naturally aligns with Principled principles, since building deep trust relies heavily on fairness and integrity. Adaptive and Resilient leaders often borrow from S&A, using frameworks or analytics to make sense of ambiguous environments. T&V leaders may anchor their ideas in ethics to ensure that significant changes are meaningful, and A&R leaders may draw on empathy and strong relational bonds to keep teams motivated through unpredictable circumstances.

## Developing Traits from Other Clusters

Overlaps between clusters are not fixed; they shift according to context. A crisis might push a typically Structured and Analytical leader to cultivate Adaptive and Resilient qualities or to rely on relational strategies that keep teams calm. A far-reaching strategic initiative might compel a Transformative and Visionary leader to incorporate ethical principles, ensuring that their high-level goals stay people-centric and morally grounded.

These transitions can be challenging. A T&V leader who loves high-level strategy might need to refine systematic thinking to become more detail-oriented. In contrast, an R&P leader who aims to sustain harmony may need Adaptive traits when profound changes demand difficult decisions. Actual growth often requires stepping outside comfort zones—sometimes with the help of coaching, supportive peers, or new experiences—and persisting through the initial discomfort. Over time, leaders find that becoming more versatile in this way makes them better prepared for a broader range of challenges.

## Borrowing Between Clusters

Here are common examples of how traits may draw from one another:

- Transformative and Visionary (T&V): May embrace structured planning from S&A or strengthen relational empathy from R&P.
- Relational and People-Focused (R&P): Can gain analytical skills from S&A or develop resilience from A&R.
- Adaptive and Resilient (A&R): Might adopt visionary inspiration from T&V or ethical grounding from P.
- Structured and Analytical (S&A): Benefits from relational intelligence or flexibility, gleaning traits from R&P or A&R.
- Principled (P): Could enhance visionary thinking from T&V or tap into adaptability from A&R.

## Ease of Adoption

Not all clusters blend with equal difficulty. Some share common ground, while others feel naturally at odds. The table below summarizes how readily someone in one cluster might adopt traits from another:

| From/To | T&V | R&P | A&R | S&A | P |
|---|---|---|---|---|---|
| T&V | - | Easy | Moderate | Difficult | Easy |
| R&P | Easy | - | Easy | Difficult | Easy |
| A&R | Moderate | Easy | - | Difficult | Moderate |
| S&A | Moderate | Moderate | Difficult | - | Easy |
| P | Easy | Easy | Difficult | Moderate | - |

## Shared Traits Make Transitions Easier

- Relational ↔ Ethical: Both center around trust, fairness, and strong relationships.
- Transformative ↔ Relational: Vision can be carried out more effectively when leaders emphasize empathy and inclusion.

## Contradictory Traits Make Transitions Harder

- Adaptive ↔ Structured: Quick pivots can clash with rigid processes or hierarchies.
- Relational ↔ Structured: Focusing on human emotion can conflict with methodical systems or data-driven processes.

## Context-Driven Adaptation

- The situation often dictates which traits are most straightforward to adopt. For example, a Structured leader might use Relational skills in a team-building workshop, while an Adaptive leader might use Structured approaches during a calmer period.

### Building Versatility

Adopting traits from other clusters demands maturity, self-awareness, and a willingness to learn. Leaders must:

- Maintain Patience: Transforming ingrained habits takes time and consistent effort.
- Be Self-Aware: Pinpoint which skills you lack and measure progress realistically.
- Stay Open: View new traits not as failings in your current style, but as strengths you can cultivate.

At its core, leadership is not about rigidly committing to one approach; it is about having enough flexibility to respond to shifting needs. The goal is to develop a unique blend: remain true to your core strengths while consciously adopting additional traits that fill gaps or suit particular challenges. A leader who achieves this balance—knowing when to lean on data-driven analysis, when to inspire grand visions, and when to show empathy or adapt quickly—is far more prepared for the realities of organizational life.

## Leadership Styles Matrices

As you grow in your understanding of leadership styles, it helps to use frameworks that visually map how different styles relate to each other. In addition to clustering styles, we can create conceptual matrices to explore the main dimensions of leadership. By placing leadership styles within these matrices, you can better understand how different qualities interact and where your strengths lie.

These matrices are practical tools—guides to help you think through when you might want to lean into one approach or pull back on another. They aren't rigid categories, but flexible guides that help with reflection, alignment, and growth.

## Matrix 1: Relational vs. Structured and Transformational vs. Adaptive

This first matrix helps you consider how your leadership style balances two key dimensions: focus more on people and relationships or on systems and structure and lean toward transformative, big-picture change or Adaptive, in-the-moment problem-solving.

**Axes:**

- **X-Axis: Relational (Left) ↔ Structured (Right)**
- **Y-Axis: Transformational (Top) ↔ Adaptive (Bottom)**

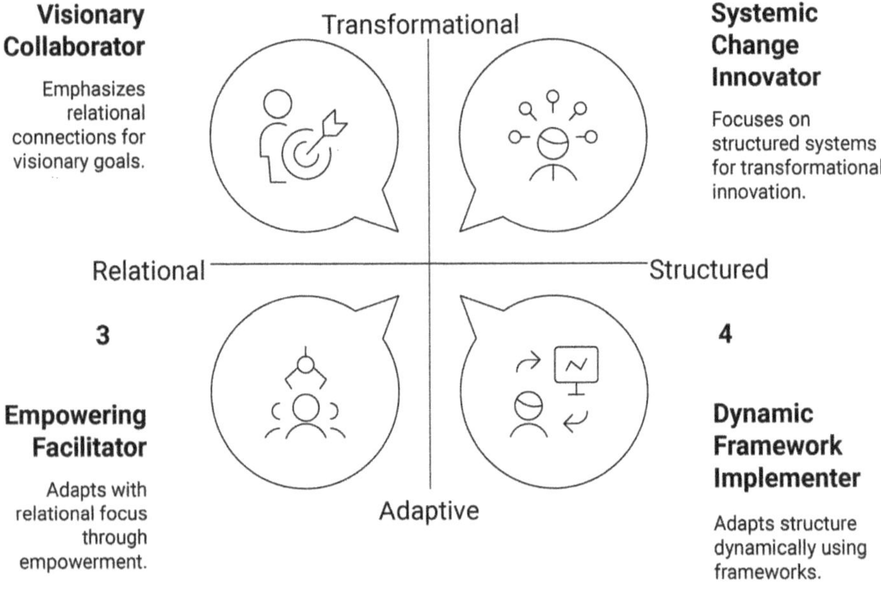


*Figure 10: Relational vs. Structured and Transformational vs. Adaptive*

### Relational and Transformational (Top Left)

These styles prioritize emotional connections, empathy, and

collaboration, while focusing on long-term, visionary, or transformational goals.

- Transformational Leadership
- Purpose-Driven Leadership
- Resonant Leadership
- Charismatic Leadership
- Transcendent Leadership
- Servant Leadership
- Empathy-Based Leadership
- Relational Leadership
- Inclusive Leadership

## Relational and Adaptive (Bottom Left)

These styles adapt to uncertainty while maintaining a strong relational and people-centered focus. They rely on flexibility and empowerment.

- Human-Centered Leadership
- Democratic Leadership
- Shared Leadership
- Co-Creative Leadership
- Maternalistic Leadership
- Paternalistic Leadership
- Adaptive Leadership
- Agile Leadership

## Structured and Transformational (Top Right)

These styles focus on leveraging systems and structures to achieve transformational, visionary outcomes, often focusing on innovation, sustainability, or systemic change.

- Innovation Leadership
- Sustainable Leadership

- Regenerative Leadership
- Biophilic Leadership
- Strategic Leadership
- Systems Leadership

## Structured and Adaptive (Bottom Right)

These styles emphasize structure and systems, but adapt dynamically to changing conditions, using frameworks, technology, or neuroscience to respond effectively to uncertainty.

- Transactional Leadership
- Crisis Leadership
- Resilient Leadership
- Hybrid Leadership
- Quantum Leadership
- Mindful Leadership
- Situational Leadership
- Holacratic Leadership
- AI-Enhanced Leadership
- Digital Leadership
- Neuroscience-Based Leadership
- Cognitive Leadership

The Relational vs. Structured and Transformational vs. Adaptive matrix provides a practical framework for leaders to evaluate their leadership styles based on two key dynamics: how they balance Relational vs. Structured approaches, and how they navigate the spectrum of Transformational change vs. Adaptive responsiveness.

This matrix serves as a reflective tool for identifying strengths and blind spots, empowering leaders to tailor their approach to the needs of their teams and organizations. Leaders can use this matrix to align their style with specific challenges, such as adopting a transformational approach during periods of growth or relying on structured adaptability during crises. By understanding where their tendencies fall within the matrix, leaders can intentionally develop complementary skills and cultivate flexibility to lead effectively across a range of scenarios.

## Matrix 2: Individual-Centric vs. System-Centric and Visionary vs. Practical

Let's dive into our second matrix, which explores different aspects of leadership. Here, we're looking at two new dimensions: how much focus a leader places on individuals vs. the broader organization and whether their mindset is geared toward big, visionary ideas or more down-to-earth, practical solutions.

**Axes:**

- **X-Axis: Individual-Centric (Left) ↔ System-Centric (Right)**
- **Y-Axis: Visionary (Top) ↔ Practical (Bottom)**

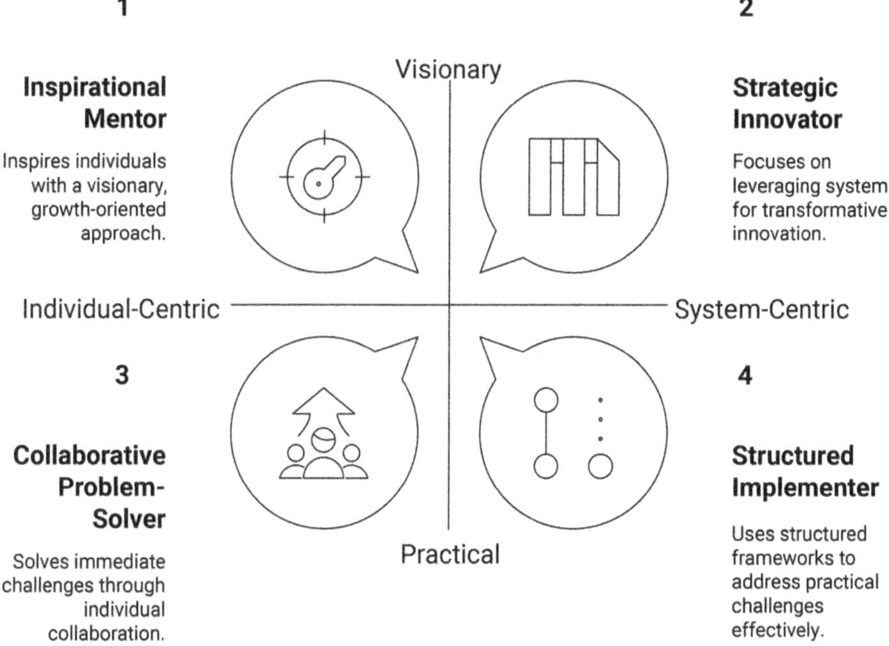


*Figure 11: Individual-Centric vs. System-Centric and Visionary vs. Practical*

## Individual-Centric and Visionary (Top Left)

These styles focus on inspiring individuals to embrace a visionary purpose, prioritizing personal growth, connection, and well-being in the pursuit of long-term impact.

- Transformational Leadership
- Resonant Leadership
- Charismatic Leadership
- Transcendent Leadership
- Purpose-Driven Leadership
- Biophilic Leadership

## Individual-Centric and Practical (Bottom Left)

These styles focus on the immediate needs, well-being, and collaboration of individuals, using a relational and people-focused approach to solve day-to-day challenges.

- Servant Leadership
- Empathy-Based Leadership
- Relational Leadership
- Maternalistic Leadership
- Paternalistic Leadership
- Human-Centered Leadership
- Shared Leadership
- Democratic Leadership

## System-Centric and Visionary (Top Right)

These styles prioritize leveraging systems, technology, and structures to achieve bold, transformative, and forward-thinking objectives, often with a focus on sustainability and innovation.

- Innovation Leadership
- Sustainable Leadership
- Regenerative Leadership
- AI-Enhanced Leadership
- Digital Leadership
- Systems Leadership
- Strategic Leadership

## System-Centric and Practical (Bottom Right)

These styles are rooted in structured and practical approaches, using frameworks, tools, and adaptability to respond effectively to immediate challenges and dynamic environments.

- Transactional Leadership
- Crisis Leadership
- Holacratic Leadership
- Neuroscience-Based Leadership
- Cognitive Leadership
- Adaptive Leadership
- Agile Leadership
- Situational Leadership
- Hybrid Leadership
- Mindful Leadership

The Individual-Centric vs. System-Centric and Visionary vs. Practical matrix offers a nuanced perspective on leadership by exploring how leaders prioritize individuals vs. systems and how they focus on visionary aspirations vs. practical, actionable outcomes.

This matrix is invaluable for leaders seeking to balance their focus between empowering individuals and optimizing systems, while maintaining the right blend of visionary foresight and practical execution. By situating their leadership styles within this framework, leaders can identify opportunities for growth, such as complementing a system-centric approach with a stronger focus on individual well-being or balancing visionary ambitions with pragmatic strategies. The matrix can guide leaders in aligning their leadership style with organizational priorities, fostering a more holistic and adaptable leadership approach that drives both immediate results and long-term impact.

## Using the Matrices for Reflection and Development

Think of these two matrices as mirrors reflecting how different leadership styles play out in real life. They don't exist in isolation, but serve as a map to help you understand why some styles excel in specific situations while others fall short. It's about giving you a practical way to assess your strengths and potential areas for growth.

Imagine you're a leader facing market uncertainty or a turbulent work environment. The first matrix can guide you: perhaps you notice that to thrive in these conditions, you need to be more Adaptive or Relational to keep your team motivated. Another scenario: maybe you're grappling with the tension between your desire to empower individuals and your need to keep the organization running smoothly. Here, the second matrix can help you reconcile these demands—finding a way to empower people while monitoring systemic outcomes.

By recognizing where your preferred styles fall within these matrices, you gain a clearer picture of where you shine and where you could stretch. For example, let's say you're most comfortable in the Transformational-Relational quadrant of the first matrix. That's great, but it might also be a signal for you to work on becoming more Adaptive—especially if the environment becomes unpredictable. Or maybe you identify strongly with being Visionary and Individual-Centric in the second matrix. This could be a cue to invest more energy in Practical or System-Centric approaches, to ensure that your grand ideas are supported by the necessary structures and grounded.

These matrices are tools that provide a road map to help you grow. They show you where you're naturally strong and point to areas where you can evolve. And remember, it's not about having a one-size-fits-all style, but about being flexible: knowing when to tap into your Relational strengths to build trust, or when to use Structured methods to ensure consistency and clarity.

## Key Takeaways from this Chapter

Leadership, at its core, is about adapting to who you are and the contexts in which you operate. This appendix has shown how different leadership clusters don't exist in isolation, but rather interact in ways that reflect the complexity of real-world challenges. Effective leaders often integrate qualities from multiple clusters, bridging vision with empathy, structure with agility, or ethical grounding with transformational goals. This interplay underscores that leadership styles are not one-note performances, but dynamic compositions—where you choose and blend elements to produce the effects your team or organization needs most.

Recognizing overlaps and understanding how traits from various clusters can enhance or balance one another, you take a significant step toward becoming a more fluid leader. Your goal is not to become someone entirely different, but to widen your repertoire so that you can shift gears with confidence and purpose. Keep refining your ability to assess the environment, reflect on your default tendencies, and step into new styles as the context demands. In doing so, you craft a leadership approach that is more agile and resilient and more deeply aligned with the evolving needs of your team, your organization, and a world where change is the only constant.

**Summary**

- **The Matrices as Maps:** Introducing two matrices—Relational vs. Structured and Transformational vs. Adaptive for the first, and Individual-Centric vs. System-Centric and Visionary vs. Practical for the second—gives a more in-depth look at where leadership styles shine and how they might overlap or diverge.

- **Overlaps and Interactions are Inevitable:** No leadership cluster or style stands alone. Recognizing overlaps helps you see how qualities can balance or enhance each other, guiding you toward a more flexible, context-driven approach.
- **Tools for Growth:** By understanding where you fit across the clusters, percentages, and matrices, you get valuable insights that help guide your personal development and enable you to make more deliberate adjustments as situations evolve.

# Chapter Workout

## Exercise 1: Exploring Overlaps and Interactions

**Objective:** To understand how different leadership clusters can complement or clash with each other, enhancing your ability to navigate complex leadership scenarios.

**Prompts:**

1. **Review Cluster Descriptions:**
   - Revisit the definitions and characteristics of each leadership cluster to refresh your understanding.

2. **Identify Potential Overlaps:**
   - Based on your primary clusters, list possible overlaps and interactions. For example, how might Transformative and Visionary (T&V) overlap with Relational and People-Focused (R&P)? In what ways do your dominant clusters complement each other? Where might they create tension?

3. **Analyze Complementary Traits:**
   - Choose two overlapping clusters and describe how traits from one can enhance the other. For example, how can empathy (R&P) strengthen visionary leadership (T&V)?

4. **Identify Potential Clashes:**
   - Consider clusters that may have conflicting traits, such

as Adaptive and Resilient (A&R) versus Structured and Analytical (S&A). How can these conflicts be managed?

## Exercise 2: Blending Leadership Clusters in Practice

**Objective:** To practice integrating traits from different leadership clusters, enhancing your versatility and effectiveness in diverse situations.

**Prompts:**

1. **Select a Scenario:**
   - Choose a real or hypothetical leadership scenario that requires blending different leadership traits. Examples include leading a major organizational change, resolving a team conflict, or launching a new innovative project.

2. **Determine Relevant Clusters:**
   - Identify which leadership clusters are most relevant to the scenario. For instance, a major change might require both Transformative and Visionary (T&V) and Adaptive and Resilient (A&R) traits.

3. **Plan Your Approach:**
   - Outline how you will blend traits from the identified clusters to address the scenario effectively. Specify which traits you will emphasize and how they will interact.

4. **Implement and Reflect:**
   - Apply your blended leadership approach in the chosen scenario. How did blending these traits influence the outcome? What worked well, and what could be improved?

## Exercise 3: Developing Traits from Other Clusters

**Objective:** To expand your leadership repertoire by consciously adopting and developing traits from clusters that are not your primary strengths.

**Prompts:**

1. **Identify Target Clusters:**
   - Based on your primary leadership clusters, identify one or two clusters from which you would like to develop additional traits. For example, if your primary cluster is Relational and People-Focused (R&P), you might choose to develop Structured and Analytical (S&A) traits.
2. **Set Development Goals:**
   - Define specific goals for developing traits from the target clusters. Ensure that these goals are SMART (Specific, Measurable, Achievable, Relevant, Time-bound).
3. **Create an Action Plan:**
   - Outline the steps you will take to achieve your development goals, including resources, timelines, and support mechanisms.
4. **Implement and Track Progress:**
   - Execute your action plan, consistently working toward your development goals. What progress have you made in adopting traits from the target clusters? What challenges have you encountered?
5. **Evaluate and Adjust:**
   - After the set timeframe, evaluate your progress toward developing the new traits. How have these new traits impacted your leadership effectiveness? Are there additional steps you need to take?

## Exercise 4: Utilizing the Leadership Matrices for Deeper Insight

**Objective:** To visually map your leadership style using the matrices introduced earlier in this chapter, and to better understand how your style plays out across different dimensions.

Use the two leadership matrices we explored to map out where you fall. This visual approach can offer unique insights and help you see where your natural tendencies are—and where you might benefit from expanding.

**Matrix 1: Relational vs. Structured (X-Axis) and Transformational vs. Adaptive (Y-Axis)**

1. **Positioning Your Style:**
   - Where Do You Fall? Based on your predominant cluster, where do you see your leadership style landing on this matrix? Mark your spot and take a moment to describe why you chose that position.

2. **Analysis:**
   - **Implications of Your Position:** What does your placement on the matrix suggest about your approach—do you prioritize relationships over structure, or transformation over adaptability?
   - **Scenario Effectiveness:** How does this positioning influence your effectiveness in different situations? For instance, are you more successful in dynamic environments where adaptability is key, or do you shine in stable contexts where clear structure and relational trust matter?

3. **Growth Opportunities:**
   - **Room for Expansion:** Look at your position in the matrix and identify areas for growth. If you lean toward

being highly Relational and Transformational, think about how adding more structure or Adaptive traits could balance your leadership style.

**Matrix 2: Individual-Centric vs. System-Centric (X-Axis) and Visionary vs. Practical (Y-Axis)**

1. **Positioning Your Style:**
    - **Your Spot in the Matrix:** Where do you think you fall on this matrix? Place your leadership style accordingly, and explain the reasoning behind your choice.

2. **Analysis:**
    - **Implications of Focus:** Consider how your focus—whether on individual empowerment or organizational efficiency—shapes your decision-making and team dynamics.
    - **Strengths:** What are the strengths that come from being in your chosen quadrant? For example, being visionary and individual-centric might mean you're great at motivating and inspiring your team.

3. **Growth Opportunities:**
    - **Expanding Horizons:** Explore ways to integrate traits from other quadrants. If you're predominantly visionary and individual-focused, how might adopting more practical, system-focused approaches improve your ability to deliver operational results?

# Chapter 8

# Gaining a Full Perspective with 360-Degree Feedback

*Feedback is not criticism; it's a mirror reflecting opportunities for growth.*

Leadership can feel like a constant balancing act—keeping your team motivated, aligning with organizational goals, and adapting to changing challenges. However, one critical piece often gets overlooked: how others perceive your leadership. While self-assessment is applicable and annual reviews provide insights, they only scratch the surface. You need a holistic view from all angles to understand your leadership impact.

This is where a 360-degree feedback approach comes in. Instead of relying on just one perspective—your manager's review, your reflections, or feedback from a select few—it gathers insights from everyone who interacts with you in meaningful ways. This includes direct reports, peers, supervisors, and sometimes external partners or clients. By taking in this broader spectrum of feedback, you better understand your strengths, the areas where you might be falling short, and the hidden aspects of your leadership that could hold you back or have untapped potential.

The 360-degree assessment often includes the Johari Window concept, a model designed to map self-awareness. This framework helps you explore how your traits and behaviors align with what others see in you. It works by expanding the "Open Area" (what you and others know about you) while shrinking the "Blind Spot" (what others see, but you don't). Over time, it can even uncover previously unknown areas of your leadership and bring hidden strengths or challenges into view.

This chapter dives into the mechanics of 360-degree feedback: why it's a valuable tool for growth, and how to interpret and act on the feedback you receive. It's not just about identifying gaps; it's about turning those insights into actions that improve your authenticity, trustworthiness, and overall impact as a leader.

## Why 360-Degree Feedback Matters

Most traditional feedback tools are limited in scope. Your own biases can skew a self-assessment. A manager's feedback, while necessary, usually reflects a narrow slice of your behavior in specific contexts. These approaches can leave blind spots—areas of your leadership that you might not even realize are affecting others.

A 360-degree approach fills in those gaps by drawing on input from various perspectives. Direct reports can shed light on how your leadership translates day-to-day. Peers bring insights into how you collaborate and share responsibility. Managers offer a higher-level view; external partners can reflect on your professional presence and accountability.

This layered feedback can reveal patterns that one source alone would miss. For example, direct reports might highlight your ability to set clear goals while pointing out that you could improve how you handle disagreements. Peers might praise your calmness under pressure, but suggest that you sometimes hold back information that others need. Managers could commend your initiative, but wish you had more involvement in the team's decision-making.

Combined, these perspectives provide a nuanced, detailed picture of your leadership. They illuminate your strengths and challenges, clarifying how others experience your approach—and what adjustments could make you more effective.

## The Johari Window: Understanding Yourself and Others

The Johari Window, developed by Joseph Luft and Harrington Ingham in the 1950s, offers a simple yet powerful way to think about self-awareness. It divides your personality and behaviors into four areas:

1. **Open Area:** These are traits you and others are aware of. For instance, you may know that you excel at strategic thinking, and your team recognizes it too.
2. **Blind Spot:** These are traits others see, but you don't. Perhaps you believe you're approachable, but your team finds your tone intimidating in certain situations.
3. **Hidden Area:** This includes things you know about yourself, but choose not to share, like doubts about a project or personal struggles.
4. **Unknown Area:** This is the untapped potential or behaviors that have yet to be identified.

## Leadership Blind Spots and Their Impact

Every leader has blind spots. These behaviors, assumptions, or tendencies go unnoticed by you, but are apparent to those around you. They often arise from overconfidence, resistance to feedback, or a lack of diverse perspectives. Left unaddressed, blind spots can harm team morale, undermine trust, and reduce effectiveness.

Some common blind spots include overreliance on a single leadership style; failing to adjust to the diverse needs of team members or the situation; or dismissing constructive feedback. For example, a leader who excels in a visionary, big-picture role might need help managing day-to-day details, frustrating their team. Similarly, a leader focusing on maintaining harmony might avoid necessary but difficult conversations, leading to unresolved tensions.

The consequences of these blind spots can be significant: lowered productivity, disengagement, and even high turnover. Addressing them requires adaptability, humility, and a willingness to experiment with new leadership approaches. Leaders who acknowledge their blind spots and actively work to overcome them are better equipped to navigate complex challenges and inspire their teams.

## How 360-Degree Feedback Works

Stepping into a 360-degree assessment can feel daunting, but it becomes a transformative experience with the right mindset. This process is not about justifying your actions or proving others wrong; it is an opportunity to learn and grow.

Before diving in, take a moment to reflect on why you are undertaking this exercise. Is it to gain a clearer view of your strengths? To uncover blind spots? Or to fine-tune your leadership style for greater effectiveness? Whatever your reasons, remember that honest feedback, even when it stings, is a gift.

A typical 360-degree assessment involves a structured survey asking about your leadership behaviors. Feedback is gathered anonymously from:

- Managers: They provide high-level insights.
- Peers: They see you in the trenches.
- Direct Reports: They experience your leadership daily.
- Stakeholders: External voices, like clients or partners, offer an outsider's perspective.

Selecting the right respondents is just as important as your mindset. A diverse mix of voices will give you the most valuable insights. Include direct reports from those who have worked closely with you, a peer who knows your day-to-day style, and a manager who can provide a high-level perspective. Consider including a long-term client or a trusted external partner who has observed how you operate in real-world situations. The more varied the input, the more nuanced your understanding of your leadership will be.

You might be evaluated on communication, adaptability, emotional intelligence, and decision-making. The results compare your self-assessment to others' perceptions, showing where you align and where gaps exist.

For example, you might think you're great at "encouraging team input," but your direct reports disagree. On the flip side, they might highlight strengths you undervalue, like your ability to calm a team during a crisis.

# ASSESSMENT 3

## 360 Degree Assessment: Leadership Style Cluster

Downloaded the assessment named "3.1 - Leadership Styles Cluster 360 Assessment for Administering" and/or "3.2 - Leadership Styles Cluster 360 Result" at:

https://leaderscrucible.com/leadership-styles-assessments/

Full instructions for completing the assessment are contained within the assessment itself.

Send 3.1 to the individuals you selected to provide the 360 assessments.

Gather the completed assessments back and transfer the results to 3.2 to obtain the results for the assessment. This must be done separately for each respondent.

To avoid the extra step, you could send 3.2 to respondents, bearing in mind that they will have access to the assessment results.

If you feel you would obtain better results from the assessments if they were returned anonymously and you do not have a way to do so, they can be sent to assessment@leaderscrucible.com with the name and company details completed on the instruction page. Please notify the same email address to expect the submissions.

See the Chapter Workout at the end of this chapter for the assessment results.

## ASSESSMENT 4

# 360 Degree Assessment: Leadership Style Within a Cluster

Download the assessment named “4.1 - Leadership Styles 360 Assessment for Administering” and or “4.2 - Leadership Styles 360 Result” at:

https://leaderscrucible.com/leadership-styles-assessments/

Full instructions for completing the assessment are contained within the assessment itself.

Send 4.1 to the respondents who have completed Assessment 3. Based on the scores in Assessment 3, instruct them to complete the specific cluster assessment in 4.1. Provide them with the clusters to complete. I suggest you include both the highest- and lowest-scoring clusters, based on aggregated scores.

Optional: You can instruct the respondents to complete all the cluster assessments, although this may lead to overprocessing.

Gather the completed assessments back and transfer the results to 4.2 to obtain the results for the assessment. This must be done separately for each respondent.

To avoid the extra step, you could send 4.2 to respondents, bearing in mind that they will have access to the assessment results.

If you feel you would obtain better results from the assessments if they were returned anonymously and you do not have a way to do so, they can be sent to assessment@leaderscrucible.com with the name and company details completed on the instruction page. Please notify the same email address to expect the submissions.

See the Chapter Workout at the end of this chapter for the assessment results.

## Receiving and Interpreting Feedback

When the results of your 360-degree assessment arrive, they can be overwhelming. One page might highlight glowing praise for your ability to strategize, while another points out consistent criticism about handling meeting conflicts. It is natural to feel a mix of emotions—pride, defensiveness, even disappointment—but the key is to focus on the value of the insights.

Find a calm, distraction-free space to review the report. Instead of zeroing in on one standout positive or negative comment, look for recurring themes and patterns.

Compare the results to your self-assessment without being defensive. Note the styles you agree on and whether there are gaps. Are there areas where feedback from different groups aligns? For example, if peers and direct reports highlight indecisiveness, it is a clear area to work on. Conversely, if multiple groups praise your ability to keep calm under pressure, this is a strength to celebrate and build on.

Resist the urge to dismiss feedback you disagree with. Even if something feels "off," try understanding why someone might perceive you that way. Often, feedback reveals how your actions—or even inactions—come across in ways you might not have intended. This process is not about agreeing with every comment, but about uncovering perspectives that can broaden your understanding.

## Acting Based on 360-Degree Feedback

Feedback is only as good as the actions you take afterward. Start by creating a personal action plan based on the insights you have gained. If the input shows that you need to develop qualities of another style, explore ways of doing so and its value to you and your team. If emotional intelligence is required to improve, consider strategies like practicing active listening, showing empathy more intentionally, or even exploring mindfulness techniques.

Sharing parts of your feedback with your team can also foster trust. Acknowledging areas where you aim to improve shows humility and genuine commitment to growth. For instance, if feedback highlights issues with your communication clarity, you might say, "I've learned that I need to be clearer when explaining our goals, and I'd appreciate your help as I work on this."

Revisit the assessment after a set time frame—perhaps six months—to reflect on your progress. Many organizations conduct 360-degree assessments regularly, so you can use these as benchmarks to track changes and identify new growth opportunities.

## Reinforcing Adaptability and Continuous Growth

A 360-degree assessment is a snapshot of how others perceive you and a tool to sharpen your adaptability. Understanding how different groups experience your leadership allows you to adjust your approach to suit varying needs. For example, you might lean into relational skills for team-building exercises while adopting a more structured, analytical style for strategy meetings.

This process reinforces the idea that leadership is an ongoing journey, not a fixed destination. Every round of feedback is an opportunity to grow. Each small or significant adjustment refines your leadership and prepares you for future challenges. Over time, receiving feedback becomes less intimidating and a natural part of your development. The continuous cycle of input, reflection, action, and reassessment can help you weave adaptability into the fabric of your leadership style.

## Embracing a Holistic Perspective

The true power of a 360-degree assessment lies in its ability to give you a fuller, more balanced picture of your leadership. Self-reflection is crucial, but it is only one side of the coin. By integrating perspectives from those around you, you can reveal hidden qualities—strengths you have overlooked and challenges you were unaware of.

This holistic perspective encourages empathy, helping you better understand how your actions affect others. It also enables you to tailor your leadership to build stronger relationships and foster deeper trust. Over time, these insights help you confidently lead, navigate complexities, and guide your team through change.

## Key Takeaways from this Chapter

A 360-degree assessment is more than a leadership exercise—it is a gateway to deeper understanding and growth. It illuminates the gaps between how you see yourself and how others experience you, offering a clear road map for improvement. With this feedback, you can refine your approach, address blind spots, and amplify your strengths.

This feedback provides a foundation for long-term adaptability when combined with other development tools like goal-setting or coaching. As you integrate these insights into your daily practices, you will find yourself leading and thriving, aligned with the needs of those you support and your organization's goals.

# Chapter Workout

## Exercise 1: Using Your 360-Degree Assessment Results

1. **Understand the Overall Picture**
   - **Review Aggregated Scores:** Start by looking at the overall rating in each leadership cluster (Transformative and Visionary, Relational and People-Focused, Adaptive and Resilient, Structured and Analytical, and Ethical and Principled). This will help you see at a glance where you excel and where there may be opportunities for growth.
   - **Identify Patterns and Themes:** Notice any recurring feedback across multiple statements or areas—for example, consistently high or low ratings that appear in different categories.

2. **Look for Strengths**
   - **Compare Self-Assessment with Feedback:** Reflect on how your perceptions align with or differ from those of others. Create a table comparing self-assessment scores with average scores from respondent groups. Note discrepancies.
   - **Celebrate High Scores:** High scores and frequent positive comments indicate areas where you're already demonstrating effective leadership. Acknowledge these strengths and think about how you can continue leveraging them to benefit your team and organization.

3. **Identify Areas for Improvement**
   - **Pinpoint Lower Scores:** Notice which behaviors were rated lower or where feedback suggests the need for

development. Reflect on whether these results were expected or surprising.
- **Consider Context:** Sometimes lower scores in one cluster may be balanced by stronger performance in another. Ask yourself whether certain organizational challenges, role transitions, or personal factors might have influenced these ratings.

4. **Review Qualitative Comments (If Provided)**
   - **Seek Clarification:** Comments often supply a richer context behind scores. Look for repeated or specific points that come up.
   - **Focus on Behavior, Not Personality:** Constructive comments should center on observable actions and their impact. Use these insights to guide changes in your leadership approach.

5. **Create a Targeted Development Plan**
   - **Select Key Priorities:** From the patterns you've identified, choose one or two leadership behaviors to focus on initially. Trying to address every area at once can be overwhelming.
   - **Set SMART Goals:** Ensure that your objectives are Specific, Measurable, Achievable, Relevant, and Time-bound. For example: "Increase clarity of communication by scheduling monthly check-ins with the team and inviting feedback on all major decisions."
   - **Identify Resources and Support:** Consider training programs, mentoring, or coaching that can help you develop specific skills. Engage your manager, HR, or a mentor in helping you find these resources.

6. **Communicate Your Plan**
   - **Share with Stakeholders:** Where appropriate, let your team or peers know that you've heard their feedback and

are addressing it through concrete actions. This transparency builds trust and shows your commitment to improvement.
- **Invite Ongoing Feedback:** Encourage people to share their observations regularly, not just in formal assessments. Continuous feedback loops will help you stay on track and make agile adjustments to your development plan.

7. **Monitor Progress**
    - **Set Checkpoints:** Revisit your goals in regular intervals (e.g., monthly or quarterly), reflecting on the changes you've made and how they are impacting your leadership.
    - **Adjust as Needed:** If something isn't working or if new challenges arise, adapt your approach. Leadership is an evolving skill, and continuous improvement is key.

8. **Plan the Next 360-Degree** (**or Other Feedback Mechanisms**)
    - **Schedule a Follow-Up:** Many organizations run 360-degree assessments annually or biannually. By comparing feedback over time, you can measure growth and maintain momentum in your development journey.
    - **Encourage a Culture of Feedback:** Beyond formal assessments, foster a work environment where constructive, candid feedback is a normal part of daily operations.

## Exercise 2: Apply the Johari Window

1. **Draw Your Johari Window:** Create a diagram with four quadrants—Open Area, Blind Spot, Hidden Area, and Unknown Area.

2. **Populate the Quadrants:**
    - **Open Area:** Traits known to you and others (e.g., strategic thinker, empathetic).
    - **Blind Spot:** Traits known to others, but not you (e.g., micromanaging under pressure).
    - **Hidden Area:** Traits you know, but keep private (e.g., doubts about specific projects).
    - **Unknown Area:** Untapped traits or behaviors (e.g., potential creativity).

3. **Reflect and Act:** Consider expanding your Open Area by addressing blind spots, sharing hidden qualities, and exploring unknown potential.

# Chapter 9

# Environment and Leadership Style Fit

*Leadership that fits the context creates harmony, fosters growth, and drives success.*

Every leader's success is influenced by how well their style fits the environment they are navigating. Like a tool that fits a specific job, leadership styles are most effective when they match the team's needs, organizational demands, and external circumstances. No single leadership approach works everywhere, and no two environments call for the same qualities.

Understanding your organizational environment—whether it's fast-paced and unpredictable, governed by strict regulations, or driven by innovation and long-term vision—helps you align your leadership with the situation. This alignment is crucial for making the right impact.

This chapter introduces a framework to identify your organization's environment and the leadership styles that suit it best. You'll start with an assessment to define the characteristics of your workplace. From there, we'll explore seven distinct environment types, each with its demands and dynamics, and show how different leadership styles can thrive in each context.

Leadership isn't static; it's about adapting to fit the moment. By identifying your organizational environment, you can align your natural strengths with the specific challenges you face, creating a leadership style that is as effective as it is authentic.

## ASSESSMENT 5

## Environment Assessment

Complete the leadership cluster assessment.

Downloaded the assessment named "5 - Leadership Environment Assessment" at:

https://leaderscrucible.com/leadership-styles-assessments/

Full instructions for completing the assessment are contained within the assessment itself.

See the Chapter Workout at the end of this chapter for using the results of the assessment

## Seven Environment Types and Their Characteristics

This section introduces the seven environment types we've identified and offers insights into their key characteristics.

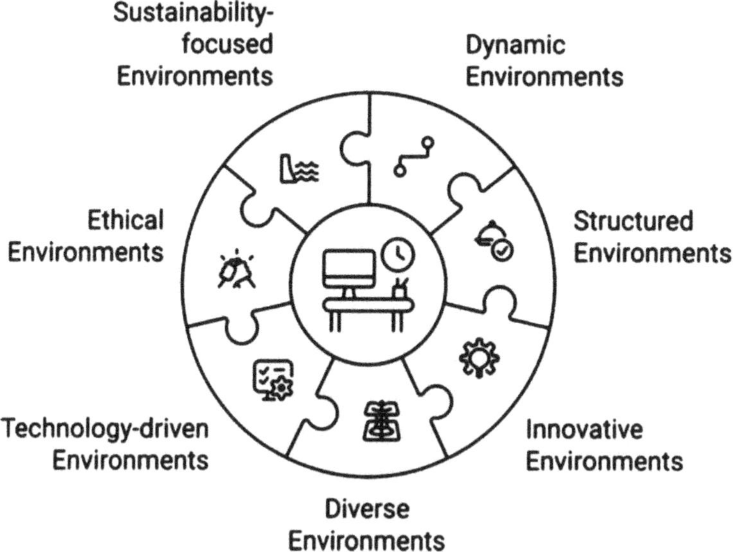


*Figure 12: Seven Environmental Types*

## 1. Dynamic, Changing, or Crisis Environments

Some workplaces feel like a whirlwind—constantly shifting, unpredictable, and full of surprises. These dynamic environments demand agility, quick decision-making, and a steady hand during turbulence. Leaders here must keep their teams grounded while steering them through challenges and recalibrating plans.

**Key Characteristics:**

- Frequent disruptions and unforeseen developments.
- A high-speed pace that rarely allows for long-term stability.
- There is a need for decisive actions under pressure.
- Strong focus on resilience and keeping the team optimistic amidst uncertainty.

## 2. Structured or Regulated Environments

Stability and compliance are paramount in highly structured finance, healthcare, or government workplaces. Rules, standards, and accountability drive success, leaving little room for improvisation. Leaders in these settings focus on precision and maintaining order.

**Key Characteristics:**

- A heavy emphasis on compliance and strict regulations.
- Clearly defined processes and decision-making frameworks.
- Stability and predictability as cultural cornerstones.
- A hierarchical structure that reinforces clear roles and responsibilities.

## 3. Innovative or Creative Environments

In workplaces centered on innovation—whether tech start-ups or creative agencies—leaders are tasked with fostering a culture where new ideas flourish. These environments celebrate experimentation, but leaders must channel that energy into meaningful outcomes.

**Key Characteristics:**

- Strong focus on creativity, experimentation, and pushing boundaries.
- A culture that encourages calculated risks and out-of-the-box thinking.
- Flexibility and autonomy within work processes.
- Collaboration that thrives on diverse ideas and perspectives.

## 4. Diverse, Inclusive, and Collaborative Environments

Teams that prioritize diversity and inclusion are rich in perspectives and creativity. Leaders in these environments must ensure that everyone feels valued, respected, and empowered to contribute. Fostering trust and equity is at the heart of effective leadership here.

**Key Characteristics:**

- A highly diverse team in terms of culture, expertise, and background.
- A commitment to inclusivity, equity, and mutual respect.
- Collaboration and teamwork as driving forces.
- Strong interpersonal relationships grounded in trust and empathy.

## 5. Technology-Driven or Digital Environments

Many organizations rely on technology in the digital age to drive efficiency and innovation. Leaders in these settings must balance a deep understanding of technical tools with a focus on the human side of technology's impact.

**Key Characteristics:**

- Heavy reliance on advanced digital tools, data analytics, and AI.
- A strong push for digital transformation and continual innovation.
- A technically proficient workforce that embraces new tools.
- Decision-making grounded in data and insights, with an emphasis on cybersecurity.

## 6. Environments Emphasizing Ethics, Integrity, and Trust

Leadership requires unwavering integrity for organizations where reputation, fairness, and moral principles take center stage. Success in these environments goes beyond profits—building trust, maintaining transparency, and honoring long-term commitments.

**Key Characteristics:**

- Clear ethical guidelines embedded in the culture.
- A strong focus on transparency and accountability.
- Fairness is a foundational value in all interactions.
- Decisions rooted in long-term impact and societal benefits.

## 7. Sustainability, Environmental Responsibility, or Long-Term Vision

In workplaces prioritizing sustainability and a long-term legacy, leaders must think beyond the immediate. These environments demand a balance between economic goals and social or environmental stewardship.

**Key Characteristics:**

- Commitment to sustainable practices and resource conservation.
- Strategic, long-term planning to drive systemic change.
- Collaborative efforts with stakeholders to create lasting impacts.
- Sustainability integrated into the organization's core mission.

## Aligning Leadership with Environment

Understanding your current or future organization's environment is only the first step. Once you've identified the context, you can develop or refine your leadership style to fit its demands. Dynamic environments may call for resilience and rapid decision-making, while structured settings require a focus on precision and compliance.

No leader is naturally equipped to excel in every environment; but with awareness and adaptability, you can grow into the leader your organization needs. Whether managing chaos, fostering innovation, or prioritizing ethics and sustainability, aligning your style to your environment allows you to lead with greater purpose and impact.

## Leadership Characteristics Required by Each Environment Type

Understanding the type of environment is the starting point. Once you've identified whether you're operating in a high-pressure, constantly shifting setting, a rules-driven organization, or an innovation-focused workspace, the real question is: What kind of leader does this situation need?

This section explores the leadership qualities and approaches best suited to each of the seven organizational environments or cultures we discussed earlier. Consider it a tool kit to refine how you lead. For instance, if your organization thrives in dynamic, crisis-prone conditions, your focus might be on quick decision-making, resilience, and transparent communication. On the other hand, precision, accountability, and ethical adherence take precedence if you're in a regulated setting.

Recognize the characteristics valued most in your context so you can make intentional choices about where to grow and how to apply your strengths.

### 1. Dynamic, Changing, or Crisis Environments

Change is the only constant in these environments, and disruptions are par for the course. New competitors pop up, markets shift unpredictably, and technology evolves in the blink of an eye. Leaders in these settings must stay steady while navigating uncertainty and rallying their teams without letting morale falter.

**Key Leadership Characteristics and Qualities Required:**

- **Adaptability and Flexibility:** Change is inevitable, so leaders must pivot quickly and keep their strategies fluid. Sticking rigidly to plans in a fast-evolving landscape only creates roadblocks.
- **Decisiveness Under Pressure:** Delaying decisions can be more damaging than making mistakes. Leaders must act confidently and clearly to keep the team moving forward, even when information is incomplete.
- **Emotional Resilience:** In chaotic situations, staying calm and composed reassures your team. Your steadiness sets the tone and helps prevent spirals of stress or panic.
- **Effective Communication:** Clear and concise updates are essential when priorities shift quickly. Leaders must also listen closely, understand their team's concerns, and respond thoughtfully.
- **Problem-Solving Skills:** Innovative thinking is a must. Whether reimagining workflows or devising creative ways to overcome obstacles, leaders in these settings rely on resourcefulness.
- **Vision and Direction:** Even in chaos, teams need a North Star. Clear goals—even flexible ones—offer stability and purpose amidst uncertainty.
- **Learning Orientation:** Every challenge is a learning opportunity. Leaders who prioritize growth for themselves and their teams emerge stronger after each crisis.

## 2. Structured or Regulated Environments

Precision and compliance are paramount in highly regulated industries. These settings value consistency, accountability, and transparent processes. Leaders thrive by providing stability while ensuring that every action meets the required standards.

**Key Leadership Characteristics and Qualities Required:**

- **Clarity and Structure:** Clear roles, responsibilities, and goals are nonnegotiable. Teams perform best when they know exactly what's expected and have a road map to follow.
- **Strong Organizational Skills:** Precision matters here. Leaders need to track processes meticulously, ensuring that nothing slips through the cracks.
- **Accountability:** Holding yourself and others to high standards builds credibility. Teams need to see that you're fair and consistent when applying rules.
- **Supportive Guidance:** Even in a structured setting, people thrive on mentorship. Providing training and development opportunities keeps the team motivated while maintaining compliance.
- **Ethical Integrity:** Adhering to regulations is just the baseline; cultivating a culture of fairness and honesty elevates the organization.
- **Reward Systems:** Celebrate adherence to processes and achievements within the framework. Whether formal recognition or a simple thank-you, acknowledging effort keeps morale high.

## 3. Innovative or Creative Environments

Creative environments buzz with ideas and thrive on experimentation. Questioning the status quo and exploring new possibilities are the norm in these settings. Leaders must balance fostering creativity and steering efforts toward meaningful outcomes.

**Key Leadership Characteristics and Qualities Required:**

- **Visionary Thinking:** Leaders must paint a bold picture of what's possible. A compelling mission inspires teams to push boundaries and think beyond conventional limits.
- **Fostering Creativity:** Encourage brainstorming and make it safe to propose unconventional ideas. Create a culture where experimentation is welcomed—and failure is seen as part of the process.
- **Empowerment:** Trust your team to take ownership of their ideas. Micromanagement stifles creativity, while autonomy sparks breakthroughs.
- **Adaptive Leadership:** Not every idea will work, and that's okay. Leaders must pivot gracefully and guide their teams to learn from missteps without losing momentum.
- **Cultivating a Creative Environment:** Provide the resources—time, tools, and spaces—that creativity needs to flourish. People are most innovative when they feel supported.
- **Recognition and Motivation:** Celebrate effort and results. Acknowledging contributions, big or small, reinforces the team's enthusiasm for exploration.

## 4. Diverse, Inclusive, and Collaborative Environments

These environments embrace differences as strengths, prioritizing inclusivity and teamwork. Leaders succeed by fostering trust, encouraging open dialogue, and ensuring that every voice is valued.

**Key Leadership Characteristics and Qualities Required:**

- **Empathy and Emotional Intelligence:** Understanding others' experiences fosters trust and connection. Listening deeply is one of the most impactful tools a leader can use.

- **Inclusivity and Cultural Sensitivity:** Creating an environment where people feel respected and valued is essential. Adapting to diverse perspectives strengthens leadership.
- **Collaborative Approach:** Decision-making is better when everyone feels ownership. Leaders should facilitate shared problem-solving and celebrate team achievements.
- **Building Strong Relationships:** Invest in building trust and camaraderie within the team. Strong bonds make navigating challenges smoother and success more rewarding.
- **Servant Leadership:** Prioritizing the needs and growth of your team inspires loyalty and performance. Supportive leaders create an environment where everyone can thrive.
- **Conflict Resolution:** Differences are inevitable, but leaders must address them quickly and fairly. Mediation and open dialogue maintain harmony.

## 5. Technology-Driven or Digital Environments

Leaders must blend technical expertise with human-centric thinking in fast-paced, tech-heavy settings. Staying ahead of trends while fostering collaboration is the key to thriving in these settings.

**Key Leadership Characteristics and Qualities Required:**

- **Technological Savvy:** Leaders must grasp the tools and systems driving their organization. Understanding digital landscapes ensures informed decision-making.
- **Strategic Vision in Technology:** Anticipate where technology is heading and align initiatives with long-term goals. Forward-thinking leaders maintain relevance in fast-evolving fields.
- **Communication Proficiency:** Virtual teams demand clear and consistent updates. Leaders must keep everyone connected and informed, no matter the platform.

- **Adaptability:** New tools emerge constantly. A learning mindset helps leaders embrace change and model resilience for their teams.
- **Data-Driven Leadership:** Leverage analytics to complement intuition. Grounding decisions in evidence ensures that strategies are robust and impactful.
- **Cybersecurity Awareness:** Protecting digital assets is a shared responsibility. Leaders must prioritize cybersecurity in every decision.

## 6. Environments Emphasizing Ethics, Integrity, and Trust

Leaders must exemplify honesty and transparency in organizations where values take center stage. Trust is the foundation of everything they build.

**Key Leadership Characteristics and Qualities Required:**

- **Integrity and Honesty:** Actions must align with words. Leading by example strengthens credibility and inspires loyalty.
- **Authenticity:** Being genuine fosters trust. Consistent, sincere leadership resonates deeply with teams.
- **Empathy:** Every decision has an emotional impact. Leaders who understand and consider these impacts build fairness and respect.
- **Purpose Alignment:** Show how daily tasks tie into larger ethical goals. When work feels meaningful, teams stay motivated.
- **Cultural Adaptability:** Honor cultural norms while staying grounded in your principles. Balancing respect with consistency is crucial.
- **Wisdom and Self-Awareness:** Reflect on your choices and stay open to feedback. Growth and humility go hand in hand.

## 7. Sustainability, Environmental Responsibility, or Long-Term Vision

Organizations prioritizing sustainability require leaders who think holistically and plan. Balancing present needs with long-term goals is at the heart of their strategy.

**Key Leadership Characteristics and Qualities Required:**

- **Strategic Vision:** Today's actions should pave the way for tomorrow's success. Leaders must balance short-term wins with enduring impacts.
- **Systems Thinking:** Understand how people, processes, and resources connect. Small changes can have ripple effects, so leaders need to see the bigger picture.
- **Environmental Stewardship:** Implement sustainable practices that prove profitability and responsibility can coexist. Lead by example.
- **Collaboration and Partnerships:** Work with stakeholders—employees and external partners—to create systemic, lasting change.
- **Education and Advocacy:** Inspire others to embrace sustainability within and beyond the organization. Awareness drives action.

As with leadership styles, environments are not cut-and-dried. They cannot simply be gathered into seven finite categories. Every environment is different and consists of a blend of these seven. However, typically, at least one environment type is strongly observable.

By aligning your leadership qualities with your specific environment, you set yourself up for success. Whether navigating constant change, fostering innovation, building inclusivity, or championing sustainability, tailoring your approach ensures that you lead with impact, authenticity, and purpose.

## Leadership Styles Clusters and Leadership Styles by Environmental Type

Having identified the types of environments and the key characteristics leaders need, it's helpful to consider which leadership styles align most effectively with a given environmental setting.

The table below provides links between our familiar leadership style clusters and leadership styles that most likely operate well in each of the seven environments.

| Environment Type Leadership Style Clusters<br>Key Leadership Styles | | |
|---|---|---|
| **Environment Type** | **Leadership Style Clusters** | **Key Leadership Styles** |
| **1. Dynamic, Changing, or Crisis Environments** | Adaptive and Resilient Leadership; Transformative and Visionary Leadership | Adaptive, Agile, Situational, Crisis, Resilient, Hybrid, Quantum, Transformational, Purpose-Driven, Transcendent, Resonant, Charismatic, Innovation, Sustainable, Regenerative, Integral Leadership |
| **2. Structured or Regulated Environments** | Structured and Analytical Leadership; Principled Leadership | Transactional, Strategic, Systems, Cognitive, Neuroscience-Based, AI-Enhanced, Digital, Mindful, Authentic, Ethical, Paternalistic, Holacratic Leadership |

| | | |
|---|---|---|
| **3. Innovative or Creative Environments** | Transformative and Visionary Leadership; Relational and People-Focused Leadership | Transformational, Purpose-Driven, Transcendent, Resonant, Charismatic, Innovation, Sustainable, Regenerative, Servant, Shared Leadership, Co-Creative Leadership, Laissez-faire Leadership |
| **4. Diverse, Inclusive, and Collaborative Environments** | Relational and People-Focused Leadership; Principled Leadership | Servant, Empathy-Based, Relational, Inclusive, Cultural Intelligence, Democratic, Shared, Co-Creative, Maternalistic, Authentic, Ethical, Social Leadership |
| **5. Technology-Driven or Digital Environments** | Structured and Analytical Leadership; Adaptive and Resilient Leadership; Transformative and Visionary Leadership | Digital, AI-Enhanced, Mindful, Adaptive, Agile, Situational, Crisis, Resilient, Hybrid, Quantum, Transformational, Innovation Leadership, Holacratic Leadership, Social Leadership |
| **6. Environments Emphasizing Ethics, Integrity, and Trust** | Principled Leadership; Relational and People-Focused Leadership | Authentic, Ethical, Transcendent, Servant, Empathy-Based, Relational, Maternalistic, Paternalistic, Biophilic, Social Leadership |
| **7. Sustainability, Environmental Responsibility, or Long-Term Vision** | Transformative and Visionary Leadership; Principled Leadership; Structured and Analytical Leadership | Transformational, Sustainable, Regenerative, Authentic, Ethical, Strategic, Systems, Cognitive, Neuroscience-Based, AI-Enhanced, Digital, Mindful, Integral Leadership |

## The Forty Leadership Styles and Environment Characteristics They Serve Best

Circumstances in a given environment are unique and it is for this reason that we cannot align specific leadership styles to an environment type with complete certainty.

This section provides a reference guide, mapping each of the forty leadership styles to the typical environments where they can have the most significant positive impact or in which they are more or less comfortable.

Each leadership style is presented with a brief description of the circumstances and environments it best serves. Keep in mind that styles can also be blended or adapted. The aim here is to understand the typical environment that resonates with your leadership styles.

### 1. Transformational Leadership

- Organizations seeking major innovation, cultural shifts, or growth.
- Motivational needs where teams must achieve beyond standard expectations.
- Innovation-driven industries are embracing continuous improvement.
- Vision-centric environments where a compelling mission aligns teams.

### 2. Purpose-Driven Leadership

- Mission-focused organizations (nonprofits, social enterprises) guided by principles beyond profit.
- Values-oriented teams are seeking meaningful work and broader societal contributions.
- Social impact strategies align business goals with ethical aims.
- Ethical marketplaces where consumer values shape success and loyalty.

## 3. Transcendent Leadership

- Purpose-driven organizations (nonprofits, social movements) elevate moral values.
- Settings focused on personal growth and higher principles.
- Ethical leadership needs to anchor grand visions in moral foundations.
- Societal-change initiatives aim for profound, meaningful transformations.

## 4. Resonant Leadership

- Emotionally demanding settings where empathy enhances team performance.
- Teams face transitions that need emotional support and understanding.
- Collaborative cultures thrive on interpersonal connections and trust.
- Customer-centric industries value emotional intelligence in client relations.

## 5. Charismatic Leadership

- Crisis management scenarios need inspirational confidence and direction.
- Motivational roles (sales, fundraising) where enthusiasm drives performance.
- Low-morale teams require a spirit boost and cohesion.
- Vision-driven organizations need a leader to embody and champion core values.

## 6. Innovation Leadership

- Cutting-edge industries (tech, biotech) where constant idea generation matters.

- Disruptive markets are requiring a redefinition of industry standards.
- Creative problem-solving efforts need unconventional solutions.
- Ambitious projects with transformative, future-oriented goals.

## 7. Sustainable Leadership

- Eco-conscious organizations prioritize environmental responsibility.
- Long-term strategic focus where sustainability shapes future success.
- Socially responsible cultures integrate ethical practices into strategy.
- Regulatory pressures mandating ecological standards and accountability.

## 8. Regenerative Leadership

- Sustainability initiatives aiming at environmental restoration and renewal.
- Agriculture and ecology sectors champion regeneration over mere maintenance.
- Long-term impact goals are prioritizing positive ecological and social outcomes.
- Collaborative ecosystems are leveraging stakeholder input for systemic improvement.

## 9. Integral Leadership

- Complex, dynamic settings require a blend of multiple leadership approaches.
- Organizational transformations (e.g., mergers, cultural integrations).

- Diverse teams with varied skills, backgrounds, and perspectives.
- Adaptive situations need tailored leadership styles for evolving contexts.

## 10. Servant Leadership

- Service-oriented organizations (nonprofits, healthcare, education).
- High employee engagement needs to boost morale, loyalty, and dedication.
- Flat hierarchies emphasize teamwork and collaboration.
- Cultures valuing empathy and putting employee well-being first.

## 11. Empathy-Based Leadership

- Teams face difficulties like layoffs, restructuring, or challenging transitions.
- Supportive cultures where the understanding of emotional needs improves performance.
- Diverse workplaces need sensitivity to multiple viewpoints.
- Customer-service industries where empathy enhances client relationships.

## 12. Relational Leadership

- Team-oriented settings where success depends on strong relationships.
- Community-focused organizations (nonprofits, social enterprises) nurturing connections.
- Service industries where interpersonal skills directly impact results.
- Collaborative projects where mutual support enhances outcomes.

## 13. Human-Centered Leadership

- Tech-heavy industries are balancing automation with human insight and well-being.
- Workplaces are facing automation where human-AI synergy must be managed.
- Wellness-focused environments prioritize employee mental health.
- Ethical consideration settings evaluating technology's impact on people.

## 14. Inclusive Leadership

- Diverse organizations leveraging multiple perspectives and backgrounds.
- Companies are addressing inequality, aiming for equity and fairness.
- Social impact goals where difference and inclusion drive better solutions.
- Cultural transformation efforts are bridging historical divides and biases.

## 15. Cultural Intelligence Leadership

- Global organizations operating across multiple countries and cultural contexts.
- Diverse workforces with varied backgrounds and traditions.
- International projects need sensitivity to local norms and values.
- Mergers and acquisitions integrate distinct corporate cultures.

## 16. Democratic Leadership

- Creative teams benefit from collective idea generation.
- Employee engagement-focused workplaces encouraging ownership and involvement.
- Collaborative decision-making environments need broad buy-in.
- Skilled professionals are eager to share expertise in guiding outcomes.

## 17. Shared Leadership

- Collaborative cultures value distributed decision-making.
- Cross-functional teams need input from multiple areas of expertise.
- Inclusive environments engage employees at all levels.
- Innovative projects flourish through diverse ideas and co-creation.

## 18. Co-Creative Leadership

- Collaborative projects demand collective ownership of solutions.
- Innovation labs are benefiting from multidisciplinary idea generation.
- Cross-disciplinary teams leveraging diverse expertise.
- Organizational change initiatives are inviting input from all levels.

## 19. Social Leadership

- Digitally engaged organizations are building online communities and brand image.
- Consumer-centric industries need transparency and public engagement.

- Reputation management scenarios require open dialogue and authenticity.
- Community building efforts fostering online and offline networks.

## 20. Adaptive Leadership

- Rapidly changing markets (tech-driven, fast-paced industries).
- Uncertain environments need quick strategic pivots.
- Crises requiring flexible problem-solving.
- Learning-oriented cultures treat challenges as growth opportunities.

## 21. Agile Leadership

- Fast-paced industries (technology, software) where rapid innovation is key.
- Changing project requirements demanding swift adaptation.
- Organizations are adopting agile methodologies (Scrum, Kanban) for iterative progress.
- Innovation-driven cultures are leveraging adaptability for competitive advantage.

## 22. Situational Leadership

- Varied skill levels among team members with different competencies.
- Dynamic workplaces where tasks and priorities often shift.
- Projects requiring distinct leadership approaches at different phases.
- Flexible organizations value leaders who tailor styles to current conditions.

## 23. Crisis Leadership

- Emergency response teams dealing with immediate threats.
- High-stakes industries where swift, decisive action is vital.
- Unprecedented challenges need to be established protocols.
- Organizational turnarounds where rapid recovery strategies are paramount.

## 24. Resilient Leadership

- Crisis and recovery phases where perseverance matters most.
- High-pressure industries face frequent challenges.
- Teams need emotional support and guidance through adversity.
- Adaptive cultures view setbacks as opportunities for growth.

## 25. Hybrid Leadership

- Distributed workforces balancing remote and on-site collaboration.
- Global teams connecting multiple locations and time zones.
- Post-pandemic workplaces are adopting flexible work models.
- Environments requiring leadership across different communication platforms.

## 26. Quantum Leadership

- Highly unpredictable markets like startups and rapid innovation fields.
- Complex problem spaces need nonlinear, Adaptive thinking.
- Creative industries where embracing complexity leads to breakthroughs.
- Emerging technologies present unknown variables and fast-paced change.

## 27. Transactional Leadership

- Structured settings like military, manufacturing, or assembly lines.
- Performance-driven cultures focused on targets and quotas.
- Regulated industries need strict compliance and adherence to rules.
- Outcome-focused projects where efficiency and measurable results are paramount.

## 28. Strategic Leadership

- Competitive industries need visionary positioning and long-term plans.
- Long-term planning scenarios focusing on sustainable growth and direction.
- Regulatory challenges requiring foresight and compliance strategies.
- Vision alignment moments ensure that daily operations reflect overarching objectives.

## 29. Systems Leadership

- Complex organizations with intricate structures and interdependencies.
- Interconnected industries (healthcare, logistics) benefiting from holistic thinking.
- Holistic challenges (sustainability efforts) need a broad, integrated view.
- Cross-departmental initiatives where system-wide coordination is essential.

## 30. Cognitive Leadership

- Intellectually diverse teams combining various thinking styles.
- Complex decision-making scenarios require multifaceted analysis.
- Conflict resolution needs to benefit from multiple perspectives.
- Innovation-oriented contexts are leveraging diverse cognitive inputs.

## 31. Neuroscience-Based Leadership

- High-stress, crisis-management settings (emergency services, rapid responses).
- Organizations are undergoing significant changes and need to manage emotional responses.
- Teams benefit from emotional intelligence and stress understanding.
- Learning cultures valuing scientific, evidence-based leadership approaches.

## 32. AI-Enhanced Leadership

- Data-rich industries are leveraging analytics and machine learning.
- Tech-adopting organizations integrating AI into operations.
- Predictive analysis scenarios inform strategic decisions.
- Innovation-focused settings gain competitive advantage through technology.

## 33. Digital Leadership

- Digital transformation efforts are modernizing technologies and processes.

- Disruptive markets where digital innovation is key to staying competitive.
- Technology-driven teams adopting new digital strategies.
- Competitive digital landscapes demand tech-savvy insight and agility.

## 34. Mindful Leadership

- High-stress workplaces where mindfulness reduces anxiety and increases focus.
- Wellness-oriented cultures promote mental health and well-being.
- Complex decision-making requires clarity, presence, and thoughtful action.
- Leadership development contexts valuing self-awareness and personal growth.

## 35. Authentic Leadership

- Ethics-focused organizations prioritize integrity and moral behavior.
- Cross-cultural settings where respect for diverse values is essential.
- Trust-building scenarios require honesty and credibility.
- Industries or roles frequently face moral or ethical challenges.

## 36. Holacratic Leadership

- Nonhierarchical organizations are experimenting with distributed authority.
- Teams value self-management and flexible structures.
- Innovative start-ups are seeking alternative governance models.
- Autonomy-focused cultures encourage individuals to lead within their roles.

## 37. Maternalistic Leadership

- Supportive environments where nurturing helps manage stress or change.
- Community-oriented organizations value unity and well-being.
- Care-focused industries (healthcare, education) prioritizing empathy.
- Resilience-building contexts fostering strong bonds and mutual support.

## 38. Paternalistic Leadership

- Traditional cultures are where respected authority figures guide the team.
- Inexperienced teams need direction and structure.
- Family businesses emphasize loyalty and long-term commitment.
- Situations demanding trust and stability through a protective leadership role.

## 39. Biophilic Leadership

- Wellness and health industries are integrating nature into work environments.
- Sustainable design contexts using natural elements to enhance creativity.
- Creative workspaces where nature helps spark innovation.
- Eco-friendly organizations emphasize environmental connections and well-being.

## 40. Laissez-faire Leadership

- Highly skilled, self-motivated teams requiring minimal oversight.

- Creative industries (design, research) benefit from maximum autonomy.
- Entrepreneurial settings encourage independence.
- Remote workplaces where micromanagement is impractical and trust is key.

This comprehensive list provides a foundation for understanding leadership approaches and the environments to which they are best suited.

## Integrating Insights for Fluid Leadership Adaptation

We have explored how leadership clusters, styles, and environmental factors interconnect to shape your leadership approach. These concepts work together to provide a complete framework for understanding and refining your leadership practice. Whether you recognize your workplace's traits, align your style with the demands of the moment, and/or adapt to new challenges, every element contributes to making you a more effective and adaptable leader.

Leadership is rarely a straightforward or static experience. Market forces shift overnight, teams evolve, technology races ahead, and societal expectations morph rapidly. Individual leadership styles can't handle such a variety of scenarios. Instead, consider the tools and perspectives presented here as a flexible guide—something you can lean on to navigate even the most unpredictable conditions. By layering these insights—from understanding your environment to identifying clusters to zeroing in on the leadership styles most suited to the situation—you create a tool kit capable of handling diverse challenges.

Being fluid in your leadership style means reading the room—or, more accurately, your organizational environment—like a seasoned navigator reading the skies. In environments dominated by change and unpredictability, you might lean into resilience, adaptability, and quick decision-making. On the other hand, structured and regulated environments demand precision, adherence to process, and a focus on ethical foundations. If your setting is people-centric, relational and empathy-driven approaches may rise to the forefront. Each scenario calls for its blend; as a leader, your ability to switch gears without losing sight of your core values is key.

One of the biggest challenges in leadership is growing beyond one's natural tendencies while remaining true to oneself. It's not about throwing away your strengths; instead, it's about expanding them.

Leadership is not about wearing a mask. Adaptability doesn't mean inauthenticity. It's about harmonizing your core values with the moment's needs. Your ethical foundation—your true north—should always remain intact. This gives your team a sense of consistency, even as you adjust your approach.

Think of your leadership journey as an experiment that never quite ends. Every project, every team, and every market condition offers new variables to test. What worked last year might need tweaking today, and that's okay. The key is to approach each experience with curiosity. Test out approaches. See how they resonate with your team, stakeholders, and yourself. Then refine.

Adaptability also requires self-awareness. After significant milestones, take time to reflect on your leadership. Were there moments where a different approach could have yielded better results? Or times when stepping outside your comfort zone paid off in unexpected ways? These reflections help you stay grounded while continuously improving.

True adaptability means striking a balance. You can adjust your style to suit the environment while keeping sight of what you stand for. For instance, prioritizing ethical decision-making doesn't change just because you're in a high-pressure, fast-moving scenario. Instead, it shapes how you approach the situation—ensuring that integrity guides every choice, no matter how quickly it must be made.

## Key Takeaways from this Chapter

The essence of fluid leadership lies in your ability to adapt without losing authenticity. By understanding your environment, aligning with relevant clusters, and tailoring your approach to the needs of the moment, you create a leadership style that is both flexible and grounded. As you refine your strategy, you'll find that leading becomes less about reacting and anticipating, less about managing and more about inspiring.

Leadership is a journey, not a destination. The tools and frameworks shared here are guides to help you navigate that journey, not rigid rules to follow. Use them to experiment, reflect, and grow. In doing so, you'll strengthen your leadership and create a positive and lasting impact on those you lead.

**Summary**

- **Environment-Style Alignment is Essential:** Effective leadership starts with understanding the landscape. Whether operating in a dynamic, innovation-driven, or regulation-heavy environment, aligning your approach to the context ensures relevance and impact.
- **Adaptive Combination of Clusters and Styles:** No single leadership style is enough. Leaders often blend multiple clusters—such as Adaptive and Resilient, Transformative and Visionary, or Relational and People-Focused—to address the complexities of their environment.
- **Intentional Adaptation Enhances Effectiveness:** Once you've mapped your environment and clusters, you can fine-tune your leadership traits to fit. This deliberate effort improves your impact as a leader and your team's overall performance.
- **Continuous Growth Through Feedback:** Leadership evolves with time. Regular reflection, combined with input from peers and teams, ensures that your style grows in tandem with the challenges and opportunities you face.

# Chapter Workout

## Exercise 1: Complete the Environment Assessment

**Objective:** This exercise helps you take a step back and objectively assess the environment in which you lead. Understanding the specific characteristics of your workplace is crucial for aligning your leadership approach with the unique demands around you.

To be most effective and avoid biased results, invite other members of a given environment to complete the assessment and consolidate the results.

## Exercise 2: Review the Environment Assessment

**Objective:** Obtain a clear understanding of the environment you are leading or will be leading in.

1. **Identify Predominant Environment(s):**
   - **Primary Environment:** The highest scores indicate the most prevalent environment type(s) in your organization.
   - **Multiple Environments:** If multiple environments have similarly high scores, or are in proximity, your organization may embody a blend of those environment types.

2. Review these environments to gain a clear understanding of their dynamics and leadership requirements.

## Exercise 3: Identifying Suitable Leadership Style Clusters and Leadership Styles

**Objective:** To pinpoint the leadership styles and clusters that best align with your organization's environment, enabling you to lead more effectively and with context.

1. **Review Environment Types and Leadership Styles and Clusters:**
    - **Action Step:** Refer to the descriptions of the seven environment types and their corresponding leadership clusters and styles provided in this chapter. Familiarize yourself with these categories.

2. **Match Environment Characteristics:**
    - **Reflection Prompt:** Considering the environment type(s) you identified, which leadership style seems best for these conditions?
    - **Journal Entry:** Write down the leadership style clusters that match your organization's environment. For instance, if your organization is constantly changing and often faces crises, you might find that Adaptive and Resilient Leadership pairs well with Transformative and Visionary Leadership.

3. **Select Primary and Secondary Clusters:**
    - **Action Step:** Determine one primary leadership style cluster that feels most critical for your environment, and a secondary cluster to complement it.
    - **Example:**
        - » Environment Type: Dynamic, Changing, or Crisis Environments
        - » Primary Cluster: Adaptive and Resilient Leadership
        - » Secondary Cluster: Transformative and Visionary Leadership

## Exercise 4: Deep Diving into Your Leadership Style

**Objective:** To dive deeper into your leadership style, explore your characteristics and qualities, and how they fit your environment.

1. **Research Cluster Characteristics:**
   - **Action Step:** Review the details of your predominant leadership style(s) and compare them to the traits required by your environment.

2. **Self-Reflection:**
   - Document your thoughts, focusing on how your leadership style addresses the demands of your organization.
     - » How do the characteristics of your predominant leadership style align with your environment?
     - » Describe a time when you effectively used your leadership style.
     - » What traits does your environment require you to develop or become stronger at?
     - » What is the worst-case scenario? Should you not strengthen these characteristics?
     - » Describe a time when these characteristics could have come in useful.
     - » What challenges could you face in adopting and applying these styles, and how will you navigate them?

# Chapter 10

# Adapting Your Leadership Style

*Fluid leadership flows like water, adjusting its course to meet every challenge with grace and purpose.*

Think back to a time when you had to change your plans on the fly—maybe a work project took an unexpected turn, or something in your personal life required a complete rethink. Sticking rigidly to one way of doing things in those moments doesn't cut it. Effective leadership is all about flexibility—much like a skilled sailor reading the winds, adjusting the sails, and navigating changing waters with finesse.

In the last few chapters, we developed your leadership self-awareness: knowing your strengths, your unique style, and where you could grow. But knowing yourself is only the first step. The real test of leadership comes when you use that self-awareness to adapt fluidly to whatever comes your way.

In this chapter, we'll dive into the art of fluid leadership—how to flex and shift your approach depending on the circumstances. We'll explore why adaptability is more important than ever in our ever-changing world and look at practical ways you can learn to adjust your style to fit different contexts.

I've learned that in mastering the art of reading your environment, understanding your team, and applying the right leadership approach at the right time, one can become a more effective leader who truly inspires those around one.

## The Fundamentals of Fluid Leadership

The term "fluid leadership" might make some people think of a leader who's all over the place, improvising decisions without a plan or letting their team run wild. That couldn't be further from the truth. Imagine driving a car—you've got the engine, the rules of the road, and a destination in mind; but how you drive depends on traffic, weather, or the condition of the road. You adapt, but you're still in control. Fluid leadership works the same way. It's about shifting gears as needed while keeping your core principles intact.

At its heart, fluid leadership is built on three essential elements: self-awareness, context awareness, and style agility. Let's break those down.

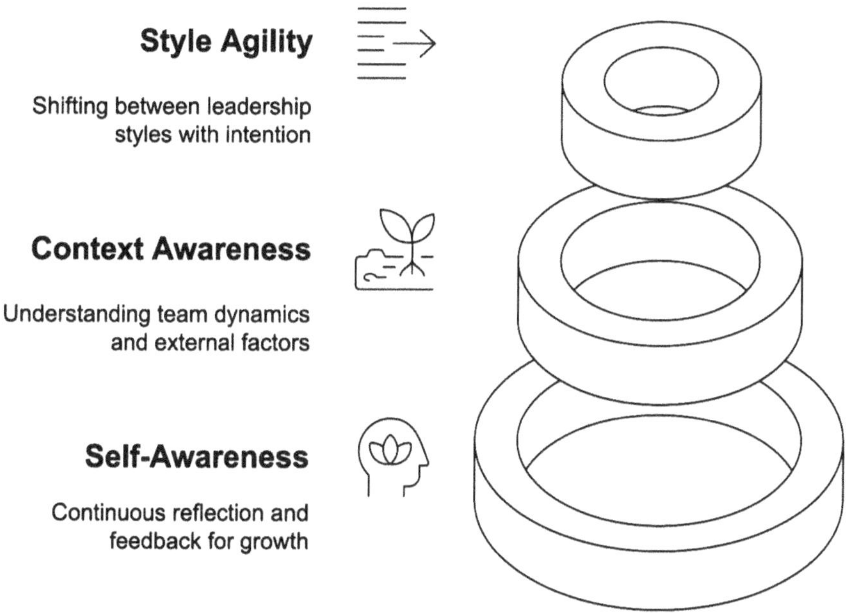


*Figure 13: Fundamentals of Fluid Leadership*

## Self-Awareness

Much of your journal work you've been doing up to now, combined with the various assessments, was about developing your self-awareness. Self-awareness is knowing your natural leadership tendencies, strengths, and areas where you might struggle. It's also about recognizing how your emotions, biases, and triggers affect your actions.

It's important to note that self-awareness isn't something you gain overnight. It's a continuous process of reflection and feedback. Journaling is an excellent way to track your interactions—what went well, what didn't, and why.

Trusted mentors and colleagues can provide valuable insights if you're open to honest conversations. There's no one-size-fits-all method. But what matters is that you commit to understanding how you show up as a leader and where you can improve.

## Context Awareness

If self-awareness is about knowing yourself, context awareness is about understanding what's happening around you. It's the ability to "read the room" and gauge the dynamics of your team, the organization, and the wider environment. For instance, a new, inexperienced team might need hands-on guidance, while a seasoned group might just want you to clear obstacles so they can get on with their work.

But context awareness goes beyond team dynamics. It also means understanding your organizational culture—whether fast-moving and open to experimentation, or more traditional and cautious. It's about being alert to external factors like market trends, regulatory changes, or competitive pressures. Missing these signals is like bringing an umbrella on a sunny day—well-intentioned, but entirely out of place.

## Style Agility

Style agility is the ability to shift naturally between leadership styles. A fluid leader knows when to step in and take charge during a crisis and when to step back and encourage collaboration once the dust settles. For example, if your team is demoralized after a setback, you might adopt an empathetic and supportive tone to rebuild morale. Later, when confidence is restored, you can return to a more performance-focused style.

The key to style agility is consistency in reasoning. People might struggle to trust a leader who swings unpredictably between approaches. But if you explain why you're changing your style—like tightening deadlines during a critical project—your team is more likely to understand and adapt with you.

When you combine self-awareness, context awareness, and style agility, you create a leadership approach that's both adaptable and grounded. You're not just reacting to situations—you're responding with intention and authenticity. Fluid leadership is about staying true to who you are, while at the same time you flex to meet the moment, ensuring that your team feels supported and inspired no matter what comes their way.

## Background to Fluid Leadership

By now you've noticed the frequent repetition of the mantra "Leadership isn't a one-size-fits-all deal" in this book. What works beautifully in one situation might fall flat in another. Just like a carpenter reaching for the right tool for the job, a leader must be able to pick the right approach for each unique challenge. This kind of flexibility is what I mean by "fluid leadership."

Daniel Goleman, known for his work on emotional intelligence, puts it well: Great leaders don't stick to one style. Instead, they move between styles, using the right one for each moment. Each style has its strengths and weaknesses, and the trick is knowing when to use which one to get the best results.

A firm, Coercive approach is sometimes necessary to bring order to a chaotic meeting. At other times, an Affiliative style, which nurtures relationships and encourages open communication, can create a more productive environment. The leader's ability to adapt her style to the situation's needs makes all the difference.

## Situational and Adaptive Leadership

As a reminder, let's briefly return to Situational and Adaptive leadership, which we previously discussed in Chapter 2. Paul Hersey and Ken Blanchard's Situational Leadership Model provides a practical framework for adapting leadership styles.

Their idea is simple: Effective leadership depends on how ready your team is—how competent and committed they are. Depending on this, a leader might need to be more directive or supportive.

Imagine that you're managing a team of software developers. One is a seasoned pro, and another is a recent graduate just getting their feet wet. With the experienced developer, you might use a Delegating style, giving them the freedom to innovate. However, for newcomers, a more directive approach—offering straightforward guidance and support—might be precisely what they need. By adjusting your leadership style to suit each individual, you help them grow and boost the project's overall success.

Ronald Heifetz introduced the concept of Adaptive leadership, which is all about tackling challenges calmly and thus being able to develop clear-cut solutions. Adaptive leaders involve their teams in problem-solving, encouraging creativity and openness to change.

Picture a company suddenly hit by a significant market shift because of emerging technology. An Adaptive leader doesn't just dictate a new strategy—they get the team involved in understanding the challenge and generating creative solutions together. This collaborative approach results in better ideas and gives team members a sense of ownership and responsibility.

Heifetz's Adaptive leadership is instrumental in constantly changing industries. By acknowledging that the old ways might not work anymore, Adaptive leaders ensure that their teams are ready to face emerging and unpredictable challenges head-on.

Fluid leaders have the skills to handle a wide range of situations, and can:

- Respond to Change Effectively: They adjust strategies as new information becomes available, keeping their teams on track.

- Engage Diverse Teams: By understanding and accommodating different needs, they motivate a wide range of people and help build strong, cohesive teams.
- Boost Performance: They apply the leadership style that best supports the team and yields circumstances leading to higher productivity and satisfaction.
- Encourage Innovation: Flexible leaders inspire creative thinking and problem-solving, allowing their teams to explore ideas freely and without fear.

By embracing fluidity, you enhance your leadership and your team's capabilities, empowering everyone to navigate change confidently.

Fluid leaders shine brightest when dealing with complex problems. They confidently navigate uncertainty by considering multiple perspectives and staying open to fresh ideas. This flexibility leads to more creative solutions and a remarkable ability to pivot when things take an unexpected turn.

## The Human Tendency toward Comfortable Styles

Let's take a moment to discuss a very human trait I have noticed that affects leadership: our natural tendency to stick with what feels comfortable and secure. Just like we gravitate toward familiar places or routines, leaders often lean on styles that align with their personalities and past experiences.

This idea of a "comfort zone" is a psychological state where things feel easy, we're in control, and there's little anxiety. It makes sense: operating from this place often means consistent performance. But it can also limit growth and prevent us from being as adaptable as we need to be.

Psychologists Edward Deci and Richard Ryan's theories on self-determination suggest that people are motivated by a need for competence, autonomy, and connection. In leadership, this often means we pick styles that fulfill these needs. A directive style gives a sense of control, and a collaborative style helps foster those much-needed connections with others.

Staying in our comfort zones has real benefits—it creates consistency in decision-making, and team members often appreciate knowing what to expect. But there are drawbacks too. If we rely too much on what's comfortable, we may struggle when faced with situations that demand something different. Leaders who thrive on consensus-building might flounder when a crisis requires decisive action. And sometimes a fixed style doesn't work for a team's diverse needs.

By sticking with what's comfortable, we risk developing blind spots. We may miss our impact on others or fail to see where we need to grow. That's why stepping out of our comfort zone is vital for effective leadership.

## The Balance between Fixed and Adaptive Leadership Styles

Being adaptable doesn't mean abandoning all consistency. Staying true to your core values and principles is just as important. If you're too fluid without anchors, it can lead to unpredictability and a lack of trust among your team members.

The most effective leaders balance consistent values with flexible methods. This balance ensures that the underlying principles stay solid, even though the approach might change depending on the situation. For example, if you're committed to transparency, you might communicate differently with a board of directors than with a junior employee, but you always strive to be open and honest.

Maintaining this balance allows leaders to:

- Build Trust: People trust leaders who are consistent in their values.
- Stay Adaptable: Flexibility in approach allows leaders to respond effectively to change without losing sight of their core beliefs.
- Earn Credibility: Aligning actions with values makes a leader credible and authentic.

## Navigating a Changing Landscape

The world is marked by constant shifts—technological advances, market changes, and evolving social expectations. What worked last year or even last week might not work tomorrow. In this environment, sticking rigidly to one leadership style can hold you and your team back.

Think about a company facing fierce competition and rapid change. A leader who clings to "the way we've always done things" may find the team falling behind. In contrast, an adaptive leader who knows when to switch things up can help steer the team toward new opportunities, foster innovation, and build resilience.

Leadership doesn't happen in a vacuum. The right style for the job depends mainly on the context—the specific challenges, the makeup of your team, the organizational culture, and even external factors like industry trends.

In a crisis, people seek a leader who can make quick, confident decisions. But if you're working on a creative project, it's often better to be the leader who opens the floor to new ideas and encourages discussion. Understanding the context that you're working in helps you select the best leadership style for that moment.

## A Spectrum of Approaches

Leadership styles abound, each with unique strengths and potential pitfalls. Knowing these different styles and when to appropriately employ each is key to being a fluid leader. Fluid leadership is about understanding the situation and choosing the most effective approach.

Great leaders mix and match to suit the situation. Combining supportive and directive behaviors, for example, can help address the emotional needs of your team and the task at hand. A leader might provide detailed instructions for a critical project while offering encouragement and resources to help the team succeed.

Leadership styles also need to evolve. As situations change and team dynamics shift, leaders must reassess and adapt. This shows team members that their leader is committed to finding the best way forward, enhancing effectiveness and building trust.

## Reading the Environment

Being fluid starts with being aware of what's happening around you. Fluid awareness means understanding external and internal factors influencing your team and organization.

Externally, staying informed about industry trends, competitive pressures, and technological advancements is essential. To keep in tune with the bigger picture, engage with stakeholders, attend industry events, and keep up with relevant publications.

Internally, consider changes within your organization—strategy shifts, policy updates, or cultural transformations. This awareness helps you foresee challenges and opportunities, allowing you to adjust your leadership approach before issues become problems.

## Understanding Your Team

You need to know your team's strengths, weaknesses, goals, and concerns to be effective. Regular one-on-one meetings are a great way to gain this insight.

Tools like the Myers-Briggs Type Indicator or CliftonStrengths (previously StrengthsFinder ) can help you understand individual personalities and preferences. Just remember, these are guides, not labels. The most valuable insights often come from simply observing and listening.

According to the Situational Leadership Model, your team's competence and commitment levels can guide your approach:

- Low Competence, High Commitment: They're enthusiastic, but still learning. A coaching style that guides and supports will work best.
- High Competence, Low Commitment: They're skilled, but could use some motivation. A supportive style can help reignite their passion.

- High Competence, High Commitment: A delegative style is ideal when the team members are experienced, motivated, and ready for autonomy.

## Assessing Task Requirements

Different tasks demand different approaches. Look at how complex, urgent, or impactful a task is. Routine tasks are handled well with a delegative approach, but complex, high-stakes projects require a closer eye and more direct involvement.

For example, launching a new product line isn't just about checking off tasks—it involves cross-functional teamwork, market analysis, and strategic planning. A transformational leadership style that inspires and rallies the team toward a shared vision can be highly effective.

## Overcoming Challenges in Fluidity

Changing your leadership style can sometimes feel like steering a ship into uncharted waters—not everyone on board will be ready for it. People often get comfortable with how things have always been, and shaking that up can create uncertainty. The best way to manage this resistance is through honest, open communication—ensuring that everyone understands why things are changing and how it will benefit them and the organization.

Being adaptable is critical, but it doesn't mean abandoning consistency. Your team needs to know that some things—like your core values and integrity—will always stay the same. They need to trust that while your tactics might shift, your principles are unwavering.

When you adjust your style, ensure that it aligns with who you are and what your organization stands for. This balance of staying true to your values while being flexible in your approach builds deep trust and genuine credibility. It shows that, even as you evolve, your leadership still comes from an authentic place.

Adapting doesn't mean swinging wildly from one extreme to the other. If you change too drastically, your team may feel confused and unsure of where you're headed. The key is to make deliberate, thoughtful adjustments appropriate to the situation.

## The Role of Trust in Fluid Leadership

Trust might be one of the most underappreciated forces in leadership. Without trust, no matter how elegantly you switch styles, your team might wonder if you are playing games or trying to manipulate them.

People need to see that your leadership approach changes come from genuine concern for the team and the organization, not from a desire to boost your ego or maintain control. That requires honesty, transparency, and consistency.

Let's say that you have decided to adopt one of the structured styles for a short period because a big client suddenly demanded urgent changes to a product. Trust-building means you explain to your team why you are taking this approach. You might say, "We must get this done by the end of next week, or the client may pull out. I know I am usually quite collaborative, but I will provide clear instructions over the next few days. I welcome questions, but to meet the deadline, we need a quick turnaround on tasks." That level of openness usually earns more respect than barking orders without explaining why everything has changed overnight.

Trust also grows when you follow through on promises. If you say you will revert to a more relational style once the crisis ends, do it. If you say you are open to feedback, respond well when someone gives you that feedback. Leaders sometimes lose trust without realizing it, simply by forgetting their commitments or letting them slip over time. A fluid leader keeps track of what they have committed to and honors those commitments.

Consider a global manufacturing company that finds itself in trouble when a significant shift in economic conditions suddenly forces it to cut costs. The leader in charge—let's call him Brian—realizes that he needs to balance two conflicting needs: (1) quick, decisive actions to reduce expenses, and (2) maintaining morale so employees do not feel like they are next on the chopping block.

At first, Brian adopts a more structured and analytical style to implement immediate, across-the-board budget cuts. This is not popular, but the company's finances demand swift measures. He calls short, tightly controlled meetings to announce the new budget limits. He does not invite much discussion, explaining that these decisions were nonnegotiable if the business is to remain sustainable. He also admits that the rapid nature of these decisions is not his usual transformational approach, but time is of the essence.

Once the immediate threat is under control, Brian switches gears. He recognizes that employees are left feeling uneasy. So he takes more of a people-focused style, booking one-on-one chats with department heads, thanking them for bearing the stress, and asking what the company can do to help teams recover. He actively acknowledges employees' fears and encourages open, honest discussions about how they can maintain motivation.

Over the following weeks, he moves into a relational style by forming a "cost-optimization committee" with representatives from all levels of the organization. Their job is to brainstorm ways to save money without harming employee well-being. The final decisions still rest with Brian, but by letting people propose and vote on various options, he fosters a sense of ownership.

Within a few months, the company stabilizes. The cost-cutting goals are met, but just as importantly, morale starts improving. Employees say they appreciated Brian's willingness to listen and adapt after the initial crisis. Brian avoided perceptions of himself as a fickle leader by openly showing why he changed styles and how each change served a specific purpose. Instead, he came across as someone who could act decisively when needed and revert to a more supportive, people-focused approach once the emergency was over.

That is fluid leadership in action: reading the room, making intentional style shifts, and staying genuine so the team understands why.

## No Single Leader Can Do It All: Building a Complementary Team

It is easy to read about all the leadership styles and feel that you must master every single one overnight. You might even feel pressure to be the ultimate renaissance leader who can pivot at will without breaking a sweat. But realize that no individual can realistically excel at all these different approaches.

We all have natural preferences, plus emotional or skill-based limitations that keep us from being perfect chameleons. The key is not to beat yourself up for having blind spots, but rather to know how to fill those gaps by surrounding yourself with people who balance you out.

Plenty of managers try to push themselves to be the commanding type when a crisis hits, the nurturing coach when someone needs development, the inclusive relational when the group is stuck, and the inspirational visionary when there is an opportunity to surpass targets. Of course, that is the dream. But the truth is, you might instinctively lean toward one or two styles because of your personality, background, or training.

Maybe you are fantastic at setting a high bar and rallying people to reach it, but you struggle to slow down and help a new team member who feels overwhelmed. Or you are a brilliant people-focuser who thrives on personal connections, yet you have difficulty taking control when deadlines loom, and everyone craves a clear directive.

What matters is knowing which styles are most natural to you and which feel like a stretch. Self-awareness is the first step—recognizing that you are not just "good at everything" or "bad at everything," but possess strengths in some areas and weaknesses in others.

Seek out people who can complement you. You are genuinely empathetic and supportive, but lack an assertive edge in high-pressure moments. It makes sense to partner with a deputy or senior team member who is coolheaded and authoritative under fire. That way, when a crisis rolls around, your team still gets a directive voice of confidence, and you can operate in a supportive role that fits your temperament.

As a leader, your job is not just to adapt your style, but to shape the environment where others can step up with theirs. Some of the best teams function almost like puzzle pieces, with each person's strengths slotting neatly into another's gaps. The result is that the team can respond more fluidly to any scenario.

You are effectively creating a leadership "ecosystem" where, if you are not the best at leading brainstorming sessions, you have someone else who is a natural facilitator and can tap into that democratic style. If you feel out of your depth when it is time to be firm and set hard boundaries, you have a teammate who is comfortable being the enforcer.

Ensuring that these complementary roles are clear often requires frank discussions about what each person brings. You might host a casual off-site, throw out hypothetical challenges, and ask each team member to discuss how they would handle it. The purpose is not to rank people from strongest to weakest, but to identify where each person feels most confident taking the lead. Over time, you build trust by letting individuals shine where they are strongest, while you focus on the areas that play to your own abilities.

No one expects you to be a flawless shape-shifter who is Transformative and Visionary, Relational and People-Focused, Adaptive and Resilient, Structured and Analytical with equal brilliance every day. You need to know yourself, see what the team needs in each situation, and ensure that you have the right people around you to fill in the gaps. Ultimately, leadership is never a one-person show anyway—it is a collective effort that thrives when multiple talents work together in harmony.

## The Journey to Fluid Leadership

The path to being a fluid leader does not have an endpoint. You do not just "complete" the journey and tick it off your to-do list. It is an ongoing practice—a willingness to keep growing, listening, and adjusting. The business world will never stay still for you or the people you lead.

Right now, you might work with one team that loves collaborating, but in five years, you might lead a different group that craves structure and direct guidance. To succeed in the long run, you must keep honing your self-awareness, context awareness, and style agility.

Being a fluid leader also involves risk. Sometimes you will pick the wrong style for a situation or communicate a shift in a way that confuses people, and you will need to step back and repair any damage. However, those mistakes can become lessons if you approach fluid leadership with humility and genuine care for your team.

Over time, you will get faster at recognizing the signals that it is time to shift your style, and you will find ways to maintain trust even when those shifts might feel abrupt. It is like learning to dance: At first, you worry about every step, but eventually you gain a sense of rhythm and can move more naturally.

The big takeaway is that leadership is not about sticking to one rigid identity—like "I am a visionary leader" or "I am a relational leader"—forever. Instead, it is about staying grounded in your values, but willing to show up differently when the moment requires it. You may have overarching principles, like respecting people, listening before judging, and valuing fairness. Those do not change.

However, applying them in high-stakes crises might differ significantly from using them in a casual, creative brainstorming session. That is the essence of fluidity: consistency in character and adaptability in action.

## Practical Tips for Becoming a Fluid Leader

Let's ground all these ideas in practical habits. Start your day by reflecting on your team's most immediate needs. Ask yourself: Do they need reassurance? More freedom? Clearer direction? Setting an intention for how you'll approach the day can help you stay focused.

Stay curious. Don't just assume you know what's going on—ask thoughtful questions, listen to people's perspectives, and be genuinely open to what they share. This habit not only deepens your understanding, but also builds trust.

Balance confidence with humility. You need to believe in your vision, but fluid leadership also means being willing to course-correct when new information comes to light. If something doesn't work, own it, learn from it, and move on. Teams respect a leader who can admit mistakes without losing credibility.

Create a culture where feedback is a regular part of the process. Maybe you introduce quick weekly debriefs where the team highlights what's working and what's not. If criticism is welcomed—not punished—you'll have a steady stream of insights to guide your leadership adjustments.

Finally, simplify complexity wherever you can. If your team is bogged down in confusing processes or excessive red tape, take the lead in clearing the path. Simpler workflows make it easier for you to adapt your style without overwhelming your team.

Fluid leadership isn't about being perfect or having all the answers. It's about staying flexible, grounded, and attuned to what your team and the situation need. When you embrace this mindset, you become a leader who can inspire confidence and steer the ship, no matter how choppy the waters may get.

## Key Takeaways from this Chapter

Fluid leadership is about reading the room, understanding what your team needs, and adjusting your approach to guide them effectively. It's about being flexible without losing what makes you you—your core values and authenticity.

In a world where change is a constant companion, adaptability isn't just a nice-to-have—it's essential. By honing your emotional intelligence, sharpening your communication skills, staying committed to learning, and practicing different leadership styles, you set yourself up to lead with agility and confidence.

Fluidity isn't a finish line you cross—it's an ongoing journey. It takes consistent effort, reflection, and a willingness to grow. As you build this capacity, you improve your leadership and empower your team to face change head-on and succeed together.

### Summary

- Fluid leadership is crucial in today's fast-paced world. It helps you respond effectively to changing situations and your team's diverse needs.
- Read the room by looking at team morale, task complexity, organizational culture, and external factors.
- Fluid leadership means being adaptable, but still anchored in your core values.
- Understanding different leadership styles lets you choose the right approach, boosting team engagement and performance.
- Developing situational awareness—knowing your team, reading the environment, and assessing the tasks—is the key to leading effectively.
- Cultivating flexibility means building emotional intelligence, improving communication, staying curious, and practicing various leadership styles.
- Overcoming challenges in adaptation involves managing resistance, balancing consistency with flexibility, and avoiding drastic shifts that might confuse your team.
- Keep building trust by being transparent, following through on commitments, and involving your team in decisions when appropriate.

The next chapter will expand on how to embed this kind of fluid mindset across broader teams and organizations so that adaptability becomes part of the culture, not just a personal trait of one leader. But I think you will find that people will notice if you start putting these principles into action for yourself—evaluating situations, shifting styles when needed, explaining your reasoning, and building trust. They will see a leader who is neither stuck in old ways nor chaotic, but someone who has the maturity to let the situation guide the style while still holding on to a consistent moral compass.

# Chapter Workout

Deepen your understanding of fluid leadership. Reflect on your ability to adjust your style based on changing circumstances and to develop strategies to enhance your flexibility and effectiveness.

## Exercise 1: Understanding Your Comfort Zone in Leadership

**Objective:** Recognize your go-to leadership styles and explore how staying in your comfort zone impacts your adaptability.

**Prompts:**

- **Comfort Zone Reflection:** Think of a time you felt completely at ease while leading. What made that situation comfortable, and how did it match your preferred style?
- **Benefits and Drawbacks:** What are the perks of sticking with your comfort zone? Conversely, when has this approach limited your ability to lead effectively?
- **Stepping Outside the Zone:** Recall a moment when you had to step out of your comfort zone and lead differently. What prompted you to do it, and what was the outcome?

## Exercise 2: Balancing Fixed and Adaptive Leadership Styles

**Objective:** Assess how well you balance staying true to your core values with being flexible in your leadership.

**Prompts:**

- **Your Core Values:** What are your core leadership values (e.g., integrity, empathy, accountability)? How do they shape your leadership, regardless of the situation?
- **Adapting while Staying True:** Describe when you adjusted your leadership style to suit a particular scenario, but stayed true to your values. How did you make that balance work?
- **The Challenges of Balance:** Have you ever faced a conflict between staying consistent and being flexible? How did you navigate that tension?
- **Balancing Act Strategies:** What strategies can help you maintain adaptability without compromising your core values?

## Exercise 3: Enhancing Situational Awareness

**Objective:** Improve your ability to understand the context of a situation so you can choose the most effective leadership approach.

**Prompts:**

- **Assessing the Situation:** How do you consider the context before stepping into a leadership role (e.g., team dynamics, the urgency of the task, culture of the organization)? Share an example of when you did this.
- **Context-Driven Decisions:** Think of a recent leadership decision you made. How did understanding the context shape the way you approached it?
- **Using Feedback:** How do you collect and use feedback to understand what your team needs? Describe a time when feedback helped you adjust your approach.
- **Steps to Improve:** How can you improve your situational awareness in future leadership roles?

## Exercise 4: Developing Style Agility

**Objective:** To cultivate the ability to switch between different leadership styles effectively, based on situational demands.

**Prompts:**

- **Create a Leadership-Style Tool Kit:** Develop a tool kit that includes key behaviors, communication strategies, and decision-making processes for each identified leadership style.
- **Practice Switching Styles:** Role-play different scenarios where you might need to switch leadership styles. This could be done with a peer, mentor, or coach. How comfortable are you with shifting between styles? What challenges do you face?
- **Implement Style Shifts in Real Situations:** Identify real-life situations where a different leadership style could be beneficial, then consciously apply the appropriate style. Document each instance where you switched styles, the reasoning behind it, and the outcomes.

## Exercise 5: Trust-Building Strategies

**Objective:** To build and maintain trust within your team, a cornerstone of effective fluid leadership.

**Prompts:**

- **Transparency Practices:** Share the reasoning behind your leadership-style shifts with your team. For example, explain why you're adopting a commanding style during a crisis and how it benefits the team. How does your team respond to increased transparency? Do they show more trust and understanding?

- **Follow Through on Commitments:** Identify key commitments you've made to your team and ensure that you honor them consistently. Document instances where you honored or failed to honor commitments and the resulting effects on trust.
- **Encourage Open Communication:** Create opportunities for open dialogue, such as regular team meetings, anonymous feedback channels, or one-on-one check-ins. Reflect on feedback received through these channels and how you addressed it.
- **Demonstrate Integrity:** Consistently align your actions with your stated values and principles, even in challenging situations. How does acting with integrity affect your team's perception of your leadership?

## Exercise 6: Building a Complementary Leadership Team

**Objective:** To create a leadership team that complements your strengths and fills in your weaknesses, enhancing overall team adaptability and effectiveness.

**Prompts:**

- **Identify Your Strengths and Weaknesses:** Based on your self-awareness assessment, list your key leadership strengths and areas where you need support. What leadership styles or skills do you excel in, and where do you need assistance?
- **Assess Your Team's Leadership Styles:** Evaluate the leadership styles and strengths of your team members through assessments, observations, or feedback. How do your team members' leadership styles complement or balance your own?

- **Fill Leadership Gaps:** Identify roles or leadership positions that require styles or skills you lack. Consider training, mentoring, or recruiting to fill these gaps.
- **Promote Collaborative Leadership:** Encourage team members to take on leadership roles that align with their strengths, fostering a collaborative and complementary leadership environment. How does a complementary leadership team enhance your ability to adapt and respond to different situations?
- **Facilitate Open Discussions:** Hold meetings or workshops where team members can discuss their leadership strengths and preferences, promoting mutual understanding and collaboration.

# Chapter 11

# Building a Fluid Organization

*Building a fluid organization means fostering a culture where every member can pivot, experiment, and lead in their own unique way.*

At this point you've already grasped fluid leadership: what it means to adapt, how to assess your environment, and why switching between leadership styles can invigorate your team's work. Until now, though, the focus has been on the individual leader—your ability to read the room, change gears as needed, and respond effectively in the moment.

But let's face it: No leader works in isolation. Even the most adaptable and self-aware person can hit a wall if the organization around them is rigid. You could bring all the openness and collaboration in the world to the table, but if the system punishes vulnerability or discourages experimentation, your efforts will only go so far.

That's why the next step is crucial: creating an organizational environment where fluid leadership isn't just a personal trait, but a shared way of operating. Think of this chapter as the natural progression from *"How do I become a fluid leader?"* to *"How do we, as an organization, build and sustain a culture of agility?"* After all, if you're the only one adapting in real time, it's a bit like trying to sprint through waist-deep water. You'll make progress, sure, but the resistance will slow you down, leaving you exhausted and frustrated.

Cultural change is no quick fix. You might have come across buzzwords about "90-day transformations" or "simple hacks to shift organizational mindsets," but those are more marketing gimmicks than reality. True change is gradual, requiring time, effort, and buy-in across multiple levels of leadership.

But it is achievable. It starts with understanding how leadership culture evolves and each person's role in that evolution. In this chapter, we'll explore the building blocks of an adaptive culture, look at examples of companies that embody adaptability, and provide practical steps to shift from rigid norms to an environment where fluid leaders can thrive.

By the end of this chapter, you'll have a clearer understanding of how individual leaders can help drive broader cultural shifts—encouraging teams to think differently, collaborate more openly, and confidently respond to change. You'll see how a fluid mindset must permeate every level of an organization, from the C-suite to frontline employees.

We'll also examine how systems, structures, and everyday practices can either accelerate or obstruct this process. While many of the values we've already covered—like self-awareness and trust—will still hold true here, we'll dive deeper into the collective dynamics of leadership. When an organization embraces fluidity, magic truly happens.

## Understanding the Organization as a Living Ecosystem

Many business books describe organizations as machines, full of parts that work together—departments, policies, procedures, and so on. While this metaphor works for understanding workflows or operations, it falls short when we talk about culture. Culture isn't a lever you pull or a cog you turn. It's more like a living ecosystem—an interdependent network of relationships, evolving norms, and subtle dynamics that shape behavior.

Thinking of an organization as an ecosystem highlights why rigid leadership styles can be so damaging. Imagine planting the same crop on the same land every year. Over time, you'd deplete the soil, reduce biodiversity, and risk losing everything if a single pest or weather event wiped out the crop. In the same way, forcing every leader in an organization to stick to a strict command-and-control approach might produce short-term predictability, but it stifles creativity, adaptability, and resilience. When a crisis or disruption hits—be it new technology, an economic downturn, or a competitor's innovation—such an environment struggles to adapt.

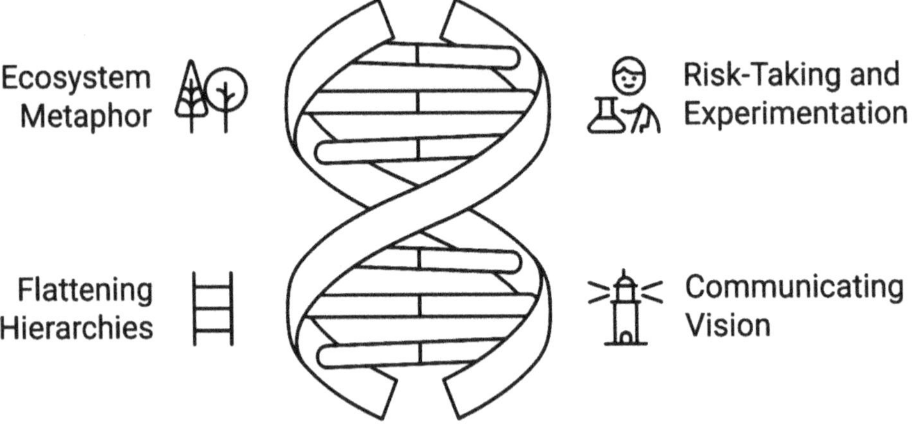


*Figure 14: The Fluid Organization*

Healthy ecosystems, on the other hand, thrive on diversity and balance. They contain a mix of species, each bringing unique strengths, and they foster resilience by enabling those species to interact and adapt together. Translating this back to leadership: An organization that encourages diverse leadership styles—principled, when necessary; relational at other times; transformative in the right moments—is better equipped to weather storms. Employees in such an organization learn to step into new roles, build fresh skills, and address challenges without being paralyzed by change.

This ecosystem analogy also reveals the importance of unspoken dynamics. Culture isn't defined by what's written in your employee handbook or splashed on your company's values page. It's shaped by how people behave day-to-day, especially when no one is looking. If those behaviors reinforce adaptability, experimentation, and openness, then your culture supports fluid leadership. However, if they prioritize hierarchy, conformity, and fear of failure, the culture becomes rigid, regardless of the official message.

Building a culture of fluid leadership means cultivating the right conditions across the entire ecosystem. This includes formal structures like reward systems and communication channels, as well as informal, unspoken beliefs about what "good leadership" looks like. Keep this ecosystem metaphor in mind as we dig deeper—it'll help you understand why partial efforts, like telling managers to "just be more fluid" without addressing the broader system, often fall short.

## Encouraging Risk-Taking and Experimentation

One of the cornerstones of a fluid-leadership culture is a healthy approach to risk and experimentation. In rigid organizations, the fear of blame or punishment can paralyze creativity. People naturally default to playing it safe, sticking to the status quo, and avoiding anything that might lead to failure. This mindset is the enemy of adaptability, as stepping into uncharted territory almost always involves some trial and error.

Encouraging risk-taking doesn't mean abandoning caution or common sense. It's about creating an environment where people feel safe testing ideas, piloting small projects, and learning from mistakes without jeopardizing their careers or reputations. In fluid cultures, leaders actively encourage experimentation by offering resources, guidance, and permission to fail. They trust that lessons from minor missteps will lead to significant breakthroughs.

Take the example of tech companies running "hackathons." These events allow employees to step outside their usual roles and tackle creative challenges, building prototypes or brainstorming new features. Not every prototype becomes a success, but the culture celebrates effort, creativity, and learning. During these hackathons, leaders often adopt coaching or democratic styles, asking questions like *"What excites you about this idea?" "How do you see this concept adding value?"* or *"What went wrong? What did we learn?"* This approach fosters a supportive atmosphere where innovation can flourish.

Contrast this with a traditional financial institution where hierarchy and risk aversion dominate. Managers might talk about wanting innovation, but employees quickly learn that mistakes can lead to embarrassment, damaged reputations, or worse. The result? People keep their heads down and stick to established practices, even when faced with changing market demands. Such organizations often struggle to pivot in crises, because their culture hasn't encouraged the skills or mindset needed for experimentation.

Shifting toward a fluid culture requires leaders at all levels to model an attitude of *"Let's learn and adapt."* This includes senior executives openly acknowledging their misjudgments. For example, when a leader says, *"We tried something new last quarter; it didn't work out as planned, and here's what we learned,"* it signals to employees that it's safe to take measured risks. Over time, this mindset seeps into the organizational fabric, freeing people to make context-appropriate decisions without being paralyzed by fear. It also encourages them to explore different leadership styles, knowing that the culture supports adaptability.

## Flattening Hierarchies without Losing Accountability

Another vital theme in a fluid-leadership culture is how the organization handles hierarchy and accountability. When we talk about "flattening" hierarchies, we do not necessarily mean dismantling all reporting lines or doing away with formal titles. Instead, we are talking about reducing the emphasis on top-down authority, while ensuring that people know who owns which decisions and responsibilities.

In a fluid culture, employees are typically encouraged to share ideas freely, rather than waiting for permission from above. Leaders adopt a more collaborative style, trusting that good suggestions can come from anywhere, whether a new intern or a veteran executive. This free-flowing exchange of ideas speeds up feedback loops and helps the organization spot inefficiencies or fresh opportunities faster. But fluid cultures do not abandon accountability. Instead, they clarify who is accountable for what, so everyone can make decisions responsibly.

An example here might be seen in companies like Spotify, which has famously experimented with "squads" and "tribes" to organize employees around products rather than keeping them locked within traditional departmental silos. Each squad is a self-contained unit that handles a specific feature or aspect of Spotify's platform. Squad members include engineers, designers, and product specialists who share accountability for outcomes. They can shift leadership styles internally, depending on what is happening—perhaps the product manager takes a relational approach when someone is struggling, or the senior engineer becomes more structured when the system hits a critical snag. The key is that decisions can be made by the people closest to the issue, rather than waiting for approval from high up the chain.

Does this mean every business should adopt a squad-based structure? Not necessarily. Each organization has its unique context. However, the underlying principle is to make it easier for people on the ground to take ownership, speak up, and adopt flexible leadership behaviors themselves. If you stifle that possibility with thick layers of bureaucracy, your culture becomes rigid. People wait for instructions instead of responding in real time to new challenges. That environment is the opposite of fluid and can be detrimental in fast-changing markets.

Sometimes larger companies fear that flattening hierarchies will lead to chaos. But fluid leadership does not translate to "no structure." It translates to "enough structure to define responsibilities and enough autonomy for people to do their best work without being micromanaged." One way to maintain accountability is to build clarity around each role's core responsibilities, deadlines, and resources, and to emphasize open feedback channels so any issue can be addressed quickly. That clarity prevents the "everyone is in charge, so no one is in charge" problem, which can happen if you flatten everything too far and never clarify who holds the final say in crucial decisions.

## Communicating Vision in a Fluid Culture

You might ask, "If leadership styles are so adaptable, how do we maintain a consistent vision or direction?" This question pops up often in discussions about fluid leadership because, on the surface, constantly shifting your approach might confuse employees who want to know what the company stands for.

The answer is separating the "what" from the "how." The "what" is your broader vision or goal—perhaps you want to be the most customer-centric online retailer or become the world's leading sustainable-energy provider. That vision remains stable. The "how" is how you lead people toward that vision, which can shift depending on the context. This distinction lets you stay flexible in day-to-day leadership, while keeping everyone aligned around a shared purpose.

In a fluid culture, leaders still articulate a clear vision, but they often do it in a way that invites feedback and ownership from the team. For instance, they might present a broad challenge—"We aim to reduce our product's carbon footprint by 50 percent in two years"—and then let teams figure out how best to achieve it. This could mean employing a relational style for teams that need support or a transformational style for highly skilled units that want to get on with it. As conditions change—maybe new regulations come into effect or new technology emerges—the teams can switch approaches accordingly, but they stay anchored to that primary objective.

However, consistent communication is vital. If employees hear about a grand vision once at a company retreat and never see it mentioned again, it fades away. Fluid cultures keep the vision front and center, weaving it into regular team updates, recognition programs, and project discussions. Leaders of all stripes—visionary, principled, or relational in the moment—remind people that their immediate goals feed into the bigger picture. This approach fosters a sense of unity, even when leadership styles vary.

A well-known illustration might be Tesla's mission to accelerate the world's transition to sustainable energy, even though they encounter obstacles at times. That purpose is hammered home in communications, strategy, and public statements, giving the company a strong North Star. In day-to-day work, though, local teams might adjust their internal leadership style depending on their immediate challenges. One part of the organization may adopt an intense, structured mode to break new ground in battery technology, while another might choose a collaborative, democratic style to refine manufacturing processes. Despite these differences, they all know the end goal and why it matters.

## Scaling Fluid Leadership through Mentorship and Role Modeling

So far, we have discussed several aspects of building a fluid culture: encouraging risk-taking, flattening hierarchies, maintaining a clear vision, etc. But how do you spread these ideas to become the norm, rather than just a new initiative that fizzles out after a few months? One effective path is through mentorship and role modeling.

Consider how employees often learn about "acceptable" behaviors. Even if they read the company handbooks, observing people around them—especially those in positions of authority—really shapes their daily actions. If executives say they value adaptability, but always cling to a single approach, employees pick up the message that the talk is just talk. Conversely, if people watch their managers truly shift styles based on the team's needs, explaining why they are doing it, that behavior becomes contagious.

This is where mentorship can play a key part. Senior leaders who have mastered fluid leadership can take less-experienced managers under their wing, guiding them in how to read a room, decide whether to be more directive or collaborative, and handle the tricky balance of trust-building and accountability.

Mentorship discussions can include real-world scenarios—such as: "Your team is facing a major conflict, and you are not sure whether it is best to step in firmly or let them figure it out themselves. How do you decide?" By walking through these dilemmas, junior managers understand how to navigate complexity rather than just reading theoretical advice from a manual.

Another possibility is peer-to-peer coaching circles, where managers at roughly the same level meet regularly to discuss challenges and insights. They might share stories about times they tried a more relational style and discovered that certain team members initially felt uncomfortable. Or they might talk about when they pivoted to a structured style during a crisis and how they communicated that shift in a way that kept morale intact.

These honest conversations, grounded in everyday experiences, demystify fluid leadership and help managers see it as a set of skills that can be learned and refined over time, rather than something you either have or you do not.

The more that leaders—both senior and mid-level—demonstrate fluid behaviors openly, the more the entire organization takes note. It creates a ripple effect. You start to see employees at all levels adopting a flexible mindset.

Perhaps a project team that does not even have a formal manager rotates who leads weekly stand-up meetings based on who has the most relevant expertise or who feels most comfortable facilitating. That does not mean they lack accountability; it just means they are experimenting with distributing leadership tasks in line with the culture's emphasis on adaptability.

## Handling Resistance and Cultural Tensions

No discussion on organizational culture would be complete without acknowledging that you will face resistance. Culture change is uncomfortable, and some people genuinely prefer a more predictable, hierarchical environment. They might believe strongly that authority must always flow from the top down, or they might worry that flexible leadership opens the door to confusion or chaos.

Sometimes these concerns come from personal insecurity—"Will I lose status if the hierarchy is flatter?"—and sometimes from past experiences—"I tried a democratic style once, and it was a disaster!"

One way to handle resistance is to give people smaller, lower-risk chances to experience the benefits of fluid leadership. If a team is skeptical, you might propose a short pilot project with a transformational style. Make it clear that you are only testing this method for a limited time and that, afterward, everyone will review what went well and what did not.

When applied correctly, people will see that this approach can lead to better outcomes or a more motivated team. If you frame it as an experiment rather than a permanent overhaul, you reduce the fear that everything is changing overnight.

It also helps to acknowledge valid criticisms and build mechanisms to prevent or minimize chaos. For instance, you might hear, "If we flatten hierarchies and let managers switch styles freely, people will never know what to expect." That can be a fair point; therefore it's important that a leader understands fluid leadership, be acutely self-aware of their own motivations and what is truly right for the situation.

Emphasize that leaders will still communicate their style choices clearly, explaining reasons for a more directive stance or an open-brainstorming approach. This transparency lowers confusion and builds trust.

Additionally, remember that cultural tensions can arise across international operations if your organization spans multiple countries. In some cultures, direct instructions from a boss are the norm, while consensus is the expectation in others.

Suppose your company has offices in places with vastly different cultural traditions. In that case, fluid leadership can either be a unifying approach (because it allows local adaptation) or a source of tension if not rolled out with sensitivity. The solution is to engage local stakeholders, ask for their input on culturally appropriate styles, and demonstrate genuine respect for regional norms. At the same time, stay consistent with the overarching principle that adaptability is beneficial in a fast-changing environment.

## Reward and Recognition Systems in a Fluid Culture

One aspect often executed poorly in organizational transformations is how people are rewarded for their behavior. You send mixed messages if you want to embed fluid leadership, but your performance reviews, bonuses, or promotions only reward those who stick to a single style.

For example, suppose a manager tries a coaching approach, invests time in developing their team, and fosters a collaborative spirit. In that case, their performance appraisal is mainly tied to short-term financial metrics, and no credit is given to people's development. Guess what happens next time? That manager will probably not prioritize coaching again.

In a fluid culture, the reward system aligns with the idea that adaptability and development matter. That might mean that performance appraisals include metrics like, "How many team members grew in their roles this year?" or "How well did the manager navigate a sudden market shift without losing morale?" or even "How open was the manager to peer or subordinate feedback?" The point is not to overload people with complicated evaluations, but to signal that the organization values a range of leadership behaviors, including effectively switching styles.

Also, recognition does not have to be purely monetary. Some companies acknowledge leadership excellence in subtle but powerful ways, like featuring fluid leaders in internal case studies or inviting them to speak at corporate events. That kind of visibility can be a big motivator for managers who want to be seen as positive contributors.

Again, though, consistency is key. Employees will sense the contradiction if the top leadership publicly praises flexible managers, but privately rewards those who follow more traditional styles.

## The Role of Training and Organizational Development

Anyone who has tried implementing a new corporate initiative will know that the best intentions can falter if employees do not receive proper training or guidance. Teaching fluid leadership at the organizational level is a multifaceted process. It can include formal workshops where people learn about different leadership styles, practice real-life scenarios, and discuss case studies from relevant industries. It can also involve informal learning opportunities like lunch-and-learn sessions, internal knowledge-sharing platforms, or cross-departmental rotations.

One challenge is that many leadership-development programs still rely on one-size-fits-all content: "Here is how to manage a team in a traditional sense." They rarely address shifting leadership styles or reading context clues in real time. So, to build a fluid culture, you must design learning experiences that emphasize these elements.

For example, in a training session, participants might role-play different scenarios—like dealing with a creative block in the product design team or responding to an urgent regulatory change in the finance department—and then discuss the best leadership style. The group can debate possible consequences, see how different styles might clash or align, and gain confidence in choosing the right approach.

Beyond structured training, there is also the ongoing organizational development (OD) process. OD experts study the "health" of an organization, looking at communication patterns, trust levels, and how effectively people collaborate. If your OD team is on board with fostering fluid leadership, they can design interventions that nudge teams toward more agility. This might include rearranging departmental boundaries, realigning incentives, or even facilitating difficult conversations where historically rigid leaders are encouraged to consider a fresh approach. OD is about continuously shaping the organizational environment, which is precisely what you need to sustain long-term fluid leadership.

## Technology as an Enabler or Barrier

Technology can be both an enabler and a roadblock to fluid leadership. On the enabling side, the rise of collaboration tools—like Slack, Microsoft Teams, Trello, Asana, and others—makes it easier for people to share ideas, coordinate projects, and communicate quickly. These platforms can flatten communication channels, reduce the dominance of rigid hierarchies, and give leaders a real-time pulse on what is happening across the company. If used well, such tools strengthen a culture of openness because people can see how projects evolve, jump in with suggestions, or offer peer coaching.

However, technology can also create barriers if implemented poorly. For instance, excessive mandatory reports or check-ins can lead to micromanagement. Employees might spend more time filling out forms or updating spreadsheets than reflecting on their leadership style or focusing on genuine collaboration. Similarly, if complicated approval processes lock down the technology, they might hamper employees' ability to respond quickly to issues. Instead of enabling fluid leadership, they can reinforce a controlling approach.

Another subtle issue is digital overload. In a hyper-connected workplace, employees and managers can become inundated with constant notifications, chat messages, and round-the-clock emails. This environment can fuel a perpetual sense of urgency and stress, making thoughtful leadership style choices more difficult. People react hastily, defaulting to the easiest style for them because they do not have the mental space to consider alternatives. That is the opposite of fluid leadership, which thrives on awareness and deliberate decision-making.

The solution is intentional tech management. Instead of adopting every new tool on the market, organizations that value agility pick tools that genuinely help people work flexibly and communicate openly. They also set boundaries around availability and response times so employees do not feel pressured to respond at all hours.

A fluid culture acknowledges that people need mental bandwidth to reflect on how they are leading. If everything is always urgent, people slip into survival mode, and creative leadership styles vanish.

## Learning from Successes and Failures

Sometimes the best way to build a culture of fluid leadership is to openly discuss what has worked and what has gone wrong in the past. In many organizations, success stories get a spotlight—like how a bold pivot into a new market saved the day—but failures are quickly swept under the rug. The problem is that ignoring failures robs you of valuable lessons. If a project collapsed because the manager insisted on a transformational style when a relational approach was needed, that is an insight worth sharing. Otherwise, people might make the same mistake in another department, repeating the cycle.

One method to make this sharing part of the culture is to establish "postmortems" or "retrospectives" after major projects or product launches. During these sessions, everyone (including the leaders involved) talks candidly about what went well, what could have been done better, and how they might shift leadership styles. The focus is not on blaming individuals, but on understanding the decision-making process and how it influences results. If leaders feel safe acknowledging that they adopted the wrong style or took too long to switch approaches, the learning can be transformative for the entire organization.

On the success side, you might identify a department that excelled in a fast-changing situation precisely because the manager displayed fluid leadership. Maybe they started with an adaptable style when the team was developing an innovative idea, then switched to a structured style when production deadlines loomed, and finally moved to a transformational approach after launch to rebuild the team's energy. Celebrating that flexibility signals that the company genuinely values the ability to read the context and shift accordingly.

These open discussions—postmortems, retrospectives, or lessons-learned meetings—are vital to embedding fluid leadership because they take abstract concepts and show them in action. They also reinforce the organization's commitment to reflection, continuous improvement, and honest communication, strengthening the cultural bedrock of fluid leadership.

## Key Takeaways from this Chapter

Embedding a fluid mindset into an organization's fabric involves much more than simply sending a memo saying, "Try different leadership styles." It is about rethinking how people relate to each other, how mistakes and experiments are handled, how hierarchy is structured (or de-emphasized), how technology is used, and how leaders demonstrate openness to learning and evolving. You might think of it as orchestrating a symphony, where multiple sections—structure, reward systems, communication, training, and culture—need to play in harmony to produce the music of adaptability.

Will it be easy? Probably not. Organizational change rarely is. However, the reward is an organization that survives unexpected disruptions and often finds ways to come out stronger. Fluid leadership, when practiced at scale, can spark more significant innovation, higher engagement, and a sense of shared purpose that helps the business stand out in a crowded, ever-changing marketplace.

The key is to keep the conversation going, to keep learning from both triumphs and failures, and to encourage everyone—from top executives to entry-level employees—to recognize that they can contribute to a more adaptable culture.

Take a moment to reflect on your organization. Where do you see signs of fluid thinking already in place, and where do you see rigid mindsets that might need more attention? Answering those questions can set you on the path to becoming a fluid leader and catalyst for cultural transformation.

**Summary**

- Think of an organization as an ecosystem where every layer and interaction can either help or hinder a culture of flexibility.
- Encourage safe experimentation and small-scale risk-taking to allow new ideas to flourish without punishing honest mistakes.
- Flatten hierarchies by giving people autonomy and transparent accountability, ensuring that they can act quickly and responsively.
- Keep your overarching vision steady, but let teams choose the best way to get there—switching leadership styles as needed.
- Use mentorship and role modeling to make fluid leadership natural and contagious throughout the organization.
- Acknowledge and address resistance by providing low-risk opportunities for skeptics to see the benefits of adaptable leadership.
- Align reward and recognition systems to promote adaptability, collaboration, and learning from successes and failures.
- Use technology to enable real-time communication and flexibility, but be cautious of digital overload or rigid reporting systems.
- Conduct regular reflections (postmortems, retrospectives) to share lessons from triumphs and setbacks, reinforcing the ethos of continuous growth.

In the next chapter, we return to you as a leader to encourage the adoption of continuous learning and development, to become the greatest leader you can be.

# Chapter Workout

## Exercise 1: Viewing the Organization as a Living Ecosystem

**Objective:** To shift your perspective from viewing the organization as a machine to understanding it as a dynamic ecosystem, highlighting the interdependence of its components and the importance of diversity and balance.

**Prompts:**

- **Organizational Mapping:** Create a visual map of your organization's ecosystem. Include departments, teams, key roles, communication channels, and external factors (e.g., market trends, regulatory bodies).
- **Identify Interdependencies:** How do different departments and roles interact? What dependencies exist that impact the organization's adaptability? Write a summary of key interdependencies and how they contribute to or hinder organizational fluidity.
- **Assess Diversity and Balance:** Evaluate the diversity within your organization in terms of skills, backgrounds, and perspectives. How does this diversity contribute to the organization's resilience and ability to adapt?
- **Identify Ecosystem Health Indicators:** Determine indicators that reflect the health of your organizational ecosystem, such as employee engagement, innovation rates, and cross-departmental collaboration. What current indicators suggest that your ecosystem is healthy or needs attention?

## Exercise 2: Encouraging Risk-Taking and Experimentation

**Objective:** To cultivate a culture where risk-taking and experimentation are encouraged, allowing for innovation and continuous improvement without fear of punitive consequences.

**Prompts:**

- **Create a Safe Space for Experimentation:** Organize an "Innovation Day" or a "Hackathon," where team members can work on creative projects outside their usual responsibilities. How did the event encourage creativity and risk-taking?
- **Implement a Pilot Project Framework:** Develop a framework for initiating and managing pilot projects. Include guidelines for selecting projects, allocating resources, and evaluating outcomes. What criteria will you use to choose pilot projects that align with organizational goals?
- **Encourage Learning from Failures:** Establish a routine for conducting postmortems or retrospectives after projects, focusing on lessons learned rather than assigning blame. How can these sessions be structured to promote open and honest discussions?
- **Reward Experimentation:** Integrate recognition programs that celebrate innovative ideas and successful experiments, regardless of their outcome. How does recognizing experimentation impact team morale and willingness to take risks?

## Exercise 3: Scaling Fluid Leadership through Mentorship and Role Modeling

**Objective:** To promote fluid leadership across the organization by leveraging mentorship programs and role modeling behaviors that exemplify adaptability and collaboration.

**Prompts:**

- **Establish a Mentorship Program:** Pair experienced fluid leaders with emerging leaders to guide them in developing adaptability and style agility. What qualities make for effective mentors in promoting fluid leadership?
- **Role Modeling Sessions:** Organize regular sessions where senior leaders demonstrate fluid leadership behaviors in real-time scenarios. How do these demonstrations influence the leadership styles of participants?
- **Peer Coaching Circles:** Create peer coaching groups where managers can share challenges, discuss fluid leadership strategies, and provide mutual support. How does peer coaching enhance your ability to lead fluidly?
- **Leadership Shadowing:** Implement a shadowing program where emerging leaders observe and learn from leaders who effectively practice fluid leadership. What specific behaviors and strategies do you observe and wish to adopt?

## Exercise 4: Learning from Successes and Failures

**Objective:** To foster a culture of continuous improvement by openly analyzing successes and failures, extracting valuable lessons, and applying them to enhance fluid leadership practices.

**Prompts:**

- **Establish Regular Reflection Sessions:** Schedule periodic meetings (e.g., monthly or quarterly) dedicated to reviewing recent projects and initiatives. What went well, and what could have been improved, in each project?
- **Conduct Postmortems and Retrospectives:** After completing a project, hold a postmortem or retrospective meeting to

discuss what worked, what didn't, and why. How can the insights from these discussions inform future leadership style adjustments and project planning?

- **Share Success Stories and Lessons Learned:** Create platforms (e.g., internal newsletters, meetings, intranet pages) to share stories of successful fluid leadership and valuable lessons from failures. How do these shared stories inspire and educate other team members about fluid leadership?
- **Implement Continuous Feedback Loops:** Develop mechanisms for ongoing feedback, such as anonymous surveys, suggestion boxes, or regular check-ins. How does continuous feedback contribute to learning and adaptability within the organization?
- **Create a Learning Repository:** Build a centralized repository (digital or physical) where lessons learned, best practices, and case studies are stored and easily accessible to all employees. How can easy access to this repository support ongoing learning and fluid leadership development?

# Chapter 12

# Continuous Leadership Development

*Leadership isn't a destination; it's an ongoing journey of learning and growth.*

By now, I trust that you've taken a deep dive into your leadership values, beliefs, and personal style—uncovering blind spots, pinpointing areas for growth, and sharpening your vision for the leader you want to become. Yet, much like a hero embarking on an epic quest, your journey is far from over. The path to leadership mastery isn't a one-time event—it's a cycle of continuous growth, learning, and transformation.

Leadership development mirrors the classic Leader's Hero Journey, where each challenge, setback, and breakthrough refines you into a more resilient and inspiring leader. By coming this far in this book, you're well into your own leadership evolution. To keep you committed on this path, it begins with the hunger for change—realizing that staying the same isn't an option. You then work the truth about your current state, laying the groundwork for transformation before crafting a Massive Action Plan to navigate obstacles and push forward. This chapter will guide you through the step of this journey—from stepping into discomfort and developing daily habits to measuring progress and raising your standards. You'll also learn the importance of celebrating your victories and giving back, ensuring that your growth benefits those you lead.

This chapter is packed with practical tools and strategies. You'll explore goal-setting techniques that turn vague intentions into concrete actions, powerful mental exercises like incantations that reinforce your inner drive, and visualization methods that allow you to see success before it unfolds. We'll also discuss the invaluable role of mentors and coaches—how they can accelerate your growth by offering guidance, accountability, and wisdom gained from experience. Finally, continuous learning—through reading, research, and reflective journaling—will equip you to navigate the complexities of modern leadership, ensuring that you remain agile in an ever-changing world.

Think of this chapter as your leadership tool kit, designed to evolve with you. By embracing the Hero's Journey and applying these practical strategies, you'll refine your leadership skills and cultivate a mindset of growth, adaptability, and meaningful impact. Let the journey shape you—one step at a time.

## The Need for a Continuous Development Mindset

The world constantly changes—markets shift, technologies disrupt, and team dynamics evolve. Leaders who assume they've "arrived" risk being left behind. A mindset of continuous development is essential to staying relevant and effective.

This doesn't mean you need to overhaul who you are. Instead, it's about small, but meaningful adjustments. Think of it as tuning an instrument—making acceptable changes so it stays in harmony. Leaders who embrace this mindset see every challenge as a learning opportunity and treat setbacks as moments to grow, not failures to fear.

By viewing leadership as a craft, you stay open to innovation and long-term success. It allows you to remain agile, resilient, and prepared for whatever comes next without losing sight of your core values.

## The Leader's Hero Journey

Inspired by Joseph Campbell's monomyth and Tony Robbins, the Leader's Hero Journey provides a timeless personal and professional transformation framework. It's about the internal evolution that makes you a stronger, wiser, and more influential leader. Let me walk through the seven stages of this journey.

## 1. Awaken Your Hunger

Every transformative journey begins with a desire for change—a deep, unshakable hunger to grow, improve, and lead more effectively. This moment is the catalyst that sets everything else into motion.

**How to Do It:**

- Reflect on what kind of leader you want to be.
- Ask yourself why these aspirations matter. Find the emotional core of your ambition.
- Use any frustration or dissatisfaction as fuel for growth.

**Key Insight:** Your hunger for growth is the force that will push you forward—especially when the journey gets tough.

## 2. Face the Truth

True leadership begins with self-awareness—an honest, unfiltered look at where you currently stand. Confronting the gap between where you are and where you want to be is the first real test of growth.

**How to Do It:**

- Periodically revisit the limiting beliefs, habits, or fears that are holding you back.
- Continuously assess what isn't working in your leadership—communication, delegation, or managing conflict.
- Take full responsibility for your current situation—no excuses, no blaming others.

**Key Insight:** Growth starts when you stop lying to yourself. Face your reality with courage.

## 3. Create a Massive Action Plan (M.A.P.)

A vision without a plan is just a dream. Here, you transform your leadership aspirations into a clear road map, outlining the exact steps to reach your goals.

**How to Do It:**

- Break your leadership goals into small, manageable steps.
- Prioritize actions that create the most significant impact—apply the 80/20 rule.
- Set firm deadlines and establish accountability.

**Key Insight:** Clarity in planning leads to power in execution.

## 4. Do What's Hard

No hero's journey is without obstacles. Challenges are worthy opponents that take you to the next level. Effective leadership means overcoming discomfort, taking risks, and facing challenges head-on.

**How to Do It:**

- Identify your personal "dragons"—fear of failure, self-doubt, or bad habits.
- Push forward even when uncomfortable—growth happens at the edges of your comfort zone.
- Reframe setbacks as valuable lessons, rather than failures.

**Key Insight:** The hardest challenges forge the strongest leaders.

## 5. Develop Daily Practices

Leadership isn't about one big moment—it's built on small, daily habits that reinforce your growth over time.

**How to Do It:**

- Create a morning routine or journaling practice to start each day with intention.
- Focus on incremental progress—small wins compound over time.
- Track your daily habits to stay consistent and disciplined.

**Key Insight:** What you do every day matters more than what you do occasionally.

## 6. Measure Progress and Raise Standards

Growth is an ongoing process, and the best leaders continually raise their expectations of themselves.

**How to Do It:**

- Regularly track measurable outcomes tied to your leadership goals.
- Ask yourself, "Am I acting in alignment with my vision and values?"
- Set new, higher benchmarks to challenge yourself continuously.

**Key Insight:** Sustained leadership growth requires continuous improvement.

## 7. Celebrate and Give Back

Leadership isn't just about personal success—it's about impacting others. The journey doesn't end with achieving your goals; it culminates in the ability to uplift and inspire those around you.

**How to Do It:**

- Take time to celebrate your milestones and your progress genuinely.
- Share your experiences—through mentorship, leadership talks, or casual advice.
- Find ways to give back, helping others grow on their leadership paths.

**Key Insight:** True fulfillment comes from achieving success and empowering others.

By embracing these seven stages, you can transform everyday obstacles into opportunities for growth and refine yourself in the process.

The journey doesn't just change what you do—it changes who you are.

## Setting Meaningful Goals

Goal-setting is one of the most impactful ways to transform vague intentions into concrete action. Instead of thinking, "I should communicate better," you might say, "I will meet with each team member individually this month to discuss their challenges and tailor my communication style accordingly."

Effective goals follow the SMART framework—they're Specific, Measurable, Achievable, Relevant, and Time-bound. For example, if you want to improve delegation, don't just aim to "delegate more." Instead, commit to delegating one key project per quarter to a senior team member, with clear objectives and regular check-ins.

Link your goals to insights you've uncovered about yourself during your journal work. If you tend to micromanage, set a goal to empower your team by handing over decision-making responsibilities. If you avoid difficult conversations, commit to addressing issues directly within a specific time frame. Goals tied to personal awareness lead to meaningful progress.

### How to Set Goals

1. **Identify a Specific Focus:** Pinpoint an area to improve, based on what you've learned about yourself. For instance, you might want to handle conflicts more effectively or delegate better.
2. **Use the SMART Framework:** Define goals like, "I will delegate one major project per month to a senior team member, with a review after completion."
3. **Break Goals into Steps:** If the goal feels overwhelming, divide it into smaller tasks. Delegating might involve identifying the right project first, setting expectations, and following up regularly.
4. **Track Progress:** Monitor your actions, review them, and adjust your approach.

### What to Include in Your Process

- A written list of goals in your journal—keeping them in your head often means they get forgotten.
- Regular check-ins are needed to measure progress (weekly or monthly check-ins work well).
- Flexibility to revise goals if circumstances change.

## Harnessing Incantations for Embodied Change

Incantations are similar to affirmations, but are much more effective. Incantations take things further by adding intense feeling and physicality. Instead of saying, "I am confident" in a calm voice, you speak with conviction, use your whole body, and repeat the words until they stick in your mind. The point is to move from simply stating a phrase to fully experiencing and embodying it, which makes the shift in mindset more immediate and powerful.

Leaders often use incantations before beginning challenging tasks—like big presentations or tough meetings—to quickly transition from doubt to certainty. By combining movement (pacing, gesturing) with vocal intensity and strong statements, you prime your mind and body for action. Over time, this practice helps reinforce new mental habits, making it easier to stay motivated and to project confidence when it counts.

## How to Practice Incantations

1. **Speak with Power:** Use a strong, clear voice and a confident posture.
2. **Move Your Body:** Pacing or gesturing energizes you, linking your words to your physiology.
3. **Repeat Consistently:** Choose a few key phrases and practice them daily or weekly until they feel natural.
4. **Stay Goal-Focused:** Tailor your incantations to your leadership aims (e.g., "I now embody clarity and purpose in every meeting").
5. **Embrace Emotion:** Channel intensity and certainty—allow yourself to feel the statements you're declaring genuinely.

## What to Include in Your Incantation Practice

- Simple, Powerful Phrases that directly address your objectives.
- Physical Expression like gestures, walking, or standing tall to connect words with body language.
- Regular Time Slots so repetition becomes routine—before a big meeting, in the morning, or whenever you need a mindset boost.

## Visualization: Seeing Success before It Happens

Visualization is a mental rehearsal technique that lets you "see" yourself succeeding before the moment arrives. Athletes use this method to prepare for competitions, and leaders can do the same for meetings, presentations, or difficult conversations.

By imagining yourself handling a challenge effectively—leading a tough meeting or resolving a conflict—you create a mental template for success. Visualization can reduce anxiety, build confidence, and help you feel more prepared when the moment comes.

Regular practice also sharpens your ability to adapt in real time. When you've mentally rehearsed different scenarios, you're less likely to be caught off guard, so the rehearsal allows you to pivot gracefully as needed.

### How to Practice Visualization

1. **Find a Quiet Space:** Eliminate distractions so you can focus.
2. **Close Your Eyes and Picture the Scene:** Imagine confidently navigating a leadership challenge. Visualize the room, the people, and the flow of the conversation.
3. **Engage All Senses:** Hear your voice speaking, feel your calm breathing, and sense the energy in the room.
4. **Focus on the Desired Outcome:** Picture the results—team members nodding in agreement, a productive resolution, or a successful presentation.

### What to Include in Your Visualization Practice

- A specific scenario is relevant to your current challenges.
- There is enough detail to make the scene vivid and believable.
- A regular habit, such as visualizing before important meetings or decisions.

## Working with a Coach: Personalized Guidance

Imagine having someone in your corner whose sole focus is helping you become a better leader—someone who can offer honest feedback without sugarcoating it, can challenge your assumptions, and can guide you toward actionable solutions. That's the role a coach plays in your leadership journey.

Unlike friends or colleagues, who might tread lightly to avoid hurt feelings, a coach provides clear, constructive input in a supportive and direct manner. They offer an outside perspective, helping you identify blind spots and sharpen your skills.

For instance, a coach won't tell you to "handle it better if you struggle with conflict resolution." Instead, they'll break down specific situations, explore alternative approaches, and teach techniques for staying calm, listening actively, and steering discussions toward positive outcomes. Over time, this tailored guidance accelerates your growth, equipping you with strategies that suit your unique challenges.

### How to Find and Work with a Coach

1. **Identify Your Needs:** Start by pinpointing the areas you want to develop—communication, strategic thinking, emotional intelligence, or conflict resolution, for a few examples.
2. **Choose the Right Coach:** Look for someone with relevant experience and a coaching style that resonates with you. Credentials are necessary, but connection and compatibility matter just as much.
3. **Set Clear Goals:** Work with your coach to define success. Maybe it's mastering delegation or improving how you handle high-pressure situations.
4. **Be Open and Honest:** Coaching only works if you're willing to be vulnerable, share your challenges, and embrace new ways of thinking.

## What to Include in Your Coaching Engagement

- Regular sessions (weekly, biweekly, or monthly).
- Specific objectives are reviewed periodically to track progress.
- A commitment to openness and trying new strategies.

## Finding a Mentor: Learning from Experience

If a coach is like a personal trainer for your leadership muscles, a mentor is more like a trusted guide who's already walked your path. They've faced challenges, made mistakes, and learned valuable lessons along the way—and they're willing to share those insights to help you navigate your journey.

Mentors offer wisdom and perspective that come from lived experience. For example, a mentor who has led through significant organizational changes might share how they balanced transparency, empathy, and decisiveness. Hearing their stories can give you a clearer picture of how to apply similar principles in your leadership challenges.

Beyond guidance, mentors can expand your professional network by introducing you to valuable connections, resources, and opportunities. Over time, these relationships often become ongoing sources of support, offering a foundation for continuous growth.

## How to Identify and Approach a Mentor

1. **Look within Your Network:** Start with seasoned leaders you admire in your field or organization.
2. **Be Clear about Your Goals:** When reaching out, explain what you hope to gain—advice on tackling a specific challenge or broader guidance on career progression.
3. **Foster a Mutual Relationship:** Mentoring is a two-way street. Show them appreciation for their time and how their advice has helped you.

## What to Include in Your Mentoring Relationship

- Regular check-ins (monthly or quarterly).
- A clear agenda or focus for each conversation, such as navigating a leadership challenge or exploring career options.
- A willingness to listen and learn from their experiences.

# Ongoing Learning: Reading, Research, and Study

The best leaders are lifelong learners. The world of leadership is constantly evolving, with new research, theories, and best practices emerging continually. Staying curious and informed ensures that you're keeping up and staying ahead.

Commit to regular reading, attending workshops, and even enrolling in courses or certifications. For example, if you're working on emotional intelligence, you might dive into books by Daniel Goleman. If you focus on leading diverse teams, look for resources on cultural intelligence. Continuous learning keeps your skills sharp and prepares you for challenges.

## How to Maintain Ongoing Learning

1. **Curate a Reading List:** Focus on topics that align with your growth areas, like negotiation, cross-cultural leadership, or strategic thinking.
2. **Engage with Thought Leaders:** Follow experts in your field, attend webinars, and subscribe to relevant publications.
3. **Consider Formal Education:** Short courses, certifications, or advanced degrees can deepen your knowledge and provide fresh insights.

## What to Include in Your Learning Plan

- Specific topics tied to your goals (e.g., conflict resolution).
- A reading schedule, attending workshops, or completing courses.
- Regular reflection on how new knowledge applies to your role.

## Journaling: Reflecting on Your Leadership Journey

We've already got you working on your journal in this book. Sometimes the most straightforward tools are the most effective. Journaling helps you process experiences, track growth, and refine your leadership style.

Set aside time each day or week to jot down what went well, where you struggled, and what you learned. For instance, you might notice that a more directive approach worked in one meeting, leaving some team members feeling unheard. Writing it down allows you to see patterns, evaluate trade-offs, and think about how to improve.

Over time, your journal becomes a personal road map, highlighting your progress and recurring challenges. This reflection fuels adaptability, helping you respond to situations with intention rather than habit.

## Additional Tools and Techniques

While the tools above form a solid foundation, there are other strategies worth exploring:

- **Self-Care and Well-Being:** A leader can't pour from an empty cup. Prioritize activities that recharge you, like exercise, meditation, or hobbies. You're more equipped to lead effectively when you're at your best.

- **Building a Personal Board of Advisers:** Assemble a small group of trusted mentors, peers, or industry experts who can offer diverse perspectives and challenge your thinking.
- **Networking and Professional Associations:** Engaging with other leaders exposes you to new ideas and methods. Attend events or join organizations where you can exchange insights.
- **360-Degree Feedback Assessments:** Periodic reviews from peers, subordinates, and superiors provide a well-rounded view of your leadership style and areas for growth.

## Making Adaptability a Habit

Being an adaptable leader isn't about abandoning your values or changing who you are. Rather, it's about staying curious, open, and willing to evolve.

At first, this might feel awkward—like learning to ride a bike or mastering a new skill. But with practice, it becomes second nature. You'll start to see challenges as opportunities and feel confident navigating unfamiliar situations because you've built a tool kit to guide you.

You'll notice tangible improvements in your leadership by regularly setting goals, using affirmations, visualizing success, seeking guidance from coaches and mentors, committing to ongoing learning, and reflecting through journaling. Your team will likely notice too, appreciating your openness, adaptability, and ability to steer them through both smooth and choppy waters.

## Key Takeaways from this Chapter

Fluid leadership is about growth. It's about recognizing that you'll never stop learning—and that's good. With a toolbox of strategies like goal-setting, coaching, mentoring, and continuous learning, you're equipped to survive as a leader and thrive.

Every challenge you face is an opportunity to sharpen your skills and deepen your impact. By approaching leadership as a journey rather than a destination, you ensure that you remain relevant, effective, and inspiring, no matter what the future holds.

### Summary

- A "leadership toolbox" of personal-growth techniques helps you systematically improve. By selecting methods like goal-setting, affirmations, visualization, coaching, mentorship, ongoing learning, and journaling, you create a structured plan for consistent development.
- Become the greatest leader you can be by stepping out on your Leader's Hero Journey.
- Goal-setting translates vague intentions into clear, measurable targets that guide your actions and progress.
- Visualization allows you to mentally rehearse desired outcomes, reducing anxiety, and increasing preparedness when facing challenging situations.
- Working with a coach provides objective, personalized guidance to address specific gaps and accelerate your growth.
- A mentor offers the wisdom of experience, sharing lessons learned, and broadening your perspective on effective leadership.
- Ongoing learning—through reading, courses, workshops, and networking—keeps your knowledge fresh and ensures that you stay relevant in a changing world.
- Journaling is a reflective practice, enabling you to analyze your experiences, recognize patterns, and refine your approach.
- Additional tools, such as caring for your well-being, forming a personal board of advisers, and utilizing 360-degree feedback, further enrich your growth journey.
- Over time, consistently using these techniques makes adaptability more natural, helping you remain compelling and inspiring as you guide your team through shifting landscapes and new challenges.

# Conclusion:

# Embracing the Journey of Fluid Leadership

*Leadership is about impact—the kind that resonates beyond organizations to touch lives and shape futures.*

By 2035, effective leaders will merge technological fluency with deep human insight in ways we're only beginning to see today. They'll navigate complex decisions with agility, using AI-driven data, yet remain firmly grounded in empathy, emotional intelligence, and a people-first mindset. This future leader will seamlessly integrate emerging technologies—without necessarily being a coder—while fostering environments that champion mental well-being, continual upskilling, and cross-cultural collaboration.

They'll bring together distributed teams across multiple time zones, promote flatter hierarchies, and emphasize societal impact over mere profit. In essence, the leader of the future will be both a master of digital tools and a nurturing human presence, demonstrating that genuine connection, adaptability, and global thinking lie at the heart of tomorrow's most effective leadership.

Leadership, as we have discussed, is not some destination you arrive at—it is more like a lifelong road trip with twists, turns, and detours along the way. Fluid leadership invites us to embrace this journey, reminding us that the best leaders adapt gracefully to changing circumstances, shifting challenges, and evolving environments.

In this final chapter, we'll take stock of the core lessons from this guide, acknowledge how far you have come, and share practical advice for continuing to grow as an adaptive leader.

## Looking Back on Key Lessons

As we have explored, leadership is not a one-size-fits-all formula or a rigid identity. Instead, it is a living, breathing practice—a balance between who you are and the unique context in which you lead. From those early chapters, focused on self-awareness and understanding your natural tendencies, to the later sections—unpacking leadership styles and situational nuances—one truth has stood out: Effective leadership requires knowing yourself and being tuned in to what is happening around you.

Leadership is about influence—encouraging others, earning trust, and making meaningful change happen. Throughout this book, we have explored how actual influence comes not from wielding authority, but from being authentic, showing character, and building connections with those you lead.

There is no single "best" leadership style. As we examined forty different styles, one thing became clear: what works wonders in one situation can completely flop in another. Adaptability and self-awareness are critical: they help you adjust and grow in response to what is needed.

Alignment is everything. Outstanding leadership comes when your style fits the organizational culture and the moment's demands. Whether you're seeking feedback, keeping a leadership journal, or reflecting on your environment, understanding this alignment enhances your ability to lead effectively.

Stories matter in leadership. The narratives you share help bring people together, communicate your vision, and build trust. This book's examples—showcasing leadership in action—are potent reminders of how stories can inspire and transform.

Leadership is not a skill you tick off as "done." It is a constantly evolving tool kit, ready to adapt and expand as new challenges come your way. By balancing self-reflection with a clear understanding of your environment, you can grow into a leader who knows their strengths, but also understands when to step out of their comfort zone.

Most importantly, leadership is never "finished." The best leaders are lifelong learners, constantly evolving alongside their teams, organizations, and the world at large.

## Why Adaptability Matters More than Ever

If there is one principle that fluid leadership hinges on, it is this: adaptability is not a luxury—it is a necessity. Today's leadership environments are increasingly unpredictable, shaped by everything from rapid technological changes to shifting societal expectations. Leaders need to approach adaptability not as a fallback, but as their default mindset. This involves:

- **Staying Curious:** Always be open to new ideas, perspectives, and skills.
- **Being Resilient:** See challenges not as roadblocks, but as opportunities to learn and innovate.
- **Fostering Collaboration:** Value diverse voices and bring out the best in collective strengths.
- **Staying Humble:** Acknowledge what you do not know and actively seek input from others.

## Blending Leadership Styles

One of the biggest takeaways from this book is the importance of blending and fluidly moving between leadership styles or their qualities. Some situations call for transformational leadership, such as rallying your team during significant changes. Other times, servant leadership is needed, focusing on the growth and well-being of your team. Combining authentic, situational, and ethical leadership approaches allows you to create tailored solutions to meet unique challenges.

Far from being inconsistent, this flexibility is a hallmark of wisdom. Great leaders understand that the "right" style depends on the context, the team's needs, and the organization's goals.

Tools like environmental assessments, which we covered in earlier chapters, help leaders identify these demands. Whether managing a crisis, working within a tightly regulated framework, or navigating a highly creative industry, aligning your leadership style to the situation boosts individual and organizational success.

## Practical Steps to Keep Growing

In the previous chapter, we explored how to maintain a continuous leadership development program. Below are some additional tips that I have found helpful in my journey to outstanding leadership.

1. **Make Time to Reflect:** Regularly review your leadership journal. Celebrate what is working, identify areas for growth, and check how well your leadership style aligns with your current goals.
2. **Ask for Feedback:** Keep those feedback channels open. Tools like 360-degree reviews can provide valuable insights into how you are perceived as a leader.
3. **Invest in Yourself:** Take advantage of workshops, coaching, or other learning opportunities to sharpen your skills and broaden your perspective.
4. **Reconnect with Your Purpose:** Every so often, pause and ask yourself: Are your actions and decisions still aligned with your core values and bigger mission?
5. **Lead by Example:** Show, do not tell. Whether it is integrity, adaptability, or empathy, model the behaviors you want to see in your team.
6. **Harness the Power of Stories:** Use personal anecdotes and historical examples to inspire, connect, and convey your vision.
7. **Revisit the Tools:** Review the leadership frameworks in this book. They are not meant to be forgotten; use them to reassess and refine your approach.
8. **Stay Future-Focused:** Monitor emerging trends and challenges, from new technologies to changing workforce dynamics, and be ready to adapt.

## The Ethical Core of Leadership

Ethics has been a recurring thread in this book, and for good reason. The best leaders achieve results without compromising integrity, fairness, or transparency. Balancing stakeholders' expectations with the broader impact of your decisions is no easy task, but it is the mark of a truly great leader.

Ethical, servant, and authentic leadership styles offer a blueprint for ethical leadership. By prioritizing honesty, trust, and team well-being, these approaches foster cultures of accountability and respect—qualities that endure.

## A Journey Worth Celebrating

Before you close this book, take a moment to recognize how far you have come. Leadership is not just a role, but a profoundly human endeavor that challenges, rewards, and transforms. By embracing fluid leadership, you have equipped yourself with the tools to face uncertainty, inspire those around you, and make a lasting, positive impact now and in the future.

Leadership is also about legacy. It is the sum of the lives you influence, the values you uphold, and the changes you inspire. Think about the legacy you want to leave—one rooted in ethics, adaptability, and genuine impact.

And remember, this is not the end of the road. Leadership is a lifelong pursuit. The insights and tools from this guide are just the start. As you step forward, know that the world needs effective—but also compassionate and forward-thinking—leaders.

The book might end here, but your journey as a fluid leader is just beginning. Go forward boldly, ready to adapt, thrive, and inspire. The future of leadership is liquid, and you are well prepared to navigate it.

Thank you for taking this journey with me. I wish you every success as you continue to grow and evolve as a leader. May you lead purposefully, inspire others with your vision, and create a lasting, positive legacy.

If you have not yet done so, I highly recommend my two books—*The Leadership Compass* and *Leading with Tomorrow in Mind*—that dive more deeply into each leadership style we have included in this book. These books adopt a unique storytelling approach that facilitates learning and are filled with tips and exercises to embrace any particular style's characteristics better.

Best regards,

Pietro Pazzi

PS: Feel free to reach out if you have any queries, require guidance on your leadership journey, or want to share your leadership experiences.

info@leaderscrucible.com

Visit the Leaders Crucible website at https://leaderscrucible.com for the latest leadership and development insights. Follow me @pietropazzi and @leaderscrucible on LinkedIn for weekly insights about leadership and growing as a leader.

# Appendix I

# Core Qualities and Competencies of Forty Leadership Styles

## Cluster: Transformative and Visionary Leadership

### 1. Transformational Leadership

- Inspiring a shared vision
- Empowerment and motivation
- Leading by example
- Building strong relationships
- Fostering a growth mindset
- Innovation as a driver for transformation

### 2. Purpose-Driven Leadership

- Acknowledging reality and internal alignment
- Developing a sustainable vision
- Engaging stakeholders and innovating for the future
- Measuring and communicating progress
- Inspiring a broader movement
- Fostering community partnerships

## 3. Transcendent Leadership

- Cultivating inner wisdom
- Redefining success and living with purpose
- Ethical use of technology
- Creating a ripple effect
- Aligning personal and organizational values with societal well-being
- Addressing spiritual intelligence

## 4. Resonant Leadership

- Emotional intelligence
- Building trust and relationship
- Inspiring a shared vision
- Empowerment and motivation
- Fostering a positive culture

## 5. Charismatic Leadership

- Charisma and presence
- Effective communication
- Vision and inspiration
- Building trust and rapport
- Leading with optimism

## 6. Innovation Leadership

- Visionary thinking
- Encouraging experimentation
- Promoting continuous learning
- Inspiring passion and purpose
- Building a legacy of innovation
- Learn from failure

## 7. Sustainable Leadership

- Balancing profitability with responsibility
- Collaboration and trust
- Ethical decision-making
- Leaving a positive legacy
- Vision for the future
- Foster environmental stewardship

## 8. Regenerative Leadership

- Innovation-driven growth
- Apply circular economy principles
- Collaborative supply chains
- Stakeholder engagement
- Phased implementation
- Balancing ecological impact with innovation

## 9. Integral Leadership

- Blends various styles as needed
- Visionary thinking
- Adaptability
- Emotional intelligence
- Systems thinking
- Resilience
- Cognitive diversity and collaboration

# Cluster: Relational and People-Focused Leadership

## 10. Servant Leadership

- Serves the needs of the team
- Prioritizes growth and development
- Empathy and compassion
- Active listening
- Building community
- Leading by example

## 11. Empathy-Based Leadership

- Building trust and solidarity
- Active listening
- Supporting emotional and psychological well-being
- Empathy for the environment
- Creating an inclusive community

## 12. Relational Leadership

- Building strong relationships
- Effective communication
- Collaboration and teamwork
- Emotional intelligence
- Creating a supportive environment

## 13. Human-Centered Leadership

- Prioritize well-being
- Embrace innovation
- Foster collaboration
- Promote ethical AI development
- Build trust and respect
- Create a vision for coexistence
- Equitable access to resources

## 14. Inclusive Leadership

- Facing uncomfortable truths
- Engaging the leadership team
- Building an inclusive culture
- Listening to all voices
- Cementing a legacy
- Building structural diversity in leadership

## 15. Cultural Intelligence Leadership

- Cultural awareness and sensitivity
- Adaptability
- Effective communication
- Building trust and relationships
- Inclusive leadership

## 16. Democratic Leadership

- Collaboration and participation
- Foster consensus-building
- Empowerment through shared decision-making
- Leveraging diverse strengths
- Shared responsibility

## 17. Shared Leadership

- Collaborative leadership
- Inclusivity in leadership
- Empowerment through delegation
- Strategic vision
- Building a shared culture

## 18. Co-Creative Leadership

- Collaboration and shared responsibility
- Adaptability and flexibility
- Emotional intelligence
- Trust and resilience
- Collective accountability
- Crowd-sourced innovation

## 19. Social Leadership

- Visionary thinking
- Digital savviness
- Content creation and storytelling
- Community building
- Addressing public perception
- Data-driven decision-making
- Resilience and adaptability
- Builds long-term trust

# Cluster: Adaptive and Resilient Leadership

## 20. Adaptive Leadership

- Flexibility and adaptability
- Collaboration and communication
- Problem-solving
- Decision-making under pressure
- Resilience

## 21. Agile Leadership

- Flexibility and adaptability
- Iterative planning

- Rapid decision-making
- Overcoming challenges
- Building a culture of agility
- Fostering innovation through adaptability

## 22. Situational Leadership

- Situational awareness
- Tailoring leadership to specific team development stages
- Adaptability
- Clear communication
- Empowerment
- Resilience

## 23. Crisis Leadership

- Clear and calm communication
- Strategic thinking and planning
- Adaptability and flexibility
- Empowering the team
- Rapid decision-making
- Resilience and determination
- Post-crisis recovery plans
- Teams support mechanism during crises

## 24. Resilient Leadership

- Assessing challenges
- Empowerment and team resilience
- Innovation and adaptation
- Celebration of success and learning from setbacks
- Develop and maintain robust contingency plans

## 25. Hybrid Leadership

- Uniting the team
- Adaptability in leadership
- Effective communication
- Empowering decision-making
- Resilience and well-being focus
- Leveraging diverse talent
- Integrates remote and on-site teams

## 26. Quantum Leadership

- Quantum thinking
- Intuition and creativity
- Adaptability and flexibility
- Building trust and connection
- Embracing uncertainty

# Cluster: Structured and Analytical Leadership

## 27. Transactional Leadership

- Structured approach
- Maintaining accountability and process consistency
- Clear expectation
- Rewards and penalties
- Focus on results

## 28. Strategic Leadership

- Strategic thinking and planning
- Balancing operational and strategic goals

- Adaptability and innovation
- Ethical considerations
- Global cooperation and collaboration
- Influence and negotiation

## 29. Systems Leadership

- Understanding complex systems
- Collaboration and stakeholder engagement
- Long-term vision
- Adaptability and innovation
- Ethical considerations

## 30. Cognitive Leadership

- Understanding cognitive styles
- Active listening and empathy
- Effective communication
- Problem-solving and decision-making
- Conflict resolution

## 31. Neuroscience-Based Leadership

- Understanding the brain's response to stress
- Calming communication
- Fostering empathy and support
- Building resilience
- Creating a positive work environment
- Applying mirror neuron principles

## 32. AI-Enhanced Leadership

- AI-enhanced decision-making
- Addresses ethical considerations in AI decision-making
- Upskill teams to work alongside AI tools

- Fosters a human-AI collaboration culture
- Strategic market analysis
- Optimizing operations
- Data-driven storytelling and engagement

## 33. Digital Leadership

- Visionary leadership
- Building digital infrastructure
- Change management and empowerment
- Strategic thinking and external engagement
- Resilience and perseverance
- Inspiring a digital-first culture
- Address digital divides
- Equitable access to digital resources

## 34. Mindful Leadership

- Practicing presence and awareness
- Encouraging reflective practices
- Creating emotionally safe environments
- Managing fear and anxiety
- Making decisions with clarity
- Fostering resilience

# Cluster: Principled Leadership

## 35. Authentic Leadership

- Authentic
- Self-awareness
- Transparency and integrity
- Ethical decision-making

- Building trust and relationships
- Leading by example

## 36. Holacratic Leadership

- Decentralized decision-making
- Empowering autonomy
- Collaboration and unity
- Adaptability and resilience
- Emphasizing conflict resolution

## 37. Maternalistic Leadership

- Caring and protective nature
- Guiding with empathy and love
- Fostering unity and solidarity
- Nurturing resilience and hope
- Encouraging personal growth

## 38. Paternalistic Leadership

- Caring and protective nature
- Building trust and respect
- Providing guidance and support
- Fostering unity and tradition
- Resilience and hope

## 39. Biophilic Leadership

- Connecting with nature
- Promoting well-being
- Fostering creativity and sustainability
- Creating a lasting impact
- Biophilic design into organizational structures
- Promoting a broader cultural connection to nature

## 40. Laissez-faire Leadership

- Trust and empowerment
- Autonomy
- Clear goals
- Effective communication
- Building a strong team

# Appendix II

# Expanded Characteristics of the Forty Leadership Styles

## Cluster: Transformative and Visionary Leadership

### 1. Transformational Leadership: Leading by inspiring change and growth.

- Inspires and motivates people to transcend their self-interests for the greater good.
- Empowers others to see their potential and purpose.
- Helps the team see beyond their tasks and understand how their work contributes to a greater goal.
- Fosters a growth mindset, encouraging the team to embrace challenges as opportunities.
- Leads with integrity, aligning actions with words.

### 2. Purpose-Driven Leadership: Leading with a mission that extends beyond profit.

- Strongly commits to aligning goals with a purpose beyond profit.
- Shows that leadership is not just about financial success, but is also about contributing to the greater good.

## 3. Transcendent Leadership: Leading by inspiring purpose and self-discovery.

- Leads relationally, acting as a guide and mentor who walks alongside others on their journey of self-discovery.
- Emphasizes empowering others to find their path and live in alignment with their highest values.
- Incorporates transcendent leadership practices, focusing on wisdom, awakening, and pursuing higher purposes.
- Encourages personal development and inner awakening.
- Redefines success by focusing on meaningful connections, wisdom, and contributions to collective well-being.
- Ensures that technology is used ethically and supports human development and inner awakening.
- Creates a lasting impact through leadership that inspires continuous growth, discovery, and connection.
- Crafts a compelling vision that addresses the profound, often overlooked needs of people.
- Communicates the vision with clarity and inspiration, resonating with the values and emotions of the audience to inspire them to join the mission.
- Leads by example, embodying wisdom, compassion, and humility.
- Develops mental and emotional resilience, embracing challenges as opportunities for growth.
- Leads with patience and persistence, understanding that profound, meaningful change takes time.

## 4. Resonant Leadership: Leading by building strong emotional connections.

- Builds strong emotional connections with employees and stakeholders.
- Leads with empathy, inspiration, and a shared purpose.
- Connects with people on an emotional level.

- Cultivates emotional intelligence and communicates with empathy.
- Practices active listening.
- Is compassionate in decision-making.
- Fosters an inclusive environment.
- Fosters a culture of collaboration, support, and shared purpose.
- Challenges established norms and inspires innovation.
- Shares their vision and insights to inspire others.
- Leads by example, demonstrating how emotional intelligence and connection can lead to innovation and impact.

## 5. Charismatic Leadership: Leading through the power of personality and inspiration.

- Uses personal magnetism and persuasive communication to inspire confidence.
- Guides the team through significant crises.
- Cultivates a strong, confident presence.
- Clearly articulates the vision and values.
- Builds trust and rapport by being approachable, authentic, and consistent.
- Communicates directly and sincerely.
- Communicates openly and honestly, especially during challenges.
- Remains visible and present, especially when the team needs leadership the most.
- Turns challenges into opportunities for growth.
- Demonstrates resilience, ensuring that the company survives and emerges stronger from crises.

## 6. Innovation Leadership: Leading by fostering creativity and driving progress.

- Sets bold, ambitious goals. Sees beyond the present and imagines a transformative future, inspiring the team and guiding groundbreaking innovation.
- Develops and executes a comprehensive plan. Breaks down complex goals into manageable tasks and deadlines.
- Provides access to resources and workshops to stay updated with the latest trends and skills.
- Recognizes and leverages the diverse experiences and viewpoints of the team to approach problems creatively and innovatively.
- Inspires passion and purpose by keeping the team focused on the purpose of their work, connecting daily tasks to a greater cause.

## 7. Sustainable Leadership: Leading with a long-term, eco-conscious vision.

- Leads by example, modeling sustainable practices and using resources responsibly, encouraging the team to do the same.
- Promotes a culture of responsibility by fostering a culture prioritizing environmental and social responsibility. Encourages sustainable, goal-aligned innovation.
- Balances profitability with responsibility, balancing success with environmental protection and prioritizing long-term environmental health.
- Aligns strategies with vision, ensuring that actions align with the overarching vision. Regularly reviews progress, adjusting plans as needed.
- Creates a legacy that benefits others beyond one's tenure and understands leadership as a responsibility to future generations.

## 8. Regenerative Leadership: Leading by leveraging social influence and online engagement.

- Demonstrates a commitment to creating systems that restore and renew the environment.
- Leads with a vision that extends beyond sustainability to regeneration.
- Considers the long-term impacts of decisions on the environment and society.
- Embraces and implements regenerative practices in the leadership style, showing that regeneration and profitability can coexist.
- Cultivates relationships with suppliers, partners, and stakeholders who share similar values.
- Promotes collaboration across different departments within the organization.

## 9. Integral Leadership: Leading by integrating multiple leadership styles.

- Combines various leadership theories and practices into a comprehensive, integrated approach.
- Adapts leadership styles to the context and needs of the situation.
- Applies situational leadership to provide the proper support and guidance to different teams.
- Recognizes the value of cognitive diversity and encourages different perspectives in decision-making.
- Articulates a compelling and clear vision for the future.
- Aligns the team's efforts with the vision to inspire collective commitment.
- Understands and manages the interconnectedness of the company's operations.
- Leads the adoption of cutting-edge technologies.
- Demonstrates resilience and adapts to challenges.

## Cluster: Relational and People-Focused Leadership

### 10. Servant Leadership: Leading by serving and empowering others.

- Demonstrates an unwavering focus on serving the crew, prioritizing their needs, safety, and well-being.
- Places the team above oneself, inspiring loyalty and dedication.
- Regularly assesses and addresses the needs of the team.
- Leads by example, showing a commitment to serving others through actions.

### 11. Empathy-Based Leadership: Leading by understanding and responding to emotional needs.

- Focuses on understanding and addressing the team's emotional and psychological needs.
- Connects personally to ensure that the team feels supported and understood.
- Fosters an inclusive community where everyone feels valued and supported.
- Creates a culture of understanding and care, strengthening the group.
- Values diverse perspectives, ensuring that all voices are heard and respected in decision-making.
- Creates an environment where everyone feels they belong and can contribute to the community's success.
- Demonstrates inclusive behavior in the leadership style, showing respect, understanding, and support for all individuals, regardless of their background or position.

## 12. Relational Leadership: Leading by prioritizing relationships and social interactions.

- Builds and nurtures relationships within the team.
- Recognizes that the strength of an organization lies in interpersonal connections.
- Models supportive behavior.
- Encourages peer support.
- Regularly acknowledges and celebrates positive interactions.

## 13. Human-centered Leadership: Leading with a focus on human well-being in a tech-driven world.

- Emphasizes empathy, negotiation, and collaboration when resolving conflicts and building harmonious coexistence between humans and AI workers.
- Demonstrates empathy and understanding toward their team members.
- Recognizes that humans are at the center of their organization's success.
- Encourages collaboration between humans and AI, fostering an environment where different entities can coexist and work together effectively.
- Respects diverse perspectives and involve all stakeholders in decision-making, creating a positive and empowering work environment for all.

## 14. Inclusive Leadership: Leading by valuing diversity and creating equitable opportunities.

- Integrates diversity, equity, and inclusion into every aspect of leadership practices.
- Creates an environment where all voices are heard, valued, and empowered to contribute.

- Confronts uncomfortable truths and takes action to address systemic issues.
- Implements initiatives to diversify leadership, creates an inclusive culture, and ensures equity, laying the foundation for a truly inclusive organization.
- Engages all employees in the transformation process, amplifies marginalized voices, and fosters open dialogue to ensure that everyone's voice is heard and valued.
- Leaves a legacy and creates a lasting impact that benefits the company and society, demonstrating that true success is measured in profits and the positive change we create.
- Cultivates empathy to understand the experiences and perspectives of others, particularly those from underrepresented groups, leading with inclusivity at the forefront.
- Embraces transparency, using uncomfortable truths as a catalyst for growth and improvement.
- Is open to feedback, even when it's hard to hear.
- Takes responsibility for shortcomings and commits to making necessary changes.
- Systematically diversifies leadership, fosters a culture of inclusion, and ensures equity, creating an inclusive workplace.
- Focuses on building a leadership team that reflects the workforce's diversity and the broader market.
- Creates initiatives and programs that support belonging for all employees.
- Regularly reviews and addresses disparities in pay, opportunity, and treatment.

## 15. Cultural Intelligence Leadership: Leading effectively across different cultures.

- Leads effectively in multicultural environments with high cultural sensitivity.
- Navigates cultural complexities and builds a shared organizational culture.

- Understands and respects cultural differences.
- Invests time learning about the cultural backgrounds of team members.
- Adapts the leadership approach based on cultural norms and values.
- Seeks to understand the perspectives of all parties before intervening in a conflict.
- Aims for resolutions that address the core needs of all parties.
- Ensures that leaders from different cultures are represented in the organization.
- Emphasizes the importance of cultural diversity in leadership roles.
- Promotes diversity in leadership.
- Fosters an inclusive culture.
- Provides training and development opportunities focused on cultural intelligence and inclusive leadership.
- Manages the change process effectively, guiding the team through the complex integration of two diverse cultures.

## 16. Democratic Leadership: Leading by involving the team in decision-making.

- Encourages team members to share insights and ideas.
- Empowers team members to take ownership of plans.
- Utilizes the diverse skills and perspectives of the team.
- Emphasizes shared responsibility and the importance of every member's contribution.
- Involves the team in decision-making.
- Actively seeks input and fosters collaboration.

## 17. Shared Leadership: Leading by distributing responsibility and collaboration.

- Involves leaders at all levels, encouraging collaboration, inclusivity, and collective decision-making.

- Empowers leaders across different departments and regions to contribute to planning and execution.
- Showcases distributed leadership, where responsibility and decision-making are shared.
- Fosters trust, engagement, and innovation by distributing leadership.
- Commits to collaboration by involving leaders at all levels.
- Encourages open dialogue across all levels.
- Builds cross-functional teams, uniting individuals from different departments and regions.
- Promotes diversity and ensures teams are diverse in background, experience, and perspective.
- Engages employees at all levels in critical decisions.
- Creates an inclusive culture, establishing a work environment where everyone feels valued.
- Empowers others by delegating authority and responsibility.
- Delegates tasks and decision-making authority, showing confidence in team members' abilities.
- Provides clear objectives when delegating.
- Supports autonomy, allowing the team to approach tasks in their own way.
- Shares information openly with the team and stakeholders.
- Invites feedback and demonstrates integrity.

## 18. Co-creative Leadership: Leading through shared leadership and collaborative creation.

- Focuses on collaboration and shared responsibility.
- Embraces the diverse strengths and perspectives of team members.
- Creates a culture of collective responsibility, ensuring that everyone feels empowered to contribute to shared goals.
- Encourages innovation through collaboration, allowing the team to co-create solutions to complex challenges.

- Models co-creative leadership and demonstrates the value of shared leadership and collective wisdom.
- Creates an environment where all voices are heard and valued, facilitating discussions to allow team members to contribute their unique perspectives.
- Distributes leadership roles based on strengths, rather than hierarchy.

### 19. Social Leadership: Leading by leveraging social media and online platforms to connect with audiences.

- This style builds influence and achieves organizational goals.
- This style emphasizes understanding consumer behavior and tailoring digital communication strategies to effectively engage target audiences and foster a sense of community.
- Social leaders use social media not just as a marketing tool, but as a platform for communication, transparency, and building genuine connections with stakeholders.
- Builds brand loyalty, managing public perception and navigating the challenges of a rapidly evolving digital landscape.

## Cluster: Adaptive and Resilient Leadership

### 20. Adaptive Leadership: Leading by adjusting to dynamic and unpredictable situations.

- Adapts to rapidly changing and unpredictable environments.
- Readily changes their strategies and plans in response to new information or challenges.
- Comfortable operating in ambiguous and uncertain environments.
- Not bound by rigid plans or processes. They embrace change,

welcome diverse input, and encourage flexibility within their teams.

- Can quickly assess situations, analyze information, and make decisions under pressure.
- Decisive and act swiftly when needed.
- Committed to learning from their experiences and their environment.
- View challenges as opportunities for growth and adapt their approach based on new insights.

## 21. Agile Leadership: Leading with adaptability and responsiveness in dynamic situations.

- Readily adjusts their strategies and plans in response to unexpected changes.
- Remains calm under pressure and pivot effectively to address new information or challenges.
- Makes informed decisions swiftly, especially in high-pressure situations.
- Prioritizes gathering essential information quickly and use frameworks or criteria to guide their choices.
- Trusts their teams to embrace change, solve problems, and take ownership of their work.
- Encourages a culture of continuous learning and development.

## 22. Situational Leadership: Leading by adapting your style to different contexts.

- Quickly assesses the unfolding situation and understands the unique needs of each situation.
- Demonstrates a keen awareness of the environment and makes rapid decisions based on evolving circumstances.
- Shifts leadership style to suit the different needs of team members and the challenges they face.

- Understands team members' strengths, weaknesses, and experience levels.
- Remains flexible and recognizes when a different approach is needed.

## 23. Crisis Leadership: Leading with composure, decisiveness, and adaptability in critical situations.

- Exhibits exceptional crisis leadership by remaining calm under extreme pressure.
- Makes rapid decisions and guides the team through unprecedented and chaotic situations.
- Practices mindfulness and stress-management techniques to remain composed during crises.
- Empowers team members by giving them the autonomy to make decisions.
- Shows trust in the team's abilities by allowing them to take ownership of tasks.
- Promotes a culture where team members feel free to suggest new ideas and solutions.
- Demonstrates the ability to make rapid, effective decisions.

## 24. Resilient Leadership: Leading with strength and determination through challenges.

- Navigates challenges, recovers from setbacks, and thrives in adversity, remaining calm, focused, and adaptive to confidently guide the team through uncertainty.
- Delegates authority, empowering leaders and teams to make decisions and take ownership.
- Supports well-being: recognizes the importance of mental and emotional health.
- Fosters a positive and supportive work environment where employees feel valued and empowered.

## 25. Hybrid Leadership: Leading effectively across physical and virtual workspaces.

- Effectively manages teams across physical and virtual spaces.
- Ensures cohesion, productivity, and well-being in a blended work environment.
- Reinforces the company's vision and creates initiatives to strengthen bonds between in-office and remote employees, ensuring that the team remains united and focused on their mission.
- Streamlines communication and empowers decision-making across physical and virtual spaces.
- Prioritizes mental health and work-life balance for all team members.
- Leverages the strengths of a hybrid work model to enhance the team's adaptability and resilience.
- Exhibits adaptability by effectively leading a hybrid team during a crisis.
- Seamlessly adjusts the leadership style to meet the demands of both in-office and remote employees.
- Embraces change and welcomes it as an opportunity for growth.
- Regularly evaluates the needs of team members, whether remote or in-office, tailoring the leadership approach accordingly.

## 26. Quantum Leadership: Leading by embracing uncertainty and interconnectedness.

- Embraces uncertainty.
- Sees the interconnectedness of all things.
- Flows with chaos, allowing intuition to guide through shifting landscapes.
- Encourages the team to see the system, not just obstacles.
- Recognizes that the world is not always linear or logical.
- Is open to trusting intuition.

# Cluster: Structured and Analytical Leadership

## 27. Transactional Leadership: Leading through structure, rewards, and consequences.

- Emphasizes clear structure, supervision, and rewards and penalties to motivate employees.
- Sets clear expectations for the team, outlining specific targets and timelines.
- Uses meticulous planning and a structured approach, leaving little room for deviation.
- Implements a system of rewards and penalties to drive performance.
- Focuses on achieving measurable outcomes.
- Uses a well-defined framework or methodology to manage projects.
- Maintains adherence to the core plan, even when flexibility is necessary.
- Regularly reviews progress against the plan.
- Offers rewards, such as bonuses, promotions, or recognition, for those who meet or exceed their targets.
- Clearly defines the consequences for failing to meet expectations.
- Uses rewards and penalties in balance.
- Defines key performance indicators (KPIs) that align with goals and regularly measure progress.
- Focuses efforts and resources on activities directly contributing to desired results.
- Keeps the ultimate objectives at the forefront of decision-making.

## 28. Strategic Leadership: Leading by balancing short-term needs with long-term vision.

- Balances short-term operational needs with long-term strategic goals.
- Navigates the complexities of conflict while maintaining a clear vision.
- Demonstrates the importance of balancing immediate tactical decisions with strategic planning.
- Addresses short-term challenges without losing sight of the broader vision.
- Establishes a strategic leadership model, balancing operational efficiency with ethical and strategic considerations.
- Defines the strategic vision early, ensuring that it aligns with the core mission.
- Keeps the long-term impact in mind while addressing immediate challenges.
- Develops contingency plans.
- Implements security measures and protocols to protect operations.
- Is proactive in legal and regulatory compliance.
- Develops a flexible operational model to withstand disruptions.
- Emphasizes the ethical implications of decisions.

## 29. Systems Leadership: Leading by understanding and managing interconnected systems.

- Understands the intricate connections within a complex system.
- Approaches challenges holistically.
- Adopts a systems perspective, understanding how different parts interact and influence each other.

## 30. Cognitive Leadership: Leading by understanding and leveraging diverse thinking styles.

- Leverages cognitive diversity and psychological insights to enhance decision-making and resolve conflicts.
- Understands and integrates different cognitive styles.
- Familiarizes themselves with different cognitive styles.
- Facilitates open dialogue and encourages team members to share their perspectives.

## 31. Neuroscience-Based Leadership: Leading by applying insights from brain science.

- Applies insights from neuroscience to leadership practices.
- Understands how the brain processes emotions, stress, and change.
- Uses this knowledge to guide decisions, particularly during a crisis.
- Develops a foundational understanding of neuroscience.
- Uses neuroscience knowledge to inform leadership decisions.
- Fosters an emotionally intelligent culture that recognizes and supports employees' needs.

## 32. AI-Enhanced Leadership: Leading with data-driven insights and AI assistance.

- Integrates AI into leadership practices to make informed decisions based on data-driven insights and predictions, anticipating challenges, and responding effectively to dynamic situations.
- Incorporates AI technologies into decision-making to analyze vast data and uncover actionable insights.
- Continuously updates knowledge of AI advancements and how they can improve leadership effectiveness.
- Bases decisions on reliable data and predictive analytics.

## 33. Digital Leadership: Leading by effectively utilizing digital tools and strategies.

- Sets an ambitious goal to transform industries through digital innovation.
- Sees beyond current capabilities and envisions a future where digital tools and strategies drive growth and progress.
- Identifies and supports early adopters of new technologies and approaches, encouraging them to mentor others.
- Recognizes and rewards progress during change to build momentum and reinforce positive behaviors.

## 34. Mindful Leadership: Leading with presence, awareness, and emotional regulation.

- Integrates mindfulness practices into the decision-making process, promoting self-awareness, emotional regulation, and presence in every interaction. This helps the leader remain calm and make clear decisions, even under pressure.
- Mindful leaders regularly reflect on their thoughts, emotions, and behaviors and understand how these affect their leadership.
- Seek feedback to enhance their self-understanding.
- Mindful leaders manage their emotions effectively, especially in stressful situations.
- Remain calm and composed, even under pressure, to model emotional stability for their teams.
- Mindful leaders are fully present in their interactions with others. They actively listen, pay attention, and engage thoughtfully in conversations.

## Cluster: Principled Leadership

### 35. Authentic Leadership: Leading with genuine self-expression and integrity.

- Prioritizes transparency, integrity, and ethical behavior.
- Respects and adapts to different cultures without compromising values.
- Leads with genuineness, building trust and respect.
- Establishes and enforces clear ethical guidelines.
- Remains firm in their principles, even in the face of ethical dilemmas.
- Fosters an ethical culture, encouraging and rewarding ethical behavior.
- Adjusts the leadership style to meet different regions' cultural and business expectations.
- Uses open forums to build trust and counter misinformation.

### 36. Holacratic Leadership: Leading by distributing authority and empowering teams.

- Empowers the team to make decisions and take responsibility.
- Creates an environment where each team member's expertise is valued, and their contributions are respected.
- Fosters open communication and collaboration, ensuring that everyone has a voice.
- Builds unity through autonomy, where team members feel empowered to lead in their areas of strength.
- Delegates decision-making power to individuals based on their expertise, allowing them to act within their domain.
- Ensures accountability alongside delegated authority.
- Builds a culture where team members feel confident in making decisions without waiting for approval.

- Empowers the team by allowing each member to lead in their expertise.
- Understands each team member's unique strengths and skills.
- Allows team members to focus on their areas of expertise, providing opportunities to develop and refine those skills.

## 37. Maternalistic Leadership: Leading with a mother's strength and compassion.

- Acts as a mother figure who guides and protects her team in a familial manner.
- Combines strength with compassion and care.
- Prioritizes the care, protection, and well-being of the most vulnerable team members.
- Fosters a sense of security to keep morale high and ensure resilience.
- Motivates through love, empathy, purpose, and a sense of belonging, rather than through fear or aggression.
- Creates a strong sense of unity, solidarity, and family within the team.
- Helps the team heal, nurtures hope, and rebuilds strength after losses or challenges.

## 38. Paternalistic Leadership: Leading by guiding and protecting like a father figure.

- Acts as a protector and guide, making decisions in the team's best interests.
- Cultivates a caring attitude, seeing the team as individuals who can be positively impacted.
- Balances authority with compassion, ensuring that the team feels protected and supported.
- Is approachable and fosters open communication.
- Builds trust and respect.
- Leads by example and invests in relationships.

- Communicates transparently, being open and honest.
- Focuses on fostering resilience and instilling hope for the future.

## 39. Biophilic Leadership: Leading by integrating nature and well-being into the workplace.

- Creates healthier, more creative, and more sustainable work environments.
- Envisions a future where nature and work coexist harmoniously.
- Promotes sustainable practices and seek to create work environments that connect people to nature.
- Values nature and understands the benefits of integrating natural elements into workspaces.
- Encourages employees to connect with nature and promote a sense of well-being.
- Encourages creativity by incorporating nature-inspired workshops and exploring biomimicry in product development.
- Sees nature as a source of inspiration and innovation.
- Commits to sustainable practices and promotes eco-friendly initiatives within their organizations.
- Aims to create work environments that benefit both people and the planet.
- Adapts their approach to different work environments, extending biophilic principles to both in-office and remote settings.
- Recognizes that a connection to nature can benefit employees in various ways.

## 40. Laissez-faire Leadership: Leading by providing autonomy and minimal direction.

- Shows profound trust in the crew, empowering them to make critical decisions.

- Fosters a culture of autonomy, where each crew member is responsible for their actions.
- Delegates responsibility based on team members' strengths and trusts them to execute without micromanaging.
- Creates an environment where team members take ownership of their roles and decisions.
- Provides guidance without solving every problem, encouraging the team to develop solutions.
- Allows the crew to operate with independence, enabling quick decision-making and adaptability.
- Empowers team members to make decisions within their areas of expertise, encouraging them to trust their judgment.
- Provides minimal supervision, allowing the team to perform duties with creativity and initiative.
- Trusts in expertise and avoids micromanaging.

# About the Author

**Pietro Pazzi** is a seasoned corporate executive, general manager, consultant, and entrepreneur with over thirty years of diverse experience across multiple industries and cultures.

Pietro's commitment to continuous learning is evident in his extensive educational background. He holds an MBA in general management and has completed various management programs, including an executive development program at the prestigious Oxford Saïd Business School. His passion for personal and professional growth has led him to obtain multiple certifications, including being a certified Lean Six Sigma Black Belt and Master Black Belt.

With a deep learning in psychology, Pietro has effectively applied his knowledge to sales and marketing, earning him the highest accreditation as a Chartered Marketer. His ability to understand and connect with people has been a key driver in his success.

Pietro has led business-transformation initiatives throughout his career, specializing in change leadership, business-process management, continuous improvement, data analytics, and business intelligence. He is recognized for his expertise in strategy development and deployment, leadership development, and driving business turnarounds.

Pietro has held significant leadership roles, including managing director and global head of Lean Six Sigma, where he led comprehensive process-improvement strategies worldwide. His extensive experience includes facilitating executive strategy and execution workshops in diverse cultures worldwide, further establishing his reputation as a global business leader.

In addition to his professional achievements, Pietro has a keen interest in AI and emerging technologies. He is also passionate about photography, having opened a gallery in Cape Town, South Africa and an online platform. Pietro values fitness and balances his professional life with his passions.

Currently residing in Munich with his wife, Pietro is a proud father of two adult children and a grandfather to four, all living in the UK.

A relentless pursuit of excellence in business and personal endeavors drives his life and work.

For more, visit his LinkedIn profile at:
https://LinkedIn.com/in/pietropazzi

# References

## Introduction

Benmira, Sihame and Moyosolu Agboola. "Evolution of Leadership Theory." *BMJ Leader* 5, no. 1 (2021): 3–5. https://doi.org/10.1136/leader-2020-000296.

Goleman, Daniel. "Leadership That Gets Results." Harvard Business Review, Mar.–Apr. 2000. https://hbr.org/2000/03/leadership-that-gets-results.

Heifetz, Ronald A. *Leadership without Easy Answers*. Harvard University Press, 1994.

Heifetz, Ronald A., Marty Linsky, and Alexander Grashow. *The Practice of Adaptive Leadership*. Harvard Business Press, 2009.

Hersey, Paul, and Kenneth H. Blanchard. *Management of Organizational Behavior: Utilizing Human Resources*. 3rd ed. Prentice Hall, 1977.

Larson, Lindsay, and Leslie DeChurch. "Leading Teams in the Digital age: Four Perspectives on Technology and What They Mean for Leading Teams." *The Leadership Quarterly* 31, no. 1 (2020): Article 101377. https://doi.org/10.1016/j.leaqua.2019.101377.

Lennon, Tania. "5 Ways Leaders Can Survive and Thrive in a Turbulent 2025." *I by IMD* (Institute for Management Development), January 8, 2025. https://www.imd.org/ibyimd/2025-trends/5-ways-leaders-can-survive-and-thrive-in-a-turbulent-2025/.

Yueh, Linda, John Dore, and Vyla Rollins. "What Will Leadership Look Like in 2025?" *Think* at London Business School, January 3, 2025, https://www.london.edu/think/what-will-leadership-look-like-in-2025.

## Chapter 1

Bandura, Albert. *Self-Efficacy: The Exercise of Control.* W.H. Freeman, 1997.

Bandler, Richard, and John Grinder. *The Structure of Magic I: A Book about Language and Therapy.* Science and Behavior Books, 1975.

Bandler, Richard, and John Grinder. *The Structure of Magic II: A Book about Communication and Change.* Science and Behavior Books, 1976.

Beck, Aaron T. *Cognitive Therapy of Depression.* Guilford Press, 1979.

Branden, Nathaniel. *The Six Pillars of Self-Esteem.* Bantam, 1994.

Clear, James. "Identity-Based Habits: How to Actually Stick to Your Goals." Chap. 2 in *Atomic Habits.* Avery, 2018. https://jamesclear.com/identity-based-habits.

Covey, Stephen R. *The 7 Habits of Highly Effective People.* Free Press, 1989.

David, Daniel, Carmen Cotet, Silviu Matu, Cristina Mogoase, and Simona Stefan. "50 Years of Rational-Emotive and Cognitive-Behavioral Therapy: A Systematic Review and Meta-Analysis." *Journal of Clinical Psychology* 74, no. 3 (2017): 304–318. https://pmc.ncbi.nlm.nih.gov/articles/PMC5836900/.

Dilts, Robert. *Changing Belief Systems with NLP.* Meta Publications,1990.

Kouzes, James M., and Barry Z. Posner. *The Leadership Challenge* (6th ed.). Wiley, 2017.

Merton, Robert K. "The Self-Fulfilling Prophecy." *The Antioch Review* 8, no. 2 (1948): 193–210. https://entrepreneurscommunicate.pbworks.com/f/Merton.+Self+Fulfilling+Profecy.pdf.

O'Connor, Joseph, and John Seymour. *Introducing NLP: Psychological Skills for Understanding and Influencing People.* Harper Thorsons, 2002.

Rokeach, Milton. *The Nature of Human Values.* Free Press, 1973.

Seligman, Martin E.P. *Learned Optimism: How to Change Your Mind and Your Life.* Pocket Books, 1998.

## Chapter 2

Amazon Web Services. "Powering Innovation and Speed with Amazon's Two-Pizza Teams." AWS Executive Insights. Accessed September 30, 2025. https://aws.amazon.com/executive-insights/content/amazon-two-pizza-team/.

Amazon Staff. "2016 Letter to Shareholders." Amazon News, April 17, 2017. https://www.aboutamazon.com/news/company-news/2016-letter-to-shareholders.

Bachelder, Cheryl A. "The CEO of Popeyes on Treating Franchisees as the Most Important Customers." *Harvard Business Review*, October 2016. https://hbr.org/2016/10/the-ceo-of-popeyes-on-treating-franchisees-as-the-most-important-customers.

Brown, Brené. *Dare to Lead: Brave Work. Tough Conversations. Whole Hearts.* Random House, 2018.

Chouinard, Yvon. "Earth Is Now Our Only Shareholder." Patagonia, Sept. 14, 2022. https://www.patagonia.com/ownership/.

Collins, Jim. *Good to Great: Why Some Companies Make the Leap...and Others Don't*. Harper Business, 2001.

Dweck, Carol S. *Mindset: Changing the Way You Think to Fulfil Your Potential*. Robinson, 2017.

Economic Club of Washington, D.C. "PepsiCo Chief Indra Nooyi on the CEO of the Future." May 12, 2009. https://www.economicclub.org/sites/default/files/transcripts/Nooyi%20Remarks%20JF%20Revised%2007%2029%2010.pdf.

Edmondson, Amy C. "Psychological Safety and Learning Behavior in Work Teams." *Administrative Science Quarterly* 44, no. 2 (1999): 350–383. https://www.jstor.org/stable/2666999.

Edmondson, Amy C. *The Fearless Organization: Creating Psychological Safety in the Workplace for Learning, Innovation, and Growth*. Wiley, 2018.

Greenleaf, Robert K. *Servant Leadership: A Journey into the Nature of Legitimate Power and Greatness*. Paulist Press, 1997.

Nadella, Satya, with Greg Shaw and Jill Tracie Nichols. *Hit Refresh: The Quest to Rediscover Microsoft's Soul and Imagine a Better Future for Everyone*. Harper Business, 2017.

Novo Nordisk. "Diversity and Inclusion in the Workplace." Accessed September 30, 2025. https://www.novonordisk.com/sustainable-business/diversity-and-inclusion.html.

Sinek, Simon. *Leaders Eat Last: Why Some Teams Pull Together and Others Don't*. Portfolio, 2014.

Sinek, Simon. *Start with Why*. Portfolio, 2009.

Southwest Airlines. "Culture." Accessed September 30, 2025. https://careers.southwestair.com/culture.

Toyota. "Toyota Production System." Accessed September 30, 2025. https://global.toyota/en/company/vision-and-philosophy/production-system/index.html.

U.S. Department of Justice. "Volkswagen to Spend Up to $14.7 Billion to Settle Allegations of Cheating Emissions Tests and Deceiving Customers." June 11, 2016. Archived February 6, 2025. https://www.justice.gov/archives/opa/pr/volkswagen-spend-147-billion-settle-allegations-cheating-emissions-tests-and-deceiving.

U.S. Environmental Protection Agency. "Volkswagen Clean Air Act Civil Settlement." Updated March 11, 2025. https://www.epa.gov/enforcement/volkswagen-clean-air-act-civil-settlement.

Valve Corporation. *Valve Handbook for New Employees*. Valve Press, 2012. https://assets.sbnation.com/assets/1074301/Valve_Handbook_LowRes.pdf.

Yousafzai, Malala, and Christina Lamb. *I Am Malala: The Girl Who Stood Up for Education and Was Shot by the Taliban*. Little, Brown, 2013.

## Chapter 3

Avolio, Bruce J., and William L. Gardner. "Authentic Leadership Development: Getting to the Root of Positive Forms of Leadership." *The Leadership Quarterly*, 16(3) (2005): 315–38. https://doi.org/10.1016/j.leaqua.2005.03.001.

Bass, Bernard M., and Ronald E. Riggio. *Transformational Leadership*. 2nd ed. Psychology Press, 2006.

Blake, Robert R., and Jane S. Mouton. *The Managerial Grid*. Gulf Publishing, 1964.

Burns, James MacGregor. *Leadership*. Harper & Row, 1978.

Carlyle, Thomas. *On Heroes, Hero-Worship, and the Heroic in History*. Wiley and Putnam, 1846.

Earley, P. Christopher, and Soon Ang. *Cultural Intelligence: Individual Interactions Across Cultures*. Stanford University Press, 2003.

Fiedler, Fred E. *A Theory of Leadership Effectiveness*. McGraw-Hill, 1967.

Goleman, Daniel. *Emotional Intelligence: Why It Can Matter More Than IQ*. Bantam,1995.

Goleman, Daniel. "Leadership That Gets Results." *Harvard Business Review*, March–April 2000. https://hbr.org/2000/03/leadership-that-gets-results.

Goleman, Daniel, Richard E. Boyatzis, and Annie McKee. *Primal Leadership: Learning to Lead with Emotional Intelligence*. Harvard Business Review Press, 2002.

Heifetz, Ronald A., and Marty Linsky. *Leadership on the Line: Staying Alive Through the Dangers of Leading*. Harvard Business Review Press, 2002.

Hersey, Paul, and Kenneth Blanchard. *Management of Organizational Behavior: Utilizing Human Resources*. 3rd ed. Prentice Hall, 1977.

House, Robert J., et al. *Culture, Leadership, and Organizations: The GLOBE Study of 62 Societies*. Sage Publications, 2004.

Marquet, L. David. *Turn the Ship Around! A True Story of Turning Followers into Leaders*. Penguin, 2013.

Stogdill, Ralph. "Personal Factors Associated with Leadership: A Survey of the Literature." *Journal of Psychology* 25 (1948): 35–71.

## Chapter 4

Adair, John. *Action-Centred Leadership*. McGraw-Hill, 1973.

Bass, Bernard M. *Leadership and Performance Beyond Expectations*. Free Press, 1985.

Fiedler, Fred E. *A Theory of Leadership Effectiveness*. McGraw-Hill, 1967.

George, Bill. Authentic *Leadership: Rediscovering the Secrets to Creating Lasting Value*. Jossey-Bass, 2003.

Goleman, Daniel. "Leadership That Gets Results." *Harvard Business Review* 78, no. 2 (2000): 78–90. https://hbr.org/2000/03/leadership-that-gets-results.

Goleman, Daniel. *Emotional Intelligence: Why It Can Matter More Than IQ*. Bantam, 1995.

Heifetz, Ronald A. *Leadership Without Easy Answers*. Belknap Press, 1994.

Hersey, Paul, and Kenneth H. Blanchard. *Management of Organizational Behavior: Utilizing Human Resources*. 3rd ed. Prentice Hall, 1977.

Goleman, Daniel, and Richard E. Boyatzis. "Social Intelligence and the Biology of Leadership." *Harvard Business Review*, 2008. https://hbr.org/2008/09/social-intelligence-and-the-biology-of-leadership.

Kets de Vries, Manfred F.R. *The Leadership Mystique*. Financial Times Prentice Hall, 2001.

Lewin, Kurt, Ronald Lippitt, and Ralph K. White. "Patterns of Aggressive Behavior in Experimentally Created 'Social Climates.'" *The Journal of Social Psychology* 10, no. 2 (1939): 271–301. https://doi.org/10.1080/00224545.1939.9713366.

Page, Trevor. "The Social Enterprise at Work: Paradox as a Path Forward." Deloitte Insights, July 2, 2020. https://www.deloitte.com/za/en/services/consulting/analysis/paradox-as-a-path-forward.html.

World Health Organization. "Mental Health at Work." September 2, 2024. https://www.who.int/news-room/fact-sheets/detail/mental-health-at-work.

## Chapter 5

Avolio, Bruce J., and William L. Gardner. "Authentic Leadership Development: Getting to the Root of Positive Forms of Leadership." *The Leadership Quarterly* 16, no. 3 (2005): 315–338. https://doi.org/10.1016/j.leaqua.2005.03.001.

Bass, Bernard M. *Leadership and Performance Beyond Expectations*. Free Press, 1985.

Blanchard, Kenneth H., Patricia Zigarmi, and Drea Zigarmi. *Leadership and the One Minute Manager: Increasing Effectiveness through Situational Leadership*. William Morrow, 1985.

Boyatzis, Richard E., and Annie McKee. *Resonant Leadership: Renewing Yourself and Connecting with Others through Mindfulness, Hope, and Compassion*. Harvard Business School Press, 2007.

Bourke, Juliet, and Andrea Titus. "The Key to Inclusive Leadership." *Harvard Business Review*, March 6, 2020. https://hbr.org/2020/03/the-key-to-inclusive-leadership.

Browning, William, Catherine Ryan, and Joseph Clancy. *14 Patterns of Biophilic Design*. 10th Anniversary Edition. Terrapin Bright Green, 2024. https://www.terrapinbrightgreen.com/report/14-patterns/.

Burns, James MacGregor. *Leadership*. Harper & Row, 1978.

Conger, Jay A., and Rabindra N. Kanungo. *Charismatic Leadership in Organizations*. Sage Publications, 1998.

Earley, P. Christopher, and Soon Ang. *Cultural Intelligence: Individual Interactions across Cultures*. Stanford Business Books, 2003.

George, Bill. *Authentic Leadership: Rediscovering the Secrets to Creating Lasting Value*. Jossey-Bass, 2003.

Greenleaf, Robert K. *Servant Leadership: A Journey into the Nature of Legitimate Power and Greatness*. Paulist Press, 2002.

Heifetz, Ronald A. *Leadership without Easy Answers*. Harvard University Press, 1998.

House, Robert J. "A 1976 Theory of Charismatic Leadership." Toronto University, 1976. https://files.eric.ed.gov/fulltext/ED133827.pdf.

Hutchins, Giles, and Laura Storm. *Regenerative Leadership: The DNA of Life-Affirming 21st Century Organizations*. Wordzworth, 2019.

Kane, Gerald C., Doug Palmer, Anh Nguyen Phillips, David Kiron, and Natasha Buckley. "Strategy, Not Technology, Drives Digital Transformation." *MIT Sloan Management Review*, July 2015. https://sloanreview.mit.edu/projects/strategy-drives-digital-transformation/.

Lewin, Kurt, Ronald Lippitt, and Ralph K. White. "Patterns of Aggressive Behavior in Experimentally Created Social Climates." *The Journal of Social Psychology* 10, no. 2 (1939): 271–299. https://psycnet.apa.org/doi/10.1080/00224545.1939.9713366.

Marturano, Janice. *Finding the Space to Lead: A Practical Guide to Mindful Leadership*. Bloomsbury, 2014.

Pazzi, Pietro. *Leading with Tomorrow in Mind*. Kindle Direct, 2024.

Pazzi, Pietro. *The Leadership Compass*. Kindle Direct, 2024.

Pearce, Craig L., and Jay A. Conger, eds. *Shared Leadership: Reframing the Hows and Whys of Leadership*. Sage Publications, 2003.

Pellegrini, Ekin K., and Terri A. Scandura. "Paternalistic Leadership: A Review and Agenda for Future Research." *Journal of Management* 34, no. 3 (2008): 566–593. https://www.researchgate.net/publication/238769495_Paternalistic_Leadership_A_Review_and_Agenda_for_Future_Research.

Porter-O'Grady, Tim, and Kathy Malloch. *Quantum Leadership: Creating Sustainable Value in Health Care*. Jones & Bartlett, 2017.

Robertson, Brian J. *Holacracy: The New Management System for a Rapidly Changing World*. Henry Holt & Co., 2015.

Rock, David. "SCARF: A Brain-Based Model for Collaborating with and Influencing Others." *NeuroLeadership Journal* 1 (2008): 44–52. https://davidrock.net/portfolio-items/

scarf-a-brain-based-model-for-collaborating-with-and-influencing-others-vol-1/.

Senge, Peter, et al. "The Dawn of System Leadership." *Stanford Social Innovation Review* 13, no. 1 (Winter 2015): 27–33. https://ssir.org/articles/entry/the_dawn_of_system_leadership.

## Chapter 6

Hersey, Paul, and Kenneth H. Blanchard. "Life Cycle Theory of Leadership." *Training and Development Journal* 23, no. 5 (1969): 26–34. https://assets.td.org/m/59759d86d1ed4390/original/LIFE-CYCLE-THEORY-OF-LEADERSHIP.pdf.

Luft, Joseph, and Harrington Ingham. *The Johari Window: A Graphic Model of Interpersonal Awareness.* Proceedings of the Western Training Laboratory in Group Development, 1955.

Northouse, Peter G. *Leadership: Theory and Practice.* 8th ed. Sage Publications, 2019.

## Chapter 8

Alimo-Metcalfe, Beverly. "360-Degree Feedback and Leadership Development." *International Journal of Selection and Assessment* 6, no. 1 (2002): 35–44. https://doi.org/10.1111/1468-2389.00070.

Antonioni, David. "Designing an Effective 360-Degree Appraisal Feedback Process." *Organizational Dynamics* 25, no. 2 (Autumn 1996): 24–38. https://www.sciencedirect.com/science/article/pii/S0090261696900236.

Bracken, David W., Carol W. Timmreck, and Allan H. Church. *The Handbook of Multisource Feedback: The Comprehensive Resource for Designing and Implementing MSF Processes*. Jossey-Bass, 2001.

Brett, Joan F., and Leanne E. Atwater. "360° Feedback: Accuracy, Reactions, and Perceptions of Usefulness." *Journal of Applied Psychology* 86, no. 5 (2001): 930–942. https://pubmed.ncbi.nlm.nih.gov/11596809/.

London, Manuel, and James W. Smither. "Can Multi-Source Feedback Change Perceptions of Goal Accomplishment, Self-Evaluations, and Performance-Related Outcomes? Theory-Based Applications and Directions for Research." *Personnel Psychology* 48, no. 4 (1995): 803–39. https://doi.org/10.1111/j.1744-6570.1995.tb01782.x.

Luft, Joseph, and Harrington Ingham. "The Johari Window: A Graphic Model of Interpersonal Awareness." Proceedings of the Western Training Laboratory in Group Development, University of California, Los Angeles, 1955. https://www.hee.nhs.uk/sites/default/files/documents/Johari%20window.pdf.

McCarthy, Alma M., and Thomas N. Garavan. "360° Feedback Process: Performance, Improvement and Employee Career Development." *Journal of European Industrial Training* 25, no. 1 (2001): 5–32. https://doi.org/10.1108/03090590110380614.

Ward, Peter. *360-Degree Feedback*. CIPD Publishing, 1997.

## Chapter 9

Fiedler, Fred E. *A Theory of Leadership Effectiveness*. McGraw-Hill, 1967.

George, Bill. *Authentic Leadership: Rediscovering the Secrets to Creating Lasting Value*. Jossey-Bass, 2003.

Goleman, Daniel. *Emotional Intelligence: Why It Can Matter More Than IQ*. Bantam, 1995.

Goleman, Daniel, Richard E. Boyatzis, and Annie McKee. *Primal Leadership: Realizing the Power of Emotional Intelligence*. Harvard Business Review Press, 2002.

Greenleaf, Robert K. *Servant Leadership: A Journey into the Nature of Legitimate Power and Greatness*. Paulist Press, 1977.

Heifetz, Ronald A. *Leadership Without Easy Answers*. Harvard University Press, 1994.

Hersey, Paul, and Kenneth H. Blanchard. "Life Cycle Theory of Leadership." *Training and Development Journal* 23, no. 5 (1969): 26–34. https://www.scribd.com/document/846614123/Hersey-P-Blanchard-K-H-1969-Life-cycle-theory-of-leadership.

Hersey, Paul, and Kenneth H. Blanchard. *Management of Organizational Behavior: Utilizing Human Resources* (4th ed.). Pearson, 1996.

Lawrence, Paul R., and Jay W. Lorsch. *Organization and Environment: Managing Differentiation and Integration*. Harvard Business School, Division of Research, 1967.

Maxwell, John C. *The 21 Irrefutable Laws of Leadership*. Thomas Nelson, 1998.

Myers, Isabel Briggs, and Katharine Cook Briggs. *The Myers-Briggs Type Indicator Manual*. Consulting Psychologists Press, 1962.

Rath, Tom. *StrengthsFinder 2.0*. Gallup Press, 2007.

Snowden, David J., and Mary E. Boone. "A Leader's Framework for Decision Making." *Harvard Business Review* 85, no. 11 (2007): 68–76. https://hbr.org/2007/11/a-leaders-framework-for-decision-making.

Stacey, Ralph D. *Strategic Management and Organisational Dynamics: The Challenge of Complexity to Ways of Thinking about Organisations.* Pearson, 2015.

## Chapter 10

Agile Alliance. "Principles behind the Agile Manifesto." Accessed September 30, 2025. https://agilemanifesto.org/principles.html.

Denning, Stephen. *The Age of Agile.* AMACOM, 2018.

Derby, Esther, and Diana Larsen. *Agile Retrospectives: Making Good Teams Great.* Pragmatic Bookshelf, 2006.

Edmondson, Amy C. "Psychological Safety and Learning Behavior in Work Teams." *Administrative Science Quarterly* 44, no. 2 (1999): 350–383. https://web.mit.edu/curhan/www/docs/Articles/15341_Readings/Group_Performance/Edmondson%20Psychological%20safety.pdf.

Edmondson, Amy C. *The Fearless Organization: Creating Psychological Safety in the Workplace for Learning, Innovation, and Growth.* Wiley, 2018.

Hamel, Gary. "Moon Shots for Management." *Harvard Business Review* 87, no. 2 (2009): 91–8. https://hbr.org/2009/02/moon-shots-for-management.

Kotter, John P. *Leading Change.* Harvard Business Review Press, 1996.

McChrystal, Stanley, Tantum Collins, David Silverman, and Chris Fussell. *Team of Teams: New Rules of Engagement for a Complex World.* Penguin, 2015.

Schein, Edgar H. *Organizational Culture and Leadership.* 4th ed. Jossey-Bass, 2010.

## Chapter 11

Denning, Stephen. *The Age of Agile.* AMACOM, 2018.

Edmondson, Amy C. "Psychological Safety and Learning Behavior in Work Teams." *Administrative Science Quarterly* 44, no. 2 (1999): 350–383. https://web.mit.edu/curhan/www/docs/Articles/15341_Readings/Group_Performance/Edmondson%20Psychological%20safety.pdf.

Edmondson, Amy C. *The Fearless Organization: Creating Psychological Safety in the Workplace for Learning, Innovation, and Growth.* Wiley, 2018.

Kotter, John P. *Leading Change.* Harvard Business Review Press, 1996.

McChrystal, Stanley, Tantum Collins, David Silverman, and Chris Fussell. *Team of Teams: New Rules of Engagement for a Complex World.* Portfolio, 2015.

Schein, Edgar H. *Organizational Culture and Leadership* (4th ed.). Jossey-Bass, 2010.

## Chapter 12

Hersey, Paul, and Kenneth Blanchard, K.H. *Management of Organizational Behavior: Utilizing Human Resources.* 4th ed. Prentice Hall, 1982.

Campbell, Joseph. *The Hero with a Thousand Faces*. New World Library, 2008.

Covey, Stephen R. *The 7 Habits of Highly Effective People: Powerful Lessons in Personal Change*. Free Press, 1989.

Deci, Edward L., and Richard M. Ryan. "The 'What' and 'Why' of Goal Pursuits: Human Needs and the Self-Determination of Behavior." *Psychological Inquiry* 11, no. 4 (2000): 227–68. https://doi.org/10.1207/S15327965PLI1104_01.

Doran, George T. "There's a S.M.A.R.T. Way to Write Management's Goals and Objectives." *Management Review* 70, no. 11, (1981): 35–36. https://community.mis.temple.edu/mis0855002fall2015/files/2015/10/S.M.A.R.T-Way-Management-Review.pdf.

Driskell, James E., Carolyn Copper, and Aidan Moran. "Does Mental Practice Enhance Performance?" *Journal of Applied Psychology* 79, no. 4 (1994): 481–92. https://doi.org/10.1037/0021-9010.79.4.481.

Locke, Edwin A., and Gary P. Latham. "Building a Practically Useful Theory of Goal Setting and Task Motivation: A 35-Year Odyssey." *American Psychologist* 57, no. 9 (2002): 705–717. https://www-2.rotman.utoronto.ca/facbios/file/09%20-%20Locke%20&%20Latham%20 2002%20AP.pdf.

Maltz, Maxwell. *Psycho-Cybernetics: A New Way to Get More Living Out of* Life. Pocket Books, 1989.

Pennebaker, James W. "Writing About Emotional Experiences as a Therapeutic Process." *Psychological Science* 8, no. 3 (1997): 162–66. http://www.gruberpeplab.com/teaching/psych3131_summer2015/documents/14.2_Pennebaker1997_Writingemotionalexperiences.pdf.

Robbins, Anthony. *Unlimited Power: The New Science of Personal Achievement*. Simon & Schuster, 1986.

Robbins, Anthony. *Awaken the Giant Within: How to Take Immediate Control of your Mental, Emotional, Physical, and Financial Destiny!* Simon & Schuster, 1991.

Robbins, Tony. "Adopt A Powerful Morning Ritual." TonyRobbins.com. 2025. https://www.tonyrobbins.com/blog/whats-your-morning-ritual/.

Sinek, Simon. *Start with Why*. Portfolio/Penguin, 2009.

Whitmore, John. *Coaching for Performance: GROWing Human Potential and Purpose*. 4th ed. Hodder And Stoughton, 2009.

## Conclusion

Baroudi, Sandra, and Miltiadis D. Lytras. "Leadership and Innovation in Higher Education in 2035." In *Transformative Leadership and Sustainable Innovation in Education*. Emerald Publishing, 2024.

Liden, Robert C., Xing Wang, and Yue Wang. "The Evolution of Leadership: Past Insights, Present Trends, and Future Trajectories." *Journal of Business Research* 186 (2024): 114–125. https://doi.org/10.1016/j.jbusres.2024.115036.

www.ingramcontent.com/pod-product-compliance
Lightning Source LLC
Chambersburg PA
CBHW021918190326
41519CB00009B/825